Clarity
in the
Classroom

Clarity in the Classroom

USING FORMATIVE ASSESSMENT
BUILDING LEARNING-FOCUSED RELATIONSHIPS

Michael Absolum

Hodder Education

National Library of New Zealand Cataloguing-in-Publication Data
Absolum, Michael.
Clarity in the classroom : using formative assessment - building
learning-focused relationships / Michael Absolum.
Includes bibliographical references and index.
ISBN: 978-1-86971-069-9
1. Effective teaching—New Zealand. 2. Interaction analysis in
education. 3. Learning, Psychology of. 4. Classroom
environment—New Zealand.
371.1020993—dc 22

A Hodder Education Book
Published in 2006 by Hachette Livre NZ Ltd
4 Whetu Place, Mairangi Bay
Auckland, New Zealand

Reprinted 2007, 2008 (twice), 2009

Designed and produced by Hachette Livre NZ Ltd
Printed by Tien Wah Press Ltd, Singapore

Front cover: Photosport
Back cover: Evaluation Associates Ltd
Page 197: Nigel Longstaff
All other photographs: Evaluation Associates Ltd

Contents

Acknowledgements

This book started life as a conversation with my colleagues at Evaluation Associates Ltd about what formative assessment really meant that teachers and students had to know and be able to do. I want to acknowledge my huge debt to them. This book came about because of their ability to think through the issues; to provide new insights and examples of classroom practice when they were needed; to trial and improve ideas through their work with teachers and students in schools; and to allow me to sneak off and write while they reviewed endless drafts with unwavering enthusiasm. My grateful thanks to them all: Ruth Hammond, Judy Munro-Keene, Angela Thorogood, Catherine Hope, Allan Powell, Sue Leslie, Adrienne Carlisle, Michelle Nell and Barbara-Anne Alexander.

Evaluation Associates has been involved in offering professional development to New Zealand schools for over 10 years. In that time, we have worked with a large number of principals and teachers who are out there, day after day, making a difference to student learning. I want to acknowledge the contribution they have made to our thinking and the ideas in this book. I hope they find it worthy of them.

I also want to acknowledge the insightful contributions of those principals and teachers with whom we have worked particularly closely over a long period of time. These people are our close colleagues with whom we develop, test and deepen our understanding of what support teachers need in order for assessment for learning to be used richly within classrooms:

- **Lin Avery, the original designer of our programme in schools and now at Glen Taylor School**
- **David Bradley, Westbridge Residential School**
- **Cherie Taylor-Patel, Flanshaw Road School, especially for her contribution to student-led conferences**
- **Karen Windross, Waitakere School**
- **Sandra Jenkins, Glenbrae School**
- **Brenna Innes, Matipo School**
- **Rachel Shamy, Birkenhead Primary**
- **Sarah Martin, Red Beach School**
- **Riverina School and Sylvia Park School for the photographs**
- **Coatesville School for the school reports**

My partner, Mary, is my greatest critic and my greatest support. That this book is here at all is testimony to her profound understanding of teaching and learning, and her patience.

Michael Absolum — June 2006

The publisher would also like to thank Cherie Taylor-Patel and the staff and pupils of Flanshaw Road School, Te Atatu for their cooperation and help while taking the cover photograph for this book.

Preface

The teachers at Lin's school have many students who have limited personal resources, making learning at school initially difficult for them. Many have underdeveloped language and inadequate personal strategies to manage themselves, their learning and their relationships with their peers. These teachers struggle on a daily basis with how to teach these students effectively so that when they leave school they are able to confidently and competently take their full place in society. The struggle is never easy. These teachers deserve all the help and support they can get. This book is for them.

'Our experiences . . . all point to the need to rethink a teacher's core aim — enhancing pupils' learning. To achieve this calls for . . . a readiness to change the parts both teacher and pupils play in supporting the learning process.'

Black et al., 2002

*'I have never before seen a school where the pupils
are so naturally responsive and independent
in their work or where the relationship between teachers
and scholars so nearly approaches the ideal.'*

Extract from McClune & Lord, 1916

OVERVIEW

We all want students who have high expectations of themselves as learners; students who feel confident about their capacity to learn, who set high goals for their learning, and who work for themselves to construct enjoyable, challenging learning pathways to their futures.

This book contains research-based principles, strategies and techniques that teachers can best use to help students to learn: to help them be the type of students we all want.

It outlines what teachers need to think about, and how they need to act towards students to encourage them to become strong partners in the teaching/learning endeavour. It also covers how teachers can teach their students the skills they need to be effective partners, and what teachers need to know in order to be effective partners themselves.

The book is about more than an approach to teaching and assessment; it is about
- the nature of student learning;
- the nature of the relationship that needs to be present to sustain that learning;
- what the teacher needs to do in order for students to learn powerfully and effectively.

When teachers use these approaches the classroom becomes one in which:

1. **Student achievement improves:** when students have a clearer understanding of what achievement looks like, they have a greater chance of achieving; and they do.

2. **Student behaviour improves:** once students really engage in learning, their behaviour improves because their attention is focused on learning.

   - *'The way I speak to the children has changed and is now more learning-focused and I've seen a real improvement in the behaviour of the kids.'*

3. **Student ownership of learning improves:** the students have a clearer idea of their learning journey because they are fully involved in every step of the process.

   - *'They tell me what they need help with, they really do. It just amazes me what they know. I thought, "Oh, they won't be able to think up how I could help them", but they do, they really do.'*
   - *'The children can see where they need help and how well they are going. It's amazing really how honest and sincere their judgements become.'*
   - *'They learn to think about how their learning is going and what else they need help with. They're more confident to ask for help. Much more willing to stay on the mat for further support.'*

4. **Student engagement increases:** the quality of work becomes more important than the quantity, and the students — being more focused on their own learning — are keen to see their own growth and progress.

   - *'They are more focused, they can see where they're going and what they're able to do. They have strategies to use, they have more confidence and can see the results of their efforts.'*
   - *'It [learning intentions] sets things out clearly in your mind, and with the success criteria it's a really good way to know what you still don't quite understand.'*

5. **Enjoyment returns to teaching:** because everything to do with student behaviour is focused on learning, the quality of the working environment is good for everyone.

- *'All my conversations with the children are about learning and I no longer have to nag.'*
- *'It's revitalised my teaching, it's given me a burst of enthusiasm. It's given me more energy and it's more rewarding and the students are far more focused on their achievement.'*
- *'I haven't felt like this about my teaching for years, it's just great.'*
- *'It brings the joy back into teaching again.'*

This book is about how you can create these conditions in your classroom. It begins by outlining a view of learning, that we see as a precondition to all of the understandings needed by teachers and students to create effective conditions for learning. It then provides a detailed description of what these understandings are, the implications for planning, and finally, how family can be brought into partnership with teacher and student to further support learning.

'Learning's the thing'

Every teacher knows a lot about the nature of learning. In our view there are two critical aspects to learning that should be highlighted from the beginning.

Learning, to be effective, must enable
the learner to 'own' the learning *process*

Owning a new skill, concept or understanding can only be achieved through a process of deep engagement with the skill, concept or understanding; practising it, trying it out, using it. Marie Clay (2005) describes how young children actively work at learning to read and write:

' . . . young constructive readers and writers work at problem-solving sentences and messages, choose between alternatives, read and write sentences, work on word after word, with the flexibility to change responses rapidly at any point. As they attend to several different kinds of knowledge, they are searching, selecting, rejecting, self-monitoring, and self-correcting.'

Most young children do learn with minimal teacher intervention; they do it because they want to learn what others know.

As teachers, we commit a grave disservice against students when we merely want them to know how others think about things. This causes us to privilege passivity over activity in learning, and removes a large part of the incentive for students to learn. If all we have to do as students is demonstrate that we have learnt how others understand things, what is in it for us? The understanding of others is of no use to us, unless it helps us to improve our understanding of the world, and we will not know this unless we, ourselves, can produce a better understanding. For example, we don't learn language merely to know what others think and understand. We learn it to enable others to know what we think. We learn it to be able to put our perspective *on* the world *to* the world. We can only practise putting our perspective by putting our perspective. To learn to be active we have to be active. To learn from others' wisdom, we have to practise interpreting their wisdom in terms of our own understandings.

The best learners are not those who follow our rules about how they should learn, but those who listen to our rules and then follow them if and as it suits them as they determinedly pursue their own learning. These people are *originators*: they ask, they challenge, they try out their own tests and ideas of what a concept or skill is really about; they constantly show initiative and are creative; they want the concepts for themselves so they can see and understand the world better. Good teaching supports all students in enhancing their ability to be originators. Too much learning in classrooms is passive.

Learning is the process of testing for a difference between what you currently do or understand, and what you want to do or be able to understand; and being able to take informed action and problem-solve to reduce the gap. If we want to write 'better', then we have to compare what we do write with 'better' writing and find ways to reduce the gap. This is what learning is about. Teaching is about motivating students to identify the gap and helping them find ways to reduce it.

As learning progresses, new gaps become visible and need to be reduced in the same way. Classroom activity is not about learning if it is not about gap reduction.

Learning, to be significant, must result in the learner 'owning' *what is learnt*

'Ownership' of what is learnt is gained when the learner can use new skills or concepts as tools for themselves to see the world better or more clearly. Real learning is about engagement with the skills, concepts or understandings to be learnt, so we are able to make those skills, concepts and understandings our own and have them become part of how we interpret and interact with the world. The process of gaining ownership — the process of learning — progresses from 'I hear the concepts of others', to 'I know and understand the concepts of others', to 'I own for myself and can use creatively for my own purposes the concepts of others. They are now *my* concepts. My voice, my interpretation, my style, is visible in the way I describe and use these concepts'. Too much learning gets no further than halfway through the process.

Think about these examples of owning new learning.

1. Learning to ride a bike
Whenever a physical skill is the focus of learning, we acknowledge that active practice is important. It is never just a matter of learning 'how to ride a bike'; you want to learn to ride a bike.

Learning 'how' is an important part of the journey, but is certainly not the end destination. You know what skilled riding looks like and you attempt to imitate it. You attempt to reduce the gap between good riding and your riding. With repeated attempts — with practice — you find that you succeed. You practise, and practise, and practise. But that is not the end of your learning. As you become more skilful you realise that riding a bike is no longer something that you can merely do, you now have a sense of deep competence. You are no longer tentative about riding across the footpath, or along a narrow walkway, or of weaving in and out of the path of other cyclists. You make adjustments to your direction without thinking about it. You can even take your hands off the handlebars, show off a little, and continue to ride with minimal risk of falling off. You see yourself as a bit of a trick-cyclist. Riding is one of the things that you can do, it is your skill.

2. Learning to write by hand

In your early days at school, handwriting lessons went on day after day. It was never a matter of just learning 'how to write'. You have to go through the 'how' to actually learn to write, but as you practised you gradually managed to reduce the gap between your marks on the paper and the exemplars that the teacher put up on the board, and you came to know that the marks meant something.

Then something else began to happen. Over time your own personal style of handwriting began to develop and emerge and you noticed that it was different from that of all of the other students in your class, and certainly different from that of your teacher and parents. Eventually you even stopped having to think about how to form letters. Somehow, as you reduced the gap between the exemplar and what you produced, your own handwriting style emerged.

No one told you to do this, you did not think about it, it just happened. The active practice *transformed* the taught script into something that you alone *own*. Uniquely.

3. Learning to be numerate

The point of learning a concept is to learn it so well that it becomes a part of how the learner views the world. We do not want students just to know the number framework in mathematics. We want them to deeply understand it so they can apply it easily, automatically, and whenever they need it in their lives. We want them to be able to toss numbers around in their heads, rearrange them, create new patterns, look at patterns in new ways, play games with them; in short, we want them to be a bit of a trick-cyclist with numbers.

We don't want them to learn 'how to add, subtract, multiply and divide'. We want them to add, subtract, multiply and divide. Learning 'how to' leaves the skill or concept as a thing external to them. That is learning, but not as we want it. They have to learn 'how', but that by itself is not enough. Teaching students so they are numerate, rather than just knowing about numeracy, so they have their own personal style and approach to numbers, requires the same conditions for learning as those we have highlighted for handwriting and bike riding. We have to provide them with extended opportunities to become deeply skilful; to own numeracy. They need repeated opportunities to engage with the manipulation of numbers to solve a wider range of different problems; the more the better. If we do this, then over time the number system will come to be second nature to them.

4. Learning to speak

Who teaches us language? Learning language is a somewhat mysterious process, but we know that as we get better at it, especially at speaking and writing it, we do bring our own style to it. We learn it largely by active practice, within our socio-cultural community of language users. We learn it by using whatever vocabulary and grammatical control we have to try to communicate, and evaluating the feedback about our attempt — did the person understand us? Did the person use more elaborate language in their reply? Is there anything to suggest that there is a gap between my language ability and that of those around me? — and practising more elaborate language to try to reduce the gap. Over time, as we get better, we develop our own style of speaking and writing, using the grammatical conventions and the lexicon of our language, creatively and imaginatively, to communicate.

5. Learning physics at university
Science education research shows that students can learn disjointed sets of 'facts' and formulae relating to science that will enable them to pass exams, but leaves them feeling less positive about science, less confident that they understand it, less able to see themselves as scientists, and less able to see the relevance of what they have learnt (Weiman, 2005). These students have learnt concepts and rules of science to the point of understanding, but not to the point of ownership. If teaching leaves students feeling like this, what is the point?

6. Learning to teach
It is difficult to use 'learning to teach' as an example of owning the learning because so many of us were in fact taught to teach in ways that encouraged passivity in students, in ways that mimicked how we were taught as students. At training college, we were taught something of 'how to teach', but we did most of our learning to teach in our first years in the classroom. We learnt to teach by teaching. And we all developed our own styles of teaching. Whatever our approach, we own our own teaching; it becomes a part of us to the point where we describe ourselves as teachers.

The simple thesis of this book is that students need to be active managers, regulators and directors of their own learning if they are to learn to the stage where they genuinely own the learning. All classroom processes need to be directed towards supporting and enabling students to be the best managers of their own learning they can be. The role of the teacher is to model and scaffold the processes of learning, in order to support students as managers — at all times.

Lessons that support student ownership

What does a lesson that supports student ownership look like in a real classroom?

Table 1 on pages 16–19 gives a generic pattern for a lesson that will enable students to be real partners in the teaching/learning process and to develop the learning through to the stage of deep ownership. We show a normal lesson sequence, the general strategies that are appropriate at each part of the sequence, and the type of reaction students will give.

This generic lesson sequence has been given a context to enhance its use as an exemplar. The learning is about making a 'balloon dog', such as a clown might make at a children's party. This is a light-hearted learning, deliberately chosen so that you don't have to worry about its significance or relevance, or particular subject-specific teaching technique, and can focus instead on the lesson processes and how they support student engagement and partnership.

Points to note about this lesson sequence

In the introduction

The key objective is to get the students really engaged with the learning and the experiencing of success and the confidence to take risks — like attempting the next task. What you are looking for is very active, buzzy engagement; enabling students to really engage with *each* aspect of the lesson helps to achieve this, even if it does take some time. For example, having them evaluate the learning intention and the relevance of the learning intention, or to think of their own ideas as to why such learning is important — individually, in pairs, in fours, and then as a class — as it really brings them fully into partnership with you. It enables them to think about it almost as deeply as you did when you were doing the planning. This motivates them and gives them a commitment to the learning intention, but you do need to check that your strategy has been successful. Sometimes you know this from the buzz, but if that is not there, then you need to check. Checking, itself, helps build a learning-focused relationship as it shows students that you are really serious about staying in step with them and their learning. Sharing the learning intention and the success criteria is not just about enabling the students to be clear — in fact it is mainly about motivation, as you can see from the student's reactions.

The amount of time it takes to achieve this type of learning sequence will vary. In the example given in Table 1, the sequence is described in some detail, and when beginning a new unit of learning all the elements will be apparent. However, not every lesson will necessarily involve an explicit discussion of each of the elements. For example, relevance for tomorrow's lesson may simply be that we found it 'tricky' today, and it may be a one-sentence discussion to establish that relevance. It would be unlikely that an observer would be able to identify each of the elements in every lesson, but that does not mean they are not there.

The sequence described in the example is not invariant either. While lessons always manage to start and finish, there are many variations on the order of events in the middle. The exact order needs to be driven by the needs of the students and the thinking the teacher has done about how to introduce the learning. For example, preparing for new learning might well come before you show an exemplar. In the example given, the teacher might have asked students just to try and make a dog shape out of a balloon before showing an exemplar.

Catering for diverse needs

Each student who does not have their learning needs catered for by the lesson arrangement becomes alienated, to some extent, from learning. Their learning comes to a halt because the conditions for them to learn are not present. Depending on their skill and assertiveness levels, over time this can build up to be a major problem.

Building our ability to support student ownership

Research has confirmed what we know from our experience. Lists of core principles for effective teaching that best support students can be located easily. Here is one such list:

- Set high expectations and give every learner confidence they can succeed.
- Establish what learners already know and build on it.
- Structure and pace the learning experience to make it challenging and enjoyable.

	TABLE 1: LESSON OR UNIT SEQUENCE FOR LEARN
	Strategy
Planning	• Plan the lesson or unit in some detail, taking into account what you know of the students' prior knowledge. (See Chapter 9 on planning; also see introduction bel for the second part of planning.)
Introduction Sharing learning intentions	• Talk with the students about what you are intending that they learn, and why: 'We are going to learn how to make a dog shape from a balloon.' Make sure you explain why you think it is an important and relevant learning.
Modelling/exemplars	• Use models, exemplars, examples, and modelling as appropriate to clarify the intended learning; distinguish between *what* you want them to learn and *how* y want them to learn it.
Checking clarity	• Check the extent to which students are clear about the learning intentions; mak you are not just checking their compliance.
Checking motivation	• Check that students are reasonably motivated to learn; this might be done verba non-verbally; real buy-in is critical and if it is not there then you need to know wl you are going to do to get it. • Check if the students are confident of the learning or if they have apprehension: may need to be allayed.
Sharing process	• Share planning for the whole lesson with the students and seek their views abou whether it will meet their needs – they may be happy to test out your planning they go along – they may know that you plan well and design powerful learning experiences for them.
Success criteria	• Introduce the idea of how students will know when they have successfully learn what is intended (success criteria). Either the teacher provides the success criteri describes what they mean and why they are there, or success criteria are built w the students from an examination of an exemplar. Each dog will have two ears, head, four legs, a body and a tail. • Check that the students understand the success criteria.

Preparing for new learning: 'roaming' in the known	• Students spend some time individually or in groups, exploring what they know a about the topic and hypothesising, visualising or attempting what is to be learn 'Take one balloon each and have a go at making a dog shape without any help from anyone.'
	 • This might mean seeing what they can already do with the knowledge or skill, a getting a feel for what is coming up, by
	   – having a quick skim read of a textbook chapter and thinking about wh bits of it are familiar and which are not;
	   – writing a description of a person (character) without prior instruction;
	   – making mind maps of what is known about the topic so far and of wha new learning might look like;

W TO MAKE A DOG SHAPE OUT OF A BALLOON

lent reaction/thinking

t is good to be included at this stage in considering what to learn next; it is respectful of me as a learner and allows me genuinely appreciate the need to learn [it]. Having examples of what we are learning to do is really helpful in giving ne a sense of the "big picture".'

When the teacher checks whether I understand it helps affirm my role in the learning and to be active in doing the work of earning. It is the same when the teacher checks my motivation. At times I'm not convinced that what is intended is worth earning and I would rather do something else. I need to be motivated and the teacher needs to know this. Sometimes I have een very nervous about my next steps in learning, especially at times like moving to another school or starting a new subject. really appreciate the teacher recognising that I feel like this. Most of the time I am happy to learn. That is what school is for.'

Having a look at the planning gives me a chance to get an overview of how the teacher is thinking about how my earning might proceed. It also lets me see if there are bits that might be extra interesting or fun.'

 like having a look at the success criteria, and I don't mind whether the teacher tells us what they are or if we derive nem with her. If we derive them we really get a good sense of the main features of what we are trying to learn, but ometimes it is more sensible just for the teacher to explain the ones she has listed to us. At these times it is pretty bvious why they are as they are and spending time deriving them would not be worth it.'

'hat she checks that we understand the success criteria is really important; just because she has explained them doesn't nean that I understand them at all. I like the way she really invites us to indicate if we don't and how she finds another vay of explaining them to those of us who are still stuck. We learn a lot like this.'

Getting us to have a go first is really good because it really focuses you on what your starting point is with the learning; gives you a chance to test out whether you know anything or not. Sometimes you can surprise yourself and discover you now a lot more than you thought. If you didn't try first of all then you are not going to be paying as much attention.'

 know intuitively that learning is an active process that consists of making new connections and new meanings: the more ction, the more learning. Speaking is better to assist with learning than listening is. Writing is better than reading. You an learn through listening and reading, but you learn more from speaking and writing because expressing your thoughts bout what you are learning forces you to make more connections with existing knowledge and therefore make new leanings, and therefore you learn.'

TABLE 1 continued:	
	Strategy
	– examining the results of a pre-test that they are aware of to see what concepts, skills or abilities they already have and which ones they don't
	– contemplating or imagining what the learning is likely to mean; a ment[a] rehearsal.
	• Roaming might take 30 seconds, or up to an hour. Occasionally it takes longer t[ ] this in order to build the confidence of the learner to be ready for a new step.
Teaching	• Explanation or demonstration of what is to be learnt:
	– Teacher says: 'Now that you have had a chance to make a dog by yours[ ] — and some of you know a lot of the tricks to doing it — I am going t[o] show you the first step and then let you have a go. It will only take a sh[ ] time so even if you know the first steps I want you to watch because yo[ ] might pick up some tips for refining what you do.'
	• Check that students have sufficient understanding to have a go themselves; repe[ ] explain in a different way if necessary.
Student activity	• Student tries to make the first part of the dog.
Self-assessment	• Student compares their effort with the relevant success criteria, the exemplar an[ ] with the efforts of their peers.
Peer-assessment and feedback	• Student seeks comment from peers, especially from peers who seem to have ma[ ] the activity better.
	• Student has another go based on the feedback from peers.
Teacher assessment and promotion of further learning	• Teacher talks through their assessment process by comparing the success criteri[a] the student's efforts:
	– 'You held the balloon with the uninflated end pointing away from you [ ] that as you squeezed the balloon to make parts of the dog the squeezed had somewhere to go. Good. That is exactly right. But now, as you squ[ ] and twist you need to stretch the balloon a bit more, like this. Okay?'
Further cycles of learning and teaching occur . . . then	
Active reflection	• Teacher reviews the lesson with the students and asks them how they found it in ter[ ]
	– their overall interest in and engagement with the lesson;
	– what the main teaching points were that they needed to pay most attenti[ ]
	– progress with learning content; understanding the tricky bits, the bits t[ ] need going over again, etc;
	– satisfaction with lesson process; what worked, what didn't, how the lea[ ] partnership worked;
	– the big picture in terms of where they should go next with further lear[ ]
	• Students are asked to reflect in ways that are suitable to the lesson process and intended learnings, with an emphasis on 'active' reflection; they might be asked
	– explain to their peers the main points about balloon-dog making;
	– write the process down and to check it with a neighbour;
	– have a brief class discussion about the process;
	– plan out how to teach it to another class.
	The teacher looks for a process that engages every student as actively as possible.

dent reaction/thinking

This sounds reasonable enough. I can be patient so that all the other kids can see the demo, but I reckon I am on top of it.'

My chance to have a go!'

This is not this easy. I thought I had it sussed but doing it is not the same as thinking about doing it.'

That is really interesting – my friend managed to do it better. She has given me some hints as to what I could try. I reckon we could all figure this out ourselves if we had time.'

like the way the teacher analyses what I am trying to do (assessment) and gives me suggestions (promotes further learning) as to how to improve. I also like that she really checks that I have found the feedback useful before she moves on to the next student.'

like the opportunity to reflect on and review my learning and to listen to how the teacher and the other students found it. I find that it deepens my understanding of what I learnt and it gives me a chance to put my own experience of the lesson into context and actually consolidate my understanding of the trickier bits as I talk or write about it and I hear other students talk about it. I can work out what I need to really focus on or practise next time.'

t also nicely rounds the lesson off and sets it up for next time; it makes me, the learner, feel central to all that happened because it is me, the learner, that is doing the reflection.'

- Inspire learning through a passion for the subject.
- Make individual learners active partners in their learning.
- Develop learning skills in the learners.

Department for Education and Skills, 2004

Who would disagree with this list? It makes sense. It has an obvious face-value to it. And it doesn't surprise anyone that this list is distilled from the extensive research into effective teaching. But just how do you make your classroom one in which all of these characteristics are present?

Clarity in the Classroom is designed to help teachers to be able to create conditions for learning consistent with all of these principles. The book has been written as a response to conversations with classroom teachers as they have worked with us to grow their capability to use formative assessment strategies. We find teachers continually grapple with 'How can I best meet the learning needs of my students?', and 'Where do I find the time to do all that is expected of me in order to do this?', and 'How do I get my students to be interested in learning?' We want this book to give straightforward and applicable answers to these questions. It is intended as an easily accessible resource for busy teachers who wish to understand and implement the key research-based concepts that underpin assessment for learning and effective teaching.

Formative assessment and organisational psychology

The basis for the ideas described in the book is sourced from two separate and significant literatures. The first comes from the formative assessment literature and the second is from the organisational psychology literature into interpersonal effectiveness.

The research into formative assessment has been compelling in helping so many teachers to rethink the strategies and techniques they use in their classrooms. Black & Wiliam (1998) define formative assessment as:

'The process used by teachers and students to recognise and respond to student learning in order to enhance that learning, during the learning.'

This definition recognises the students as central participants in the teaching/learning endeavour. We see this as critical.

'Assessment for learning involves using assessment in the classroom to raise pupils' achievement. It is based on the idea that pupils will improve most if they understand the aim of their learning, where they are in relation to this aim and how they can achieve the aim (or close the gap in their knowledge).'

Qualifications & Curriculum Authority, 2005

The formative assessment literature is where our thinking began and this origin can be seen in the title of this book. The core strategies most commonly described in this literature now form the basis of most descriptions of good teaching and have caused a transformation in the relationship between teacher and student. For example, Black & Wiliam, in their seminal publication in 1998, *Inside the Black Box*, identify five key factors that improve learning through assessment, that can be summarised as:

1. Recognition of the profound influence the motivation and self-esteem of learners have on learning.
2. Active involvement of learners in identifying learning goals and criteria for knowing when these are achieved.
3. Adjustment of teaching to take account of the results of assessment.
4. Provision of effective, timely feedback to learners.
5. Support for learners to be able to assess themselves, reflect on their learning and to understand how to improve.

However, by itself, this literature amounts to a set of valuable approaches and techniques about how to teach and about how to learn; it lacks an adequate underpinning theory of learning within the context of a teaching/learning relationship.

Teaching is about relationship management as much as it is about anything else and guidance is needed about how to ensure that that relationship is conducive to learning. A theory about learning-oriented relationships can provide structure and coherence — a philosophy, a direction — that provides teachers with a set of rules for when to use particular strategies and techniques within the context of such a relationship. To meet this need we turned to literature on increasing professional effectiveness, in particular the work of Argyris & Schön (1974). Their work is based on an examination of human action in social systems, particularly professional organisations. They have developed a theory of learning that describes the conditions necessary for increasing the capacity of all people to learn, and in particular, how to learn to build relationships through identifying and solving relationship problems that would otherwise sink the relationship or cause it to become ineffective. A theory of learning that improves the capacity of teachers and learners to nurture the quality of the relationship, as well as the quality of the actual (curriculum) learning, provides a solid platform on which to build practical classroom-based formative assessment strategies and techniques. That the two literatures sit comfortably with one another can be seen from the following two quotes. The first is from Royce Sadler (1989) who describes the process of formative assessment as one in which:

> '. . . the learner has to (a) possess a concept of the standard (or goal/reference level) being aimed for, (b) compare the actual (or current) level of performance with the standard, and (c) engage in appropriate action which leads to some closure of the gap.' (p. 121)

The second is from Argyris & Schön in an introduction to their 1974 book:

> 'We identified two outcomes of learning: first, creating a match between intentions and effect. . . . and second, detecting and correcting a mismatch. In both cases, the criteria for learning include not only the framing of an idea or design but also its implementation. How do you know when you know something — when you can produce what you say you know?'

Both literatures are about the nature of learning, about the nature of *inquiry*. Learning is about making and *testing* attributions about the world, increasing the discussability and testability of propositions, and creating the conditions to make informed choices that reduce the gap between where the learner is and where the learner wants to be.

We have used these two literatures to build a comprehensive approach to describing what both teachers and students need to be able to know and do in order to maximise student learning. This description is shaped as an integrated set of principles, strategies and techniques grouped into two parallel sets of six capabilities; one for teachers, one for students.

We define a capability as the ability to meet demands or carry out a task successfully. It consists of cognitive and non-cognitive dimensions. A capability has an internal structure that includes knowledge, cognitive skills, practical skills, attitudes, emotions, values, ethics and motivation. We like to think of each capability as a tidy package of principles, knowledge, skills and understandings, which teachers and learners progressively develop to deeper and deeper levels of understanding throughout their careers and lives.

We see each set of six capabilities linked together and configured as an arch that supports and protects learning. (See Figure 1 on page 24.)

The archway of teaching and learning capabilities

We have used a stone archway as a metaphor for the capabilities needed in teaching and learning, because of the inherent strength of the arch structure. In architecture, an arch is a curved structure used as a support over an open space, as in a doorway or room, usually made from cut stone blocks forming interlocking wedges. When it is well constructed it stands by itself; it is a protective structure. Whatever is within the arch is shielded from the outside — and can therefore get on with its business — in this case teaching and learning. There are two fundamental parts to the archway; the foundation and the keystone.

Capability one: building a learning-focused relationship

An archway is a solid structure and needs a solid foundation. Teaching and learning is founded on the quality of the relationship built between teacher and student. This relationship is the foundation for learning upon which all else rests. The teacher must know how to manage the motivational climate of the classroom, and how to foster and build a learning-focused relationship with students, so that students have optimal opportunity to build their own motivation to learn. To play their part in this relationship, students themselves need to develop certain capabilities. The greater their possession of these capabilities, the richer the learning relationship will be, and the more effective the learning.

Capability two: clarity about what is to be learnt

At the top of the arch is the keystone which closes the arch and locks the entire structure together. Without the keystone the arch will collapse, irrespective of the quality of the foundation and of the other blocks. The keystone represents clarity about what is to be learnt; unless both teacher and student are clear about what is to be learnt, why it is to be learnt, and how it is to be learnt, then teaching and learning will collapse.

In addition to these two key components there are four other major blocks in the archway.

Capability three: assessment for learning

Assessment for learning is about the understandings and strategies students and teachers need in order to

- involve students richly in the assessment of their learning;
- be able to gather dependable information about the status of a student's (or group of students') learning;
- share this information and co-construct the implications for the current learning status and what might be learnt next;
- gather and aggregate information dependably about the needs of groups of students;
- skilfully interpret and evaluate information for individuals and groups of students in order to decide on what might be done next to support learning;
- know how to build students' self- and peer-assessment strategies;
- contribute evidence to partnerships of learning (parents, colleagues, boards, etc).

Capability four: promoting further learning

Promoting further learning is about the strategies and techniques used to close the gap between the current state of learning and the current desired goal. It naturally follows on from assessment; it is what you do once you have assessed.

There are five different strategies that promote further learning:

1. **Explanation:** where either a new explanation of a phenomenon is given, or additional information is provided.
2. **Feedback:** to focus attention on aspects or features of the learning context, to increase the salience of those features, to reduce the gap; this can be given as statements or questions — verbal or non-verbal — and uses modelling, exemplars, reminders and scaffolding.
3. **Learning conversation:** where a concept or argument is examined through extended discussion where both learner and teacher are equal participants; this encourages participants to reflect and think independently and critically, so that self-confidence in one's own thinking is enhanced.
4. **Reinforcement:** where affirmation is given for any closing or narrowing of the gap in a way that is appropriate for the learner (may be extrinsic, more likely to be intrinsic).
5. **Feedforward:** where pointing to the next learning steps illuminates aspects of current performance.

Both students and teachers need to develop skills in using the strategies. Students also have to develop the skill of prompting teachers when they need help, or when the strategy the teacher used didn't work for them.

Capability five: active reflection

Both teaching and learning are more effective when teacher and student take time to think about, review and enhance the learning process, and when the learner reviews and rehearses the understanding of what was to be learnt.

Capability six: clarity about next learning steps

Being clear about the possible next learning steps is critical for any teacher serious about co-constructing deep learning experiences with students. This is dependent on the teacher having a deep knowledge of the subject and a good understanding of the progressions of learning within that. Teachers then need to be able to expose this subject knowledge to students and enable them to be co-collaborators in constructing their next learning step.

The archway

This book is about these capabilities; what they are, how they are applied, and what results you can expect when you apply them to the classroom.

As our understanding of formative assessment has grown, we have come to see that emphasis has to be placed on enabling the learner to be active in every aspect of the teaching/learning process. Teaching is only about motivating and supporting the student to make considered and reflective decisions about his or her learning. The learner is at the heart of it all.

Figure 1: Archway of teaching and learning capabilities

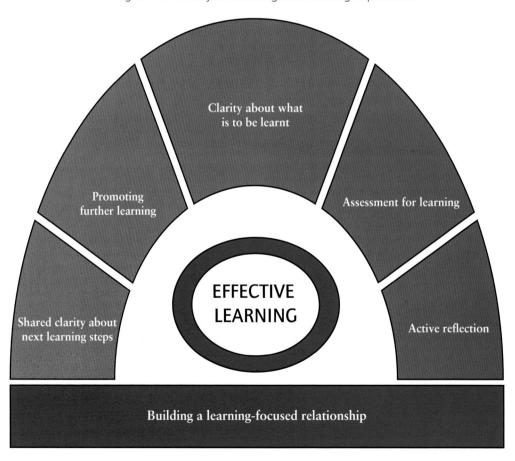

TRY THIS!
— within the first week with your new class

Tell your students that you want a class in which each and every one of them is going to learn and feel like a learner all year. You want everyone to learn what it means to learn, and to be a learner, so that everyone can learn all year.

Tell them that for this to happen all of them need to explore what it means to learn and come up with a joint understanding of what this means for them and for you — together you need to unpack the idea of learning — to develop the success criteria for learning how to learn. You then need to develop some activities that will assess how good everyone (including you) is at learning, and then help them (and you) to become better learners.

Some ideas for shaping the success criteria
As a class:

* Brainstorm 'What is learning? What does it mean to be a learner?'
* Use your brainstorm to write student definitions of what learning means; combine these to write a class definition.
* Read together the dictionary definition and review what the thesaurus has to say about learning.
* Use a Y chart to discuss what students think learning looks like, sounds like and feels like.
* What gets in the way of us learning?; What are our fears about learning?; How might we overcome, and help each other overcome, these fears?
* Summarise all of the above into 4 to 6 criteria that would define a learner.
* Have everyone, including yourself, assess themselves against the criteria.
* Have everyone, working individually and in small groups, develop activities and routines that will help each individual learn to be a better learner; have each student write these up for themselves; what about an overall class action plan?
* Decide on when you are going to reassess the success of this learning plan.

Possible activities to support learning plans

* Have a class competition to come up with a learning slogan for their room; for example, in one classroom that did this, the slogan was 'learning is mission possible' and it was displayed above the whiteboard, where most new learning was introduced.
* To differentiate between playtime and learning time, have a class sign on your door; for example, Welcome to Room 11: you are now entering a learning zone. Discuss with your class what you expect to hear and see inside, compared with what would be acceptable in the playground; you may discuss the difference between a learning conversation and a conversation that might be overheard in the playground.
* On your door or written on the whiteboard may be a learning question or a thought for the day, to get the class thinking before the day begins.
* Display quotes which are related to learning and discuss what it means to them as individuals and as a class, for example:

- Do more than just exist — live!
- Do more than just touch — feel!
- Do more than just look — see!
- Do more than just hear — listen!
- Do more than just talk — say something!
- Every piece of work is a self-portrait of the person who did it. Autograph your work with quality.
- Set learning goals as a class, display them and regularly reflect on them.
- Have a class photo board, with photos showing learning in action pinned up or a photo album of learning achievements.
- Display 'bling' moments, where as a class you celebrate learning and share good practice. (Bling moments are times where individuals have exciting insights; 'blings', 'eureka' or 'ah-hah' moments about their own learning. These are jotted on a display board and time is given to enable the student to talk about and celebrate the moment.)

Chapter 2

LEARNING-FOCUSED RELATIONSHIPS

What is a learning-focused relationship?

What it is

A learning-focused relationship is a relationship between a teacher and a student the sole purpose of which is to support student learning. The student's role in the relationship is only to learn. The student focuses on 'what has to happen *now* that will best help me learn?' The teacher's role is only to help the student learn. The teacher focuses on 'what do I need to do *now* to best help this student learn?'

A learning-focused relationship is one where *both* the student and the teacher know that by working together, the quality of student learning will be much better and the standard of achievement will be much higher.

It is one where *both* the teacher and the student *want* to work together on the learning.

It is one where *both* the teacher and the student know *how* to work together on the learning. Picture this:

You are an outdoor education teacher taking a group of learners for their first lesson in abseiling. They have all agreed to take part. Every member of the group has agreed that they will abseil down the cliff at the conclusion of the lesson. None of them have done this before. Some are very anxious, not seeing themselves as outdoor types, or 'having done anything like this before'. Others are more confident.

You begin your instruction. What you immediately notice is that ALL members of the group have given you their complete attention. Some have questions based on clarifying their understanding of what they are about to learn how to do: jump off a cliff.

As you model and describe how to attach the safety harness you can see members making small body and hand movements that imitate the movements that you are making as you fit your own harness. They are attending as closely as they can and are checking their interpretation of what you are doing through their mental imitations.

Then it is their turn to fit their harnesses. All of them want you to personally check that they have fitted it correctly. *All* that get stuck ask for help. None are too shy in these circumstances to just stay quiet at the back. They keep asking for help and for feedback until they are confident that they are doing it right. Some do it correctly first time. Others are very anxious and you have to take them through very small steps and provide them with much assurance, as they practise, that they have got each step exactly right. You move from person to person, helping them with whatever they are stuck with. They might want a repeat demonstration, or the demonstration broken down into sections, so that they can practise each section. Or they might want you to scaffold in some way just the small section they cannot quite get. They also watch their peers and learn from the ones who seem to have it sussed.

But none of them are happy to have their peers do the final check for them; they want you, the teacher, the expert, to do the final check.

You pause for a short time and ask them as a group how their learning is going, if they are finding some bits difficult or if there are some things they would like you to do differently. They reflect on what they have done, make mental assessments of where they have got up to and there is some comment about how you have sequenced the teaching. You adjust what you do next accordingly.

When everyone has mastered attaching the safety harness you begin to describe how to manage the interplay between the ropes and the carabineer, and how to tie the knot to secure the rope. Despite what you see as the awesome clarity of your explanation, you find a number of the group quite assertively asking you to repeat your demonstration and to do it slower.

They all start trying to imitate your procedure. Many get stuck at different points and, as with the safety harness, they want your individual attention to sort it out, although they also watch their peers carefully and seek help from any that seem to have it sorted: the anxious ones doubly so. If you had provided them with diagrams that show how the knots looked, they may well have referred to them and discussed these with their peers. They each keep practising until each of them is happy that both you and they believe that they have mastered the routine as much as they possibly can before the final test of going down the cliff.

The relationship between the teacher and the students in this example *is* a learning-focused relationship; both parties are motivated to ensure high-quality learning. They know what is to be learnt and how they will know when they have learnt it. All the learners differ in their confidence about their ability to learn to abseil, and differ in their prior knowledge and experience. Both parties recognise the contribution the aggregate of these differing backgrounds makes to the whole teaching and learning experience. There is a sense of urgency and importance about the teaching and the learning. The learner is actively controlling and adjusting the learning, and the teacher is actively responsive to the learner. Both parties are reflecting on how the learning is going and adjusting the teaching and/or the learning accordingly.

Why a learning-focused relationship is so important
Research (for example, Black & Wiliam, 1998) conclusively shows that students who are active in their learning, who are motivated to learn, who manage the amount of new information they get at any one time, who practise, who seek descriptive feedback, who test their learning and reflect on their learning, learn much better than those who experience passive learning situations. Given that this is the case, then the role of the school and of the teacher is to manage the teaching/learning environment to maximise active and self-regulated learning. A foundational step in establishing this type of environment is the creation of the right type of relationship — a learning-focused relationship — with the student.

Active learners in a normal classroom
The abseiling scenario is an ideal learning situation (it is easy to get learners to listen and learn when they feel their lives are at stake), but what it does is bring into sharp relief the way strongly motivated learners are assertive about their learning and the significant expectations they have of their teachers.

Getting a student, who has no option but to be at school whether they like it or not, to be as motivated and as self-regulating about learning in the classroom as the (older) students who have opted, for whatever reason, to learn to abseil, is the subject of the next chapter. But imagine for a moment that you are the teacher and that you do have highly motivated students arriving for you to teach this morning. What would it be like? What would their expectations be?

- The first thing you would notice is an obvious keenness from the students; they would be eager and buzzing about their expectations for learning; there would be a slight nervousness and tension; and they would turn up on time with all the resources they need.
- They would have high expectations of your energy, commitment, knowledge and ability.
- They would expect you to be very clear about what you thought they might need to learn and why; they would expect you to have planned how the lesson and the learning might go.
- They would expect you to like them; to respect who they are as people, whatever their background and culture.
- They would expect you to be able to support them if they still needed to build motivation or confidence.
- They would expect you to support them if they still needed to learn the skills to be self-regulating, without your attention to their special needs excessively compromising the learning of all the other students.
- They would expect you to be able to talk through your intentions for the lesson and to be happy to negotiate changes that seemed to better meet the learning needs of the whole class.
- They would expect you to have planned to give them sufficient time to learn.
- They would expect that you would establish mechanisms that would enable both them and you to monitor learning progress so that difficulties could be identified and changes could be made to the learning activities if this seemed warranted.
- They would expect you to help them identify and celebrate significant achievement of important learning goals.
- Finally, they would want to respectfully, but assertively, raise any gap between what they expect from you and what they perceive you are giving so that, with you, the gap can be closed.

To be able to do all of this in a learning situation as formal as compulsory schooling requires significant motivation and skill on the part of the student. To be able to meet expectations like these from your students requires significant skill on your part; and even more skill to be able to teach the learners to be assertive and respectful. But if the goal is a genuine learning-focused relationship, then this is what must happen. And in the first instance it is up to the teacher to bring it about.

'My [six-year-old] students had been taught last year by a teacher who had learnt to use assessment for learning strategies. When they came to me at the beginning of the year, one of the first things they asked me was "What are we going to learn this year?" They were very inquisitive and asked me why

I thought they should learn those things and how it might all happen. I thought that was fantastic because it also put me on the spot. I knew that they were not going to be satisfied with doing any old thing. They had high expectations of me as their teacher! They wanted to learn and they expected that I would have what it took to teach them. Fantastic!'

Year 2/3 Teacher

'In my school this year, as teachers have engaged their students more fully in co-construction, especially in Years 7 and 8, the kids are looking lighter, not as burdened. Get the learning right and the behaviour will largely take care of itself.'

School Principal

What it is not
Controlling

What gets focused on, flourishes. We want learning to flourish. It will not flourish if the teacher focuses primarily on controlling the student. 'Being controlled' is not what abseiling students who are desperate to be taught before they go down the cliff want or need.

In a relationship that is about power and control the teacher explicitly organises the classroom arrangements and the teaching to minimise the ability of students to exercise any agency (decision-making power) about their learning without the express permission of the teacher. Classrooms used to be very clearly about the teacher controlling the students and the learning. Learning in a classroom was seen as, essentially, an activity in which the role of the student was to passively and obediently receive the wisdom and knowledge of the teacher. We can have sympathy for this approach in classrooms, no physically bigger than today's, when they held 60 students or more and many of the students did not conform to the comparatively gentle school social norms of today. Playground fights were a regular part of playtime entertainment, and corporal punishment was just a part of the culture.

A teacher who believes that students need to be controlled limits the extent to which a deep and rich learning relationship can be developed with students. Even when the teacher only controls the classroom organisation so that learning can occur efficiently, there is a reduction in the motivation and capacity of the students to learn. Why? Because the most effective and intense learning relationship comes from the circumstance where both student and teacher share the construction of the entire environment. This does not need to be prolonged, or require both parties to endure endless discussion. The teacher should offer an initial structure, sequence and process, but should also offer genuine opportunities for the students to renegotiate any of it if they have good reason, in terms of its suitability, for their learning. All limitations that the teacher imposes on what can be co-constructed reduces the efficacy of the learning relationship and increases the extent to which the student experiences any learning that occurs as a reactive and passive process.

A controlling relationship can be established in very subtle ways. For example, research (Delpit, 1988) shows that teachers can act to exercise power in ways that are very subtle, and confuse students rather than helping them to understand the processes of learning and the different learning-oriented roles within the classroom. Often (controlling) teachers favour indirect communication that doesn't tell students clearly what is required of them.

For example, teachers might say things like, 'would you like to sit on the mat?' when it would be far clearer to use the directive, 'come and sit on the mat' which is what the teacher wants the students to do and is entitled to tell them to do. By expressing themself indirectly, the teacher is suggesting that the students have a choice, and therefore have agency with regard to that choice, when in fact they don't. The teacher knows that there is no choice, but she has suggested to the students that there is. Therefore they know less about the situation than she does, which puts her in the (controlling) position of being able to unilaterally judge what they do.

> **Question:** How do you know that you do *not* have a learning-focused relationship with a student?
> **Answer:** When you demand of a child, 'Where are your manners, boy?' and the answer comes back, 'Up there on the wall, Miss.' (Pointing to a laminated poster.)
>
> Not only do you have a controlling relationship in which you exercise control through playing the game of 'guess what is in my head so that I can tell you whether you are right or wrong', but you have not taught the boy an understanding at all of what you mean by manners.

TABLE 2: DIFFERENT PERSPEC'

1. Controlling perspective	2. Learning-focused perspective
The teacher sees Allan as someone	The teacher sees Allan as someone
• who has to learn to do what he is told, when he is told; he doesn't know how to behave;	• who has more to learn than many of his peers about how to be a focused learner in a classroom. (If he is to learn these things they must become an explicit priority of his learning agenda with regular monitoring by the teacher and Allan of his progress. The teacher may need upskilling in how to teach Allan some of these things.);
• who has little interest in learning;	• who will be interested in learning if compelling ways to show him 'what's in it for him' can be found, and if he has success at learning things that do matter to him;
• who has tantrums and angry outbursts which are very disruptive for the rest of the class and they need to be managed firmly;	• whose tantrums and anger outbursts are something he needs to be taught strategies to monitor, manage and eliminate in a classroom;

The two left-hand columns in Table 2 below show how the differences between a controlling perspective and a learning-focused perspective of a student might look. Allan's parents have drug addictions and there is some history of violence towards the children.

Caring

What gets focused on, flourishes. We want learning to flourish. It will not flourish if the teacher focuses primarily on the care of the student. Caring is not the purpose of the relationship. Of course, there is absolutely nothing wrong with caring for your students. For some students, the teacher may well be the only person that *does* care for them and that relationship may be highly valued by the student, but it is quite different from teaching them. Caring is not what is wanted by abseiling students who are about go down the cliff for the first time.

To teach you don't *have* to care for your students; you do *have* to care for their learning. To care for their learning you do have to respect them as people, and respect their capacity to learn. There is a big difference between respect for a person and caring for a person. When you genuinely respect someone as a (young) person you simply offer them exactly what you would want them to offer you: a reciprocal, mutual, deep sense of equality in your 'personness'. You want to think as well of them as you would want them to think of you. By consistently offering this respect you also build their capacity for self-respect and esteem.

TEACHERS CAN HOLD OF A STUDENT	
3. Caring perspective	**4. Activity-focused perspective**
The teacher sees Allan as someone	The teacher sees Allan as someone
• who has huge learning needs but has so many barriers to his learning because of his home circumstances;	• who finds it very hard to settle;
• who you have to tiptoe around so that he does not get upset. He is often not on task and doesn't complete work. Not too much can be expected because of how he is: 'Hopefully he will improve in time if I am patient with him and affirm him, as much as possible.';	• who has a short attention span and needs to be kept engaged in activities; • who needs activities that he can enjoy and that keep changing in some way so that he does not get bored;
• who needs opportunities to talk about what has upset him and why he gets angry;	• for whom the tasks usually need to involve gross motor and manipulation: he is not too good with fine motor or cognitive tasks;
• who has tantrums and outbursts which are evidence of how needy he is; • who seldom does homework because it is too difficult for him given his home circumstances;	• whose tantrums and outbursts are evidence of how needy he is;

TABLE 2 continued:	
1. Controlling perspective	2. Learning-focused perspective
The teacher sees Allan as someone	The teacher sees Allan as someone
• who it is good to get out of the classroom at times because he can be a nuisance in it, make the rest of the class harder to manage, and disrupts the learning of the rest of them;	• who cannot afford to spend any more time than any of his peers in the playground, helping the caretaker, running messages or sitting outside the principal's office unless these are used as learning opportunities;
• who needs firmness and consistency to keep him in line; • who, when he is taught, needs to listen, and do as he is told;	• who needs firmness and consistency when helping him learn how to behave in the classroom in ways that are consistent with being an active learner;
• about whom they know what he needs to learn;	• about whom they know what he needs to learn but can't be sure that it is actually right for him until it has been discussed;
• who you can only give as much choice as he is capable of exercising responsibly;	• who needs them to be very clear about their role in the learning relationship, and to help him find his role and learn to be comfortable with his role as learner;
	• who wants to make choices about his learning. They have to co-construct his learning pathway together so that they are both confident it will work for him, and they have to revise it often as his needs change;
• who some days is a complete disaster, right from the time he arrives;	• who, when he arrives in an emotional storm at the beginning of the day, sometimes has to be helped to learn strategies to put it to one side so that he can focus on learning;
• whom other children are expected to tiptoe around. But he can be a disruptive influence on them as well;	• whom other children are expected to 'use' as a source of information and feedback about their own learning, and to provide with feedback about his own, including modelling of appropriate classroom behaviour;
• for whom the expectation is, unfortunately, that he will turn out like his older family members;	• for whom the expectation is that he will learn to be a learning-focused member of the class and will learn as much of the curriculum as any of his peers and that, if anything, it is even more important that he does so;
• who could learn if he would sit still, do as he was told, and listen.	• with low self-esteem that will rise as he learns, begins to experience success, and be able to affirm himself as a learner.

3. Caring perspective	4. Activity-focused perspective
The teacher sees Allan as someone	The teacher sees Allan as someone
• who needs extra time in the playground to 'let off steam';	• who needs extra time in the playground to 'let off steam';
• who some days is so upset from home that he is better off helping the caretaker because then, at least, he is not causing trouble;	• who some days is so upset from home that he is better off helping the caretaker because then, at least, he is not causing trouble;
• whom other children are expected to tiptoe around to try not to upset him, but also include him as much as possible;	• whom other children are expected to tiptoe around to try not to upset him but also include him as much as possible;
• for whom the expectation is, unfortunately, that he will most likely turn out like his older family members;	
• with low self-esteem who needs opportunities to build this before he can really be a learner. His self-esteem can be strengthened by affirming who he is and through strengthening his cultural identity through cultural music/dance practices and activities.	• with low self-esteem who needs opportunities to build this before he can really be a learner. His self-esteem can be strengthened by giving him tasks that he can succeed at.

On the other hand, if you 'care' for them you tend to see yourself as having some advantage over them in life circumstances (which may be true), and as offering them some (loco-parental) support to enable them to overcome their disadvantage, their deficit. There is nothing necessarily wrong with this, but it is not respect for their essential 'equalness' and it does not provide the best basis for supporting them with their learning. It can undermine learning. In a learning-focused relationship, nothing gets in the way. The teacher does not focus on the student's socioeconomic or ethnic background or circumstances if it is not directly important for the learning at hand.

Columns 2 and 3 in Table 2 on pages 32–35 show how the differences might look between a caring perspective and a learning-focused perspective for our student, Allan.

Activity-focused

What gets focused on, flourishes. We want learning to flourish. It will not flourish if the teacher focuses primarily on providing tasks and activities designed to hook the students in; that they will enjoy. The purpose of the classroom is not to entertain the students, although learning is not incompatible with enjoyment. It does not matter how orthodox the reading programme might be, how much it conforms to a 'balanced programme' recommended by the literature and approved by senior staff. It doesn't matter if the physical education programme is really enjoyed by students who participate enthusiastically. It doesn't matter if the students can't wait to get to school in order to spend time on the computers. It doesn't matter if the health unit is delivered by external facilitators each year because the students really enjoy it. School is not primarily about what students do or enjoy. Unless both the teacher and the students clearly understand and can state what the intended learning is, and distinguish this from the tasks and activities, the activities are of limited value and over time reduce the likelihood that students will continue to value school.

In an activity-based relationship both teacher and student are focused on *doing* work. The language of the classroom is the language of work, activity and entertainment: 'What are we *doing* today? Have you *done* your writing yet? Sit down and *do* your work. Think harder, Allan. Try harder, Cheryl. You will find that this is a fun activity once you give it a go, Alex. Let's see if we can all have a really enjoyable day today. Have you finished your *worksheet*?'

An activity-focused relationship is very hard work for the teacher and is one-sided. The teacher is the one who has to design or supply the activity to the design criteria set by the students. The student's role is to engage with the activity to the extent to which they enjoy it. If they judge it to be not to their liking, they do not engage. Motivation is based on enjoyment and novelty. It is up to the teacher to provide the entertainment. A good teacher is a superb entertainer.

Columns 2 and 4 in Table 2 show how the differences might look between an activity-focused perspective and a learning-focused perspective, for our student, Allan.

The message from the research literature

Within education, we are developing a considerable body of well-researched knowledge about the conditions for effective learning.

We are becoming

- more interested in raising achievement levels for all students;
- less tolerant or expecting of failure of any student, more accepting of an accountability link between student achievement and the quality of teaching;
- more clearly research-driven in shaping further pedagogical improvement.

All of this, in fact, amounts to a revolution in education. Along with this revolution, largely as a consequence of the impact of the research (Alton-Lee, 2003), there has been a major transformation in the professional beliefs about the nature of effective teaching and learning, and the nature of the relationship between teacher and student. Table 3 (below and overleaf) demonstrates these shifts. The shift is away from either a caring or a controlling relationship towards one that is learning-focused and mutually respectful.

Table 3: Adapted from Alton-Lee, 2005

TABLE 3: SHIFTS TOWARDS TEACHING BASED ON LEARNING-FOCUSED RELATIONSHIPS

Historical beliefs	Emerging beliefs
teaching is a craft practice (each teacher rediscovers the wheel as they develop their craft knowledge);	emphasis on evidence-based approach (valid information) that attends to data about student learning and effective pedagogy to inform professional teaching practice;
teaching is a common-sense endeavour that involves transmission of content/skills;	professionalism of pedagogy derived from solid and growing research and theory base;
the learner is a sponge to soak up knowledge or a bucket to be filled;	the learner is a knowledge constructor within a community of learners;
teachers have low ability to significantly support learning of students with socioeconomic disadvantage;	teachers have significant ability to support learning of students with socioeconomic disadvantage (teacher agency accounts for at least 42 per cent of variance in scores in available NZ evidence);
learning depends on readiness of learners;	teacher's ability to build on learners' prior experiences and scaffold effective learning opportunities is crucial;
teacher as facilitator; relatively shallow understanding of some content/subject matter;	teacher has deep understanding of content/ subject matter taught and purposes for teaching;
good teaching is teaching that results in busy, happy classrooms (teacher feel-good factor);	good teaching is teaching that has a positive impact on diverse students' achievement and well-being;

if a teacher is caring, this is enough to ensure positive outcomes.	→ caring must be about the learning — teacher must respect students and build respect amongst student community — but must also care about effective teaching (evidence shows negative impacts on learners via deeply caring teachers with low expectations of students).

Recognising socially-situated reality of students

culture and socio-economic context of student not relevant or is invisible;	→ recognition of student as socially situated is integral to effectiveness of teaching and learning;
focus on social well-being and cultural identity too much to ask given size of other teaching responsibilities;	→ social well-being, cultural identity and health of the peer culture shaped through everyday educational practices; teachers must do this intentionally and knowledgeably through effective pedagogy;
academic focus — social incidental, teacher responsibility and accountability for academic only.	→ academic, cultural and social inextricably intertwined; teacher responsibility and accountability in all three.

Responsive pedagogy

disciplinary and compliance focus to classroom management;	→ learning and self-regulation focus to classroom management;
learning dependent on teacher's ability to teach each individual child;	→ learning dependent on teacher enabling students to be self-motivated and self-regulating learners;
emphasis on the teacher and the child and teaching without differentiation to needs of particular learners;	→ highly responsive to diverse needs of learners in different curricular areas in different contexts;
little continuity between teaching approaches for learners of different ages in different curricular areas;	→ generic principles of quality teaching across all ages and curricular areas in tension with subject-specific pedagogical approaches;
focus on teacher's responsibility for curriculum coverage with respect to specific academic objectives;	→ focus both on teacher's curriculum coverage with respect to what is actually learnt and ability to structure a learning environment and design effective learning tasks;
teachers infer student engagement from student behaviour.	→ teachers use systematic strategies to reveal, understand and be responsive to students' thinking and metacognitive strategies.

Role of peers

peer culture seen as a (negative) force independent of the teacher;	→ evidence shows teacher agency instrumental in developing peer culture to create learning community;

overt classroom 'culture of niceness'; peers reluctant to challenge or contradict, hidden peer conflict.	→	learners empowered to allow cognitive conflict to flourish and to develop skills to use cognitive conflict to support learning.

Role of assessment

assessment is prerogative of teacher;	→	assessment becomes a collaborative activity between student and teacher, includes student self-assessment and peer-assessment as students take increasing responsibility for own learning and become more autonomous with respect to own learning;
assessment disconnected from teaching and learning; emphasis on evaluative assessment;	→	predominant use of assessment practices that are diagnostic, descriptive, formative, designed to improve learning;
assessment information not available in a form that is useful for informing teaching.	→	aggregation and disaggregation of assessment data purposeful to improve teaching for diverse learners.

Role of parents

teacher has little agency in parental support for learning.	→	teacher agency critical in enabling parents to support learning.

In total, these changing beliefs about what it is to teach and what it is to learn illustrate the shift from a teacher-student relationship, where learning is seen as an essentially receptive exercise by the student and where the teacher creates the conditions for greatest receptivity by the most students — quiet, attentive classrooms — to one where the relationship is defined and refined by the results of research into what works best; where students are active partners in co-constructing the entire teaching/learning endeavour.

In a learning-focused relationship, the express intention of the teacher is to support and teach students to exercise as much agency as the teacher within the teaching/learning context. In other words, the intention is to create a classroom in which there is no power differential between teacher and students, where both have equal agency and the locus of control is jointly maintained so that the learner is able to maximise his/her ability to regulate his/her own learning; to be an active learner.

The teacher is not a student! Keeping the difference clear

These changes in belief, of what teaching and learning is about, should not be taken to suggest that there is a shift towards both teachers and students having the same rights and responsibilities. Co-construction of, and concurrence about, the teaching/learning process does not mean equal roles and responsibilities, or that teachers have given up any responsibilities.

Teachers still have responsibility to
- teach;
- be highly skilled in teaching;

- be highly knowledgeable about their subject area;
- have responsibility to arrange for highly effective learning opportunities and tasks;
- model appropriate relationship principles and strategies;
- monitor and support student motivation for learning;
- guide students' development of relationship strategies and abilities;
- arrange for dependable assessment opportunities; (Note: Dependable assessment is assessment that has sufficient degrees of validity and reliability to usefully inform the judgements that need to be made. Assessments used entirely within one class, where any one result can be triangulated with other information about what a student knows, can be less technically reliable than an assessment in which the results will be used to make judgements about school-wide trends, where it is critical to have good inter-teacher reliability; for example, in the way reading ages are assessed between classes.);
- monitor and manage class engagement with learning.

In fact it is not appropriate for teachers to be tentative and hesitant about these legitimate roles. The clearer and more direct they are about them, the easier it is for students to also understand how their roles are differentiated from that of the teacher.

What sort of relationship have you got with your students?

Try this simple test with your students. Ask your students to anonymously complete the survey on the opposite page, or some of it; or use it as a basis for a discussion with your students about the nature of teaching. Or reword it to suit the age of your students.

Talk with them about what the results mean to you: how you feel, what you are thinking of doing as a result. See what they say. Look for patterns in the results. One teacher who tried this found that one group of students saw her as controlling and another group as caring. On 'average' she *appeared* to have a learning-focused relationship. It was only when she looked closely at the results that she discovered she was seen as controlling by one group and caring by another! She found this fascinating and a rich source of information for future discussions with her Year 5 class. Beware of simple interpretations.

When a learning-focused relationship is present in classrooms the following examples are the sorts of things students and teachers do say.

How students and teachers see it

Student: 'I'm the one who does the learning. Not my teacher. My teacher is there to explain things to me, to help me to keep challenged, to keep me going in the right direction, and learning at the right pace. Together, and with the others in the class, we work out what I am going to learn and why. My teacher knows her stuff; she is on top of the subjects we learn with her, can tell us why it is important for us to learn it, and is skilled at explaining stuff to us and in then supporting us as we try to understand it. We let her know when we get stuck or puzzled by things and she finds ways of getting us unstuck! Everything we do is focused on our learning. In our class, control is not an issue because everyone is there for learning. We haven't got time for control!'

Circle the answer that you think best fits what happens in our class

1. Who decides what you are going to learn? Your teacher You Both of you

2. Who has the responsibility to make sure you learn? Your teacher You Both of you

3. Should naughty children be

   given a big hug because they must be sad
      to have misbehaved?
   punished for being naughty?
   asked what they need help to learn so that
      they become good learners?

4. Circle the words that best describe your learning
   at school:

   hard and fun;
   hard and boring;
   just right;
   easy and fun;
   easy and boring.

5. Do you think learning at school should be mostly

   hard and fun?
   hard and boring?
   not too hard and not too boring: just right?
   easy and fun?
   easy and boring?

6. Do you generally know what you are learning at
   school:

   always?
   sometimes?
   hardly ever: no one ever tells you, they just get you to
      do things?

7. For most things you are asked to learn at school,
   do you

   already know them and have to learn them again?
   still not know them by the end of the lesson or unit?
   learn them by the end of the lesson or unit?

8. When you find something hard to learn, does your
   teacher help you get over that hard part:

   hardly ever?
   some of the time?
   almost all of the time?

9. What does your teacher believe about you:

   dumb and can't learn?
   dumb but can learn if you try?
   that you are a learner?

10. Is your teacher mostly someone who

    is a nice, kind person?
    will help you learn?
    will keep the class quiet and busy?

11. Does your teacher mainly make you feel

    proud of who you are?
    ashamed of who you are?

12. Does your teacher worry more about

    making you feel good?
    how you are learning?
    how you are behaving?

Teacher 1: 'My job is to keep the students profoundly motivated and challenged with their learning. The students who join the class during the year often need to learn how to take charge of their own learning before they can really start to make good progress. To do this they need to know what values they need in order to drive positive learning. They need to learn how to be clear about what it is they are intending to learn, how to actually do the learning, how to assess their progress, how to enlist support from their peers, parents and me, and how to assess and modify when appropriate the quality of the learning process. It is my job to make sure that every student in my class learns these values and understandings.

'Students need to know that positive learning is based on genuine respect for themselves, those around them, and what it is they are intending to learn. This respect is seen by the openness with which they ask about things that concern or puzzle them, and the mindfulness they have towards the needs of others.'

Teacher 2: 'Never before have I thought about students needing to be on board. We said it, but we didn't allow them to have the ownership. I was negative at the beginning [of the professional development]: who's going to teach me about learning? I used to be a principal! I thought, "I'm going to get exposed." I read everything and did stuff because you [the facilitator] were coming, then I saw the kids coming on board. I saw the kids wanting to have discussions about learning. Now they come to me and I'm relaxed and we're in a partnership.'

Teacher 3: 'What more can I learn after 18 years? It's [assessment for learning professional development] been the greatest, most exciting, tiring learning of my whole career. It made me reflect so much on my own teaching practices. It has strengthened the relationship I have with my students; we're all learning. The students and I have an equal partnership in the learning.'

Student: 'We used to be little ratbags. We used to fight with each other for incredible reasons; like when Sione gave me a look that I didn't like I used to get really, really upset and want to punch him. It took me quite a while to learn that I am in charge of what I do and that I choose whether to get upset by how other people look at me, what they say to me, or what they do to me. With Sione now, I don't mind at all how he looks at me. If he gives me a look I don't like, I ignore it. If he has some problem with what I have done or not done, he needs to tell me what it is, why it upsets him, what he expects me to do, why, and then ask me what I think about all of that.

Sione has grown up too, so he is also now much more in charge of his behaviour and does not mind the distractions of others so much. He is more confident of himself, sure of who he is, confident that he is safe at school and he is respected here. He doesn't need to act tough at school. We have all learnt how to be in order to show each other respect, how to be mindful of each other, how to support each other and how to learn from each other. When we get angry we know what to do to get over it without making it worse. We go and sit in time-out until we feel calm and then we go and either talk with the teacher or one of the peer mediators. We see how our teacher is with us and we try to be like her.'

Learning-focused relationships and trends in society

The quality of the relationship between teacher and student is the key to the successfulness of the teaching. Nobody wants to learn from someone who doesn't like them or who doesn't want to teach. Nobody wants to teach someone who doesn't like them or who doesn't want to learn. If the relationship is not right, the learning is slow, at best. All too often teachers, at every level, find themselves obliged to work with students who don't want to be there, who don't want to learn. All too often it is difficult to work out how to engage with a student who doesn't appear to like you and who obviously doesn't want to learn. If you can't solve this, you know that little learning will ever take place in your class with that student. Your best chance of solving it is to use strategies that the research tells us are our best bet at building a learning-focused relationship.

Learning-focused relationships are about using the considerable potential in the relationship between teacher and student to maximise the student's engagement with learning; about enabling the student to play a meaningful role in deciding what to learn and how to learn it; and about enabling the student to become a confident, resilient, active, self-regulating learner.

Western democratic societies and their education systems have been changing markedly over the last 30 or so years, shaping more and more adequate understandings of social participation where concepts such as equality of participation, co-construction, collaboration and inclusiveness are highly valued. These concepts apply to all citizens and in all political, social, family, organisational and educational contexts.

Schooling is no exception. We now eschew hierarchy and place, in all situations not related to legitimate task or organisational performance. We want to be respected as people, not for our title, rank, class, culture or wealth. This sense of equality and respect pervades most schools and classrooms. The more we, as a society, come to understand what it means to have a right to agency as an individual, what it means to actually have agency (and what it means not to have agency), what it means to be genuine initiators of social meaning-making (and to be recipients of others' initiations), the more we understand how we want schools to be and how we want the learning within those schools to be.

The more we understand of this, the more we also understand what schools need to teach students about how to be in society, so that they themselves come to have legitimate agency and be active, positive participants in democratic society. Learning-focused relationships are in fact models of the participatory relationships needed to sustain democratic citizenship.

The characteristics of teachers and students who are in a learning-focused relationship

If the abseiling example earlier (see page 28) is analysed, the ways in which both teacher and students act — what they bring to the relationship — can be characterised under a number of headings. (See Table 4 below and overleaf.) If you were the student learning to abseil, would this capture how you might feel and act? If you were the teacher, would this capture how you might feel and act?

TABLE 4: DEFINING A LEARNING-FOCUSED RELATIONSHIP	
The student	**The teacher**
Motivated	**Motivated**
• is strongly motivated to learn and gets even more motivated as success with the learning is experienced; • is able to manage their anxiety and/or stress and motivation so that readiness to learn is optimal.	• is motivated to enable all the students to achieve the learning in the time allowed; • believes that all the students are capable of achieving; • is able to manage their stress and motivation so that teaching is optimal; • supports students so that their stress/anxiety/motivation is optimal.
Collaborative	**Collaborative**
• views the 'lesson' as a collaborative exercise between self and teacher in which the purpose of the relationship is to learn; • works with the teacher to build the motivation of the teacher to teach: thanks them, shows pleasure at progress made, at the skill of the teacher in guiding the learning.	• views the 'lesson' as a collaborative exercise between self and students in which the purpose of the relationship is to enable the students to learn and that all that they do must advance this and be seen by the students to advance this; • works with the student to build the motivation of the student to learn; checks with the student that they are experiencing success, helps them overcome difficult bits, boosts motivation by rewarding success, by introducing a range of motivational devices: jokes, interesting examples and illustrations of points.
Respectful of self	**Respectful of self**
• sees self as a learner and as someone who is relaxed about advocating for own needs when necessary (such as asking other students to be quiet so that they can hear the teacher, or asking the teacher to explain a point again).	• sees self as a learner and as someone who is relaxed about advocating for own needs when necessary (such as asking students to be quiet so that they can talk with them).

Respectful of teacher	Respectful of student
<ul><li>is willing to learn from the teacher;</li><li>respects the expertise of the teacher and believes that the teacher can teach;</li><li>uses the teacher to confirm that the learning has been mastered: provides the final assessment or check.</li></ul>	<ul><li>is respectful of the learner as a learner – recognises that they bring their own unique background to the learning and that they will use this background and prior knowledge to build the new learning;</li><li>conscious of their responsibilities as a teacher to be seen by the students as the effective source of expertise and support;</li><li>accepts the responsibility to provide the final assessment and confirmation that the student has learnt what was intended.</li></ul>

Clarity about what is to be learnt	Clarity about what is to be learnt
<ul><li>knows what is to be learnt and knows what they will be able to do when the learning is achieved;</li><li>is very conscious of the need to complete the learning in the time allowed for the learning and therefore does not want any distractions; very focused on the learning.</li></ul>	<ul><li>knows what is to be learnt;</li><li>is aware of the need to achieve a tight focus on the learning; that distractions must be avoided except as a way of spacing practice attempts.</li></ul>

Self-regulating	Responsive
<ul><li>Is able to regulate their own learning<ul><li>to manage the pace of learning to fit with the time allowed; accepts that sometimes it will be rather pressured, but that is how it is;</li><li>to have the teacher break the learning into manageable bits;</li><li>to engage in repeated opportunities to learn, through repeated explanation, modelling, practice, etc;</li><li>to assess the progress of the learning by com-paring their efforts against those of a model or a set of criteria or the efforts of their peers;</li><li>to seek teacher and peer feedback to confirm or change their own assessment;</li><li>to seek help and guidance about the bits that they are stuck on;</li><li>to be able to independently continue to practise some bits or to move on to the next bit of learning.</li></ul></li></ul>	<ul><li>Is able to regulate their own teaching<ul><li>to optimise the pace of teaching to fit with student needs and the time allowed for the learning;</li><li>to be able to offer multiple representations of what is to be learnt so that students are offered more than one way of coming to understand constructs or to develop skill;</li><li>to offer repeated opportunities to learn: through repeated explanation, modelling, practice, etc;</li><li>by assessing where the students are at with their learning and then modifying the intended programme;</li><li>on the basis of assessment to provide prompts, scaffolds, feedback as appropriate.</li></ul></li></ul>

Reflective	Reflective
• uses reflection on the learning to build a meta-cognitive map to contextualise the learning; • uses own, peer and teacher reflection on the progress of the learning to assess effectiveness of the learning and modify accordingly.	• uses own and student reflection on the progress of the learning to assess effectiveness of the teaching and modify teaching accordingly.
Next steps	**Next steps**
• to 'use' the teacher as a resource to guide the learning.	• to remain clear about further progressions of learning and when they might be introduced.

You can see that this analysis of the abseiling lesson has been arranged to fit with the capabilities archway introduced in Chapter 1 (but using slightly different language), and how the capabilities in the archway interrelate to support learning. The foundation of the whole arch is the ability to form and sustain a learning-focused relationship, and we now turn to a close examination of the structure of this relationship.

Chapter 3

LEARNING-FOCUSED RELATIONSHIPS MODEL

Understanding the structure of a learning-focused relationship

Describing all that a teacher has to do in order to achieve a learning-focused relationship in the classroom is complex. It is hard to follow complex advice about how to build a relationship and then apply it proficiently in the vastly differing circumstances we find ourselves in. For example, if you are told how to act in this specific circumstance with these students, you will not necessarily know how to act in a different circumstance with different students. It will be more helpful if you are given a broadly applicable strategy that will provide sensible guidance, for a range of circumstances and a range of different types of students.

The strategy itself has to be based on a set of assumptions or principles about how to act in order to achieve successful outcomes (in this case a learning-focused relationship) and there has to be reasonable research evidence that the principles and the strategies, when properly applied, do result in the desired outcomes. When the principles, the strategies and the outcomes are put together they form a causal model. This is shown in Table 5, pages 50–51. The point of a causal model, based, as it is, on research, is that it describes the actual outcomes that *will* occur if you act according to the principles and strategies described by the model. The model provides a powerful tool for guiding how you shape your relationships. It also enables you to check to see if what you actually say and do with students really does conform to the principles and strategies necessary if you are to build a learning-focused relationship.

Once you have deeply understood the model you will be able to use it and apply it to the full range of circumstances you meet in teaching.

The Model

Motivation

Underpinning everything we do is our motivation for doing it. This is particularly true in a teaching and learning context. The teacher must have a motivation to enable the students to learn, and the students must be motivated to do the learning. Within the context of a school, school leadership has a responsibility to nurture the motivation of teachers (and students), and the teacher has a major responsibility to manage and nurture the motivational climate of the classroom so that the students want to learn. Motivation is represented in the model as the background against which everything else sits.

The guiding principles

Assuming that a positive motivational climate is present, then actually building a learning-focused relationship with your students is dependent on the principles that guide and underpin your interactions with them. Guiding principles are the values that guide your actions and conversations in everything that you do. Common themes in current research into teaching and interpersonal relationships suggest that there are three principles that guide all effective teaching. We label these guiding principles, 'openness', 'honesty' and 'respect', but the research we have mainly drawn on terms them 'valid information', 'free and informed choice' and 'internal commitment'.

Figure 2: Interrelationship of guiding principles

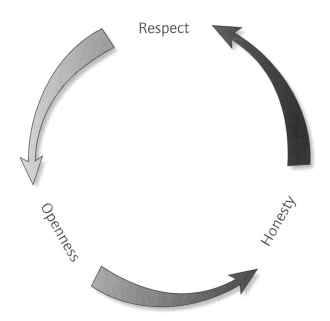

Respect

Openness

Honesty

Openness (or valid information): letting the kids know what is going on (and why)

It is not possible to make good and consistent decisions about teaching or learning (or much else) without good and sound information. Valid information is information that is normally independently confirmable and relates directly to the subject at hand. It includes all types of information: thoughts, opinions, facts, data, and reasoning. All parties to decision-making need access to all the information relevant to an issue. No parts of the information can be held back, including your own feelings and assumptions that influence how the issue may be addressed. This principle encourages the use of specific examples that help illustrate the issues being discussed, so that all involved can understand what is meant. An important element of this principle is to share the reasoning about why you believe that the conclusions you have reached are valid and true. A good test for sharing information might be, 'If I am thinking it, I probably ought to share what I am thinking, even the things I feel unsure about.' On the other hand, if you are thinking it, but you think that it is not true, stop thinking it.

Quick tips for giving valid information in the classroom
- Make sure kids really know what you are intending them to learn and why.
- Tell them how you intend to organise the classroom programme and ask them what they think of it.
- Ask them if there are improvements they could suggest.

		TABLE 5: A MODEL FOR BUILD
Guiding principles	**Guiding strategies**	**Possible teaching strategies**

Openness
(increase valid information)
	• design everything that happens in the classroom so that both students and teacher can be originators and experience high personal causation:
	  – share control of the learning/ teaching process;
	  – share control of the content.
		• share with students the intentions for the lesson content, sequence and process;
		• explain clearly the reasons for the lesson or activity, in terms of the learning objectives;
		• share the specific assessment criteria with students;
		• help students to understand what they have done well and what they need to develop;
		• show students how to use the assessment criteria to assess their own learning;

Respect (enhance free and informed choice)	• protection of self is a joint enterprise and oriented towards growth.	• check understanding and acceptability of the intentions; • if not understood or accepted, probe problem and try alternative technique to communicate; • monitor and assess what is being learnt using techniques suitable to the content and selected pedagogy; • if learning not happening try another technique; • provide feedback that is relevant to the learning, compatible with the particular pedagogy selected, and helps to construct the way forward;
Honesty (internal commitment to the choice and constant monitoring of the implementation)	• bilateral protection of others.	• check that feedback has enabled the student to take a new learning step. If not use a different technique; • determine what to teach next on the basis of what is now known.

NING-FOCUSED RELATIONSHIPS

Examples of possible teaching techniques	Consequences for students and teacher	Consequences for learning

learning intentions or objectives and success criteria listed on board, orally described;
 	
show exemplar;
 	
show standards or assessment criteria;
 	
discuss how students will know when they have learnt;
 	
discuss how students can monitor their learning;
 	
ask students to put their thumbs up if they feel they understand the learning objectives, down if they don't;
 	
ask 'Is anyone not comfortable with what we are intending for this unit?';
 	
use exemplars to show end product of learning;
 	
have students work in small groups to derive defining characteristics of exemplars;
 	
have students produce their own version of exemplar;
 	
use peer-to-peer-assessment of product against criteria;
 	
diagnostic testing;
 	
self-assessment;
 	
teacher verbally contrasts exemplar characteristics against student work with student;
 	
self and peer feedback;
 	
teacher seeks student's view of work and of feedback: 'Did that feedback/mark/comment tell you what you needed to know?'; 'How is the process going for you?'
	• teacher experienced as minimally defensive;
	
	• students more focused at the beginning of the lessons;
	
	• students able to describe the learning intentions and learning process;
	
	• students indicate commitment and support of learning process — motivation improves;
	
	• students have greater ownership of the lesson as responsibility shifts from teacher to student for learning;
	
	• teacher expectations rise;
	
	• the quality of the work improves
	  – in the amount done;
	  – in adherences to the learning intention and success criteria of the task;
	  – in students' ability to do their best.
	
	• students persevere on-task for longer;
	
	• behaviour improves;
	
	• students begin to automatically self-evaluate.
		• a learning culture develops as students start to use the language of learning rather than the language of activities.
		
		• both single and double-loop learning takes place: both teachers and students are able to jointly and independently evaluate the quality of their thinking and the assumptions underpinning it;
		
		• minimally defensive interpersonal relations and group dynamics;
		
		• the quality of the teaching and learning improves with a greater focus on understanding and concepts rather than the surface features and superficial skills;
		
		• frequent public testing of what is working for the students and what is not;
		
		• learning-oriented norms;
		
		• strong internal commitment to learning; evidence of students, ability to articulate their learning or otherwise demonstrate evidence of learning;
		
		• stating learning intentions makes a subsequent reflection against intentions a necessity.

This model is an adaptation of one developed from research into effective interpersonal relationships by Argyris & Schon, 1974.

Respect (or free and informed choice): supporting and respecting kids to make informed choices

Free and informed choice relies on the first value: valid information. When you have access to valid information it is possible to make a decision that is free of outside pressures. When you and your students make a decision or commitment within this framework, you are all confident that the choice is one that you can carry out, because the decision is truly yours and has been made on the best information available.

Respect involves ensuring that both parties (you and the student) have the opportunity to make free and informed choices. Respect is modelled by the way you interact with students, and in the setting of clear standards of how you expect students to interact with them. It is apparent in the way you speak to your students, how you model attitudes and behaviour, the energy and effort you put into your teaching, and your enthusiasm for learning. Respect is held as a sense of essential equality, of mutuality, with the students; that as people they are deserving of the same respect as you offer yourself.

Respect is also shown through notions such as patience and perseverance, where you believe in your students and do not give up on them. This requires making it clear to students that learning new things is challenging and that not understanding is sometimes part of the learning process. Part of making this clear, of respecting them, is constantly checking on students' understanding and being willing to re-teach some concepts, or employ a different teaching method to assist better understanding. Palmer (1983) describes a classroom environment which operates on this principle as a 'hospitable learning space which does not set out to make learning painless but to make the painful things possible . . . things like exposing ignorance, testing tentative hypotheses, challenging false or partial information and mutual criticism of thought. [None of these] can happen in an atmosphere where people feel threatened and judged.' Because of the nature of compulsory schooling, and school workplace rules and regulations, all decisions are not necessarily free in the strict sense of the word. It is very important that these rules and regulations are made known, so that informed choices within those constraints are possible.

Quick tips for supporting free and informed choice in the classroom
- Ask the students what they think of what you want them to learn; ask how many want to learn it (once you have told them why you think they should).
- Ask the ones who don't want to learn it why not and what they might need, or what they might need you to do, in order to develop some motivation to learn it.
- Don't accept a 'don't know'; keep exploring their choices (within the bounds of compulsory schooling).

Honesty (or internal commitment): sticking with what has been decided unless there is new information

The logical consequence of free and informed choice is internal commitment. This internal commitment to the decision happens because you know that you have all of the relevant information that was necessary to make the decision and that you made it knowing all of the restraints and consequences. Because of this you own and willingly live with the decision. There is another component of internal commitment that might not be obvious at first: being internally committed to seeking valid information in relation to the decision. This component keeps the decision a dynamic one. It means that it is not possible to make a decision and never have to think about it again. It means being open to (new) information that might not support your decision.

Quick tips for supporting internal commitment in the classroom
- Tell the students you believe in being committed to decisions that have been made by the class.
- Ask them to tell you when they think you have ignored these decisions.
- Ask them if they also believe in being committed and if they think it is right if you tell them when you think they have ignored a decision.

These three guiding principles work together in a reinforcing cycle. You first seek and share valid information, use that valid information to make an informed decision, and then become internally committed to the decision; and then to continuing to seek further valid information and subject the decision to ongoing testing. Teachers who construct teaching approaches, or strategies, that are consistent with these principles will create and experience learning-focused relationships with their students and will support optimally effective learning for their students. Students can also frame approaches to their learning that are consistent with these principles. For example, this is how these principles might frame the thinking of a student about what he or she might learn next.

- *'If you want me, as your student, to be really keen on what is to be learnt next then you have to be able to tell me not only what you think I should learn, but you also need to be able to tell me why you think that, or be able to offer me an experience where I can test for myself the value of learning it. You also then need to be able to give me an opportunity to think about what you have said or what I have experienced and then let me tell you how I evaluated it all, and why I evaluated it in that way. If I then agree that your reasons for learning it are good reasons, I will be committed to the learning. But if not, then it will be your turn again to explain again. [If you can't give me legitimate reasons for learning things, and it is not apparent to me, why should I be committed to doing the work of learning? Would you if you were in my place?]'*
- *'If each of us can do these three things properly – say what you think, say why you think it, and check how the other person sees it each time it is our turn to speak – then we will each be doing our bit to ensure that both of us have an opportunity to deeply understand how each of us thinks about or understands what is to be learnt [openness], that each of us has equal opportunity to co-construct a learning path forward [mutual respect], and be committed to whatever plan we decide on [honesty]. We will both be making our decision, freely chosen, on the basis of open, valid and tested information about what each is thinking.'*

However, the principles by themselves do not give us enough guidance to be able to consistently act and converse with students in a way that will sustain a learning-focused relationship. We need some strategies and rules to provide a fuller guiding structure.

Rules for building skills in learning-focused relationships

There are three straightforward rules that you can use to think about how you might guide yourself to greater consistency with the principles of honesty, openness and respect.

Rule one: share the good stuff in your head
- Say what you think.
- Say or demonstrate why you think it.
- Check how the other person understands what you have said and what they are thinking.

What we tend to do instead of these three things is *ask* the other person what they are thinking. This allows us to keep an eye on what they are thinking without really letting them see inside our heads, but makes it very difficult for the other person to feel that they are equal participants in the discussion with us; they know that we have deliberately kept our views hidden. They often become defensive. If they tell us, we then either ask them to justify themselves or we tell them why they are wrong, or use Socratic methods to attempt to have them prove themselves wrong. Alternatively, we tell them bits of what are in our heads; we do a lot of self-censoring. For example, we seldom show students our passion for their learning. We *do* want them to learn the very important stuff that we have available, but we don't ever really let them know that. We should.

Rule two: get rid of the bad stuff in your head
- Don't *say* anything that you do not believe is based on valid information.
- Don't *think* anything that you do not believe is based on valid information.
- If you are not sure that what you think is valid, say what it is and also say that you are not sure that it is valid, why you are not sure, and then check with the other person what they think.

For example, if you really don't think that your students are capable of achieving to a high standard, tell them. Go on, I dare you! I bet you won't because you know all the research that says that students tend to rise to meet expectations. Get rid of that thinking because it does not help you. Your students can guess that that is what you think because they know that you don't expect too much of them. How did you get on with that survey of your students earlier?

Rule three: help others to discard their junk
- If the other person says something that you think is not valid, or *doesn't* say something that you think is in their mind, tell them what you think, why you think it, and see what they think.
- Be prepared to be careful about your reasoning, and how well you have based your conclusions (what you think) on valid information and sound assumptions. Be prepared to test it all.

The guiding strategies

The three guiding strategies are the fundamental 'big picture' ways in which we design all our teaching and learning interactions with students, so that our interactions are consistent with the guiding principles.

Design everything that happens in the classroom so that both students and teacher can be originators and experience high personal causation
- Share control of the lesson content.
- Share control of the teaching/learning process.

This strategy requires effective concurrence by the students with everything to do with the teaching and learning. It means that, often, you will want to actually construct aspects of the lesson with the students. It does not mean that the students have to plan half the lesson and do half of the teaching, but that they need to be able to indicate the extent to which what you have designed is likely to work, or is working, for them.

Our description of the strategy uses two little jargon terms that we want to introduce, because we cannot find clear alternatives for them. Effective learners are those who best control or regulate their learning. For a person to be an 'originator' means that they are capable of causing or initiating a set of events, that they can start something rather than react to things others have started. Many people do not have the ability to be originators in many areas of their lives. Instead of 'causing' events, they react to the actions of others. Being an originator as a student contrasts strongly with the traditional view of formal learning where the learner is the recipient of, and reactive to, the teacher's regulation and control. To experience high personal causation means that the person, be it student or teacher, has a strong sense that when they speak, cough, look annoyed, run, or write an essay, others will notice. They will have a sense of themselves as being visible to others, of emanating (a pleasant) presence.

Originators have a measured belief in their own worth and their own right to contribute and be heard. They deeply respect themselves, know themselves, and have the ability to be assertive advocates for themselves first and foremost. Originators will act, rather than be acted upon, shape rather than be shaped, choose rather than accept choices decided by others (Rychen & Salganik, 2003). You cannot be an originator if you are passive or reactive. You have to actively learn to be an originator. You have to be actively taught to be an originator. A teacher who tries to meet the whims of all students, with ever more elaborate attempts to entertain them (better videos, or faster computer games), or ever more elaborate attempts to bribe them to behave, is not an originator. They are reacting to the demands of the students.

Teachers need to become originators themselves, first and foremost, before they can understand the concept of student as originator. Knowing valid information about yourself is a prerequisite to contributing valid information to others on other topics. If you are not aware of your assumptions, values and biases, how can it be known what biases you will bring to discussions and interchanges with others? To be able to be consistent with a guiding principle of valid information requires self-knowledge and a clear psychological separation between self and others. Waterman (1981), in a review of research literature, shows clearly that individuals who have the clearest sense of free choice, personal responsibility and universality of respect for others, are also individuals who have the clearest sense of their own identity, as expressed by measures such as identity, internal locus of control, self-esteem, and principles of moral reasoning. Black and Wiliam (1998) also stressed the importance of self-esteem in learning. Self-esteem refers most generally to an individual's overall evaluation of the self as capable, efficacious and of value. High self-esteem is viewed as an adaptive personality characteristic, associated with a greater capacity for self-regulation, including recognition of situational contingencies and task demands, higher expectations of success, persistence, and successful performance (Bandura, 1986).

The more a person sees themselves as capable of initiating or originating action on their own behalf, the greater their self-esteem. The more learners initiate actions on their own behalf for learning (the higher their self-esteem), the more they will really engage in the work of learning, and the more they will learn. Passive learners learn less. The more we can teach students to actively manage their learning, the higher their self-esteem will go and the better their learning will be. An example of what a student-originator might be like, and what they might expect about the teaching/learning experience in a classroom, was given on page 30. The teacher-originators must teach their students to gain the same sense of origin. The main strategy for doing this is by explicitly sharing control of the lesson content and lesson process. Explicitly inviting students to comment on and put forward modifications, for both the content and the process, provides the opportunity for students to originate ideas and possibilities. If the teacher then models, supports and scaffolds attempts, and provides good feedback on attempts, then students will learn to be originators. Once this begins to happen, the whole classroom culture changes for ever.

Some students come with no sense at all of origin, no sense of how to co-construct, and no motivation to participate in this way. The most extreme examples are students who are autistic, who have a marked inability to relate to others at all, let alone in the sophisticated manner we are suggesting here. Inviting them to co-construct will be completely ineffective and will not motivate them at all — and modelling how it is done will not work either.

The difficulties experienced in teaching these students highlight an important issue extremely well. Learning to be an originator is a *must* for every student. Teaching every student to be an originator is a *must* for every teacher. As adults we have an absolute obligation to try very hard to have students learn the skills and abilities of adult society. It is not an option for them or for us. How to relate to others is a critical ability for competent participation in adult society. All students must develop these skills as much as possible. The most extreme students can learn some ability to originate when it is made a very explicit focus of the learning, the teacher is strongly motivated that they learn (relentlessly determined), and there is extensive and explicit scaffolding of the learning, with much modelling and behavioural prompting (and there is an appropriate teacher-student ratio).

How to check for shared control
Ask, ask, ask, check, check, check . . .

If you think that you have planned a lesson that will cater really well for the diverse learning needs in your classroom, check to see what the students think. Ask them, really ask them, to tell you how it will meet their needs. Ask them if there is a better way of enabling them to learn what is intended. The biggest single difficulty with shaping genuine concurrence and co-construction is detecting when we have acted on assumptions (about how well students have agreed with us) without checking those assumptions. We cannot detect errors in our thinking if we do not check our thinking. In the heat of teaching, it is hard to do. It is quite easy to ask students if they have understood something and to assume that the desultory 'Yes, Miss' is genuine agreement, rather than just compliant habitual nodding in response to your habitual question. Quite often we will check that students are with us on some parts of the lesson and completely forget to check other parts. And we can't check everything. As we will see later, it is the plenary part of a lesson which allows us to discover when we should have checked but didn't, and whether we sort of checked but not very well.

Protection of self is a joint enterprise and oriented towards growth/learning

This strategy is extremely difficult to engage with for teachers who are not confident in themselves because it requires us to do what we are least inclined to do: expose our weaknesses and fears when we feel under threat and would normally be frantically trying to cover them up. It requires us to hold to our values under conditions where, if we do not have a strong sense of origin and personal causation, we will worry about the reactions of others. To take a mild example: you are partway through a lesson and it is not going well. Students are misbehaving, you feel stressed and irritable. It is highly likely that by this time you have already acted in ways that have violated at least one of the principles of openness, honesty and respect. For example, you may have shouted and demanded that the naughty boys at the back of the class do their work.

In order to keep your actions within the boundaries of these principles, this strategy says that you should do something like call for the attention of the class, and then

- tell them that you think the lesson is going badly, and why you think that;
- tell them that this distresses you;
- ask them if they see it the same way;
- if they do confirm that it is going badly, share what might need to happen to get it back on track — make sure there is listening and understanding on both sides;
- rigorously implement an agreed solution and any fall-back mechanisms built in (for example, students go to time-out if they misbehave);
- check in with students again at a later time — at the end of the lesson or later — and jointly evaluate the implemented solution;
- plan for modifications if needed.

We find actually doing this sort of straightforward, collaborative problem-solving hard to do because it requires us to share negative emotional material (the stress and upset caused by the bad lesson), and our strong, natural inclination is to hide or disguise that emotion. We also fear (negative emotion) that we will lose even more control if we admit to the students that we are having control problems.

Quick tips on how to enlist the help of the students in stopping you becoming defensive and controlling

- At the end of the lesson or day or week do a mental check of how you are feeling.
- Do you feel stressed, under pressure, annoyed at the kids, worried about your classroom management?
- If you do, plan how to start the next lesson by sharing how you feel with the students and what you intend to do about it.
- Then *check* that they see your analysis and problem solution as one that they can commit to also.

Bilateral protection of others

This strategy is the reciprocal to the previous one, and much easier to action because it has to do with how we respond when others are likely to be feeling under threat. It requires us to develop sensitivity towards events that cause us to lose bilateral control of the teaching and learning process. This can occur when the student withdraws from active participation because of a sense of threat or defensiveness. It does require us to be sensitive to the emotionality that situations might hold for the student.

Quick tip on how to keep students feeling they are in a learning-focused relationship

- Students often find it very difficult to articulate their learning processes. Many are not good at thinking about their learning, let alone speaking about it. You can help them by modelling what they might be thinking, especially about a stuck bit. For example, with a student who appears to be stuck and embarrassed about being stuck, you might say:
  - 'This is often a hard bit to learn. Sometimes it can be embarrassing when most of the class get it and you don't. And if we get embarrassed we usually want to stop learning. That might be happening for you, I don't know. But if it is, then what I suggest is that we go over it very carefully and I have another go at showing you how to do it. How does that sound?'

For example, a student might feel embarrassed or ashamed about finding it difficult to understand a concept that needs to be learnt, particularly if they know that others have understood it easily; or with receiving critical feedback, even when skilfully given, if they are not used to having any critique of their work at all. If they do not have a strong sense of origin, this embarrassment might cause them to try to disguise their difficulty. The teacher needs to be able to support them to enable them to share their embarrassment and difficulty, and to feel less embarrassed in similar situations over time and welcome 'stuck bits' as a sign of genuinely grappling with new learning.

Consistently using these three key strategies to have what we do characterised by openness, respect and honesty through our modelling, helps students begin to approach their learning with the same values. As their ability, commitment and sense of personal origin grows, so our ability to genuinely co-construct and co-own effective, strongly motivated learning experiences with them grows. And so does the power of their learning.

Teaching strategies

Everything that happens in the classroom needs to be consistent with the guiding principles and strategies. As teachers, over time, we develop our own specific strategies for different parts of a lesson. These also need to be consistent with the model. The strategies suggested in Table 5 (see pages 50–51) are reasonably high-level, generic and can be tailored to fit individual style. For example, when we want openness and co-construction, we can begin to achieve this by disclosing to the students what we are intending for the lesson and why. It makes extra sense if we can show how our thinking has arisen from prior assessment of where the students were at that was carried out with the students.

If we want to enhance their ability to freely choose and build commitment to the results of their choice, we can ask them what they think of our reasoning and ask them if they have ideas that will make the learning activities more powerful for them.

If we want them to be able to evaluate their own progress we need to share assessment or success criteria with them, make sure they understand them and how to use them, and recognise their attempts to self-assess.

Much of the rest of the book is about specific strategies for ensuring that all phases of the teaching/learning sequence are consistent with the model.

Teaching techniques

Specific techniques for applying the strategies will vary from teacher to teacher, lesson to lesson, and subject to subject. The difficulty is to ensure that any particular technique does continue to be consistent with the model. There are many classrooms now where 'learning intentions' are listed, even laminated and put on classroom walls. Making lists of what you think you want them to learn is absolutely no indication, by itself, of the students making any connection at all with what is on the list or of what they think they are learning. We have found many occasions where the writing up of learning intentions has become just another classroom ritual that clearly guides neither the teacher nor the students' thinking about what is actually to be learnt. When the list of intentions are in fact a list of activities, or when the students can point to their list of *learning intenders* but cannot tell you why they are there, then something is fundamentally missing from the teaching/learning endeavour.

Consequences for the class, the teacher, the student

The consequences listed in Table 4 (pages 44–46) and on page 60 are predicted from the logic of the model and are also typical of the impact assessment for learning has on classrooms. These are not only described widely in the literature, but are absolutely typical of what we find teachers say happens in their classrooms.

Teacher experienced as minimally defensive

If the teacher can remain open to the students even when things might be going badly, then students will see the teacher as minimally defensive. This in itself will encourage the students to display similar qualities.

Teacher expectations rise

As students become more self-regulating and their achievement improves, the teacher will raise their own sense of what learning can be achieved.

Students more focused at the beginning of the lessons

Students become accustomed to the classroom being a place where there is a tight focus on learning. When they arrive they expect to begin learning; other, less learning-focused behaviour falls away.

Students have greater ownership of the lesson as responsibility shifts from teacher to student

Students become more assertive about what they need in order to learn. This is done genuinely and not as a strategy for gaining attention.

Students persevere on-task for longer; quality of work improves

As students start to learn and their motivation for learning improves, their desire to generate work of quality improves.

Classroom behaviour improves

In a classroom with learning-oriented norms, there is little motivation for 'misbehaviour'. Teachers can report major shifts in academic engagement, in attention, in co-operative skills, as the motivation to learn rises.

Consequences for learning

A learning culture develops as students start to use the language of learning rather than the language of activities. The classroom culture shifts tangibly. Parents can be the first to really notice the shift as their children begin to talk about what they have learnt at school, rather than what they have done.

Both single- and double-loop learning takes place

Both teachers and students become able to jointly and independently evaluate the quality of their thinking and the assumptions underpinning it. Double-loop learning refers to situations where major guiding strategies, beliefs or assumptions are found to be wrong, and better, more adaptive beliefs or strategies are adopted. An example might be when teachers learn that their assumptions about the need to exercise control in the classroom are incompatible with the type of independent, self-regulating learning they want their students to engage with.

Minimally defensive interpersonal relations and group dynamics

As students learn to publicly assess and evaluate their work and that of their peers (and the teaching) to enhance learning, then students become more relaxed and open to critique; to see such comment and feedback as useful. Students begin to take greater risks with their learning, becoming more willing to try things out, knowing that only critique, not criticism, will follow.

There is a focus on understanding and concepts rather than the surface features and superficial skills; of owning what is learnt rather than understanding what others know

As both teacher and students begin to really examine the relevance and significance of what needs to be learnt, the understanding grows of the importance of owning the results of learning rather than learning to do or to recall. For example, learning to write to powerfully communicate becomes more important than learning to write sentences that are grammatically correct. Learning to use algorithms to correctly solve problems becomes a part of learning to understand how the algorithms have been constructed and the limits on their use. Describing what researchers say about a discipline is not as important as being able to use their concepts for your own research.

Frequent public testing of what is working for the students and what is not

Testing and checking that there is a shared understanding of what is happening becomes the norm for both teachers and students together, with enhanced ability to appropriately signal when something is not working.

Strong internal commitment to learning; evidence of students' ability to articulate their learning or otherwise demonstrate evidence of learning

A student's commitment is shown by their ability to generate evidence of learning; partially for their own testing of the extent to which they have learnt, partially for celebration of achieving something that they value.

Stating learning intentions makes a subsequent reflection against intentions a necessity

Both teacher and students retain a sharp focus on what is to be learnt and repeatedly review the extent to which learning is occurring.

Using the model to help build your relationship

You can use this learning-focused model to check how you are getting on with your relationships with your students. You can use it to detect where you might be being inadvertently too controlling or caring, and it provides pointers as to how you might go about changing bits of what you do. The model describes the outcomes you can predict if the principles and strategies are employed. Check with the students about the extent to which all of you currently experience these outcomes. If there are any missing, then ask the students why this might be and what you would have to do differently in order to achieve those outcomes.

Uppers and downers of a learning-focused relationship

Building up student motivation

Without motivation to learn, there is no learning. It must be the starting point for a teacher building a relationship with a class. The very first thing to do is to check the motivation for learning of the students. If they are not happy to learn, keen to learn, then the first job of the teacher is to find ways of motivating them. If you don't do this, then everything else you do will fail and you will not create a learning-focused relationship. And your students won't learn what you want them to learn.

We know that students are motivated to learn by one or more of the following motivational categories:

- Blatant extrinsic reward: food, toys, stars, points . . .
- Personal betterment or empowerment or intellectual curiosity: getting better at language, knowledge, skills, behaviour, habits . . . in a subtle but real way. (Our experience of first language learning was done without any formal discussion about why we should learn to speak — we couldn't anyway — we just did it, mainly with the unfailing support and intuitive skill of our mothers, and without any other explicit incentive.)
- Personal advancement: I want to make a difference, I like setting and working to targets (competitive), I want this qualification (career imperative, more money).
- Community participation: being able to have the skills to 'be' within society: for example, drivers licence, form-filling, banking, voting.
- Excitement, challenge, fun: for example, abseiling, hobbies, interests, sports.
- Cognitive dissonance: where there is experience, conflict or anxiety resulting from inconsistency between our beliefs or understandings and our actions — this acts as a driving force that compels the human mind to acquire or invent new thoughts or beliefs, or to modify existing beliefs, so as to *minimise* the amount of dissonance.
- Sense of belonging, being part of a group: this is where *we* are going, this is what *we* are learning, I want to be a part of that.
- Moral imperative: it is the right thing to do.

The issue of motivation in learning is peculiar to the schooling sector because of the compulsory nature of it. Kids don't have a choice. They are required to attend and this creates a problem. We know that we can write a curriculum and require students to attend schools to be taught it. What we cannot require is that they learn it; and they will not learn it unless they are motivated to do so. It is also largely up to the teacher to ensure that they are motivated. Let's look at some examples of managing student motivation.

In the abseiling example earlier, motivating the students was not a problem for the teacher. The students had chosen to be there. They were motivated — highly and obviously motivated — presumably by a sense of excitement and challenge.

Another example where the learning is undeniably effective, but the motivation is not obvious, is with first language learning. We all learn from our mothers and other significant adults. No one threatens us with our lives, or offers us special rewards, for learning language: we just do. We don't even need to be able to express ourselves in order to come to understand the language of others; and we do it quickly. Mere exposure to words, grammar and syntax is almost enough for us to become competent in our first language. We don't get formally assessed and reported on, there are no parent-teacher interviews where our progress is discussed and worried about, we don't 'pass' or 'fail' or have homework, no one gets cross if we over-generalise tense rules or say words incorrectly or put them in the wrong order. They normally don't even point out that we have made a mistake. At most, they just give us a correct model that we can understand. But we do get feedback and encouragement. They try their best to understand what we are trying to communicate. They help us to communicate the thoughts better by providing an elaborated form of what they think we want to say, and then checking to see that is what we meant. We get a buzz out of being heard and we learn from the modelling provided.

If motivation is important to learning, what is the motivation for us to learn language? Is it there? It is, but it is subtle — it is not life-threatening — but it is there. We learn language because it is what we do as humans. We learn language because the more we know of it the more we become entwined in the meaning-making of our family and community, and that is motivating because it is emotionally and intellectually enriching. Kids often will say, 'I don't know how to say what I want to say, I don't know the words'. We help our children to find ways of saying what they are thinking or feeling, and as we do this we are also helping them to develop language: painlessly, enjoyably, engagingly, with no punishment for failure apart from occasional frustration. The motivation is merely to do with personal betterment and less frustration from not being misunderstood. It is not conscious. We are not really aware that we are getting better, we just have richer conversations with others as we increase our language ability and understand the world better.

Avoiding destroying intrinsic motivation

Learning, in the examples given above, is pretty much its own reward. In fact, the motivation to learn is naturally present in all students. Students are learners. Students will learn at school as well as they learnt language at home, provided they do not experience punishment or embarrassment for learning in their own bumbling way, there are no competing motivations that make doing other things more attractive, that they do not get confused as to what schooling is actually about, and they have the skills to learn in the formal learning environment of school. Classrooms need to be organised to

- ensure that no student is humiliated, embarrassed or punished for attempts to learn anything, but rather supported to take risks with their learning;
- ensure there are no other competing attractions to intrude;
- build and nurture the motivation of students to *learn at school* so that it becomes a habit;
- teach students the skills they need to succeed as learners at school.

Learning at school is quite different from learning your first language at home. Even if no one yells at you, tells you off, tells you that you have failed or makes you feel silly, to be good at learning at school requires a range of skills that you might not have acquired in the close confines of a loving family. You may not have learnt how to manage your own anxiety about novel social situations, you might not have shaped any sense of being an originator of action (perhaps having left this to your parents), you might be shy and retiring, and you might not have learnt how to assert your needs as a learner in a formal teaching/learning situation.

To be as successful at school with your learning, you need to learn a number of strategies and skills to be able to manage the new context and relationships of the classroom. At home you learnt how to communicate. At school you develop this further but you also need to *use* your communicative ability to communicate your learning needs within a more social environment, to adults and peers that do not know you nearly as well as your parents. It is difficult learning, and if you do not learn 'how to learn' well, you will always find aspects of schooling, and the curriculum, difficult or unpleasant and have limited success.

It is up to the teacher to ensure that you do this learning. A major source of information that the teacher has as to how well you are doing with this learning, is your motivation for school. If it is low, there is a problem. A learning-focused relationship is the type of relationship that enables the teacher to best detect problems.

Let's take another look at a student who has really learnt the skills of how to learn and is using them within the context of a healthy, learning-focused relationship. This boy is learning how to improve his ability to write a paragraph about a graphic characterisation.

What would he ask of you as the teacher? First of all he would want to be as clear as possible about what writing a characterisation looked like; he would want to know what its distinguishing features were and to see a number of exemplars of characterisation. He may well ask you to write one for him so that he could see what the process was. He would want hints as to how to start the writing and how to proceed. He would look to his peers to see how they were understanding and progressing with the task and learning. He would be actively comparing his draft with the critical features of good characterisation, and he would be asking his peers what they thought. He may make alterations as a result of this discussion and reflection. Then he would ask you. He would expect you to go through the same assessment process of his work and to tell him what you thought he had done well and what he still needed to work on. If it was really important to him that he learnt to write characterisations well, he would want to manage the feedback from you so that it felt that it helped with his further learning. He would want to be clear about what you thought. If you indicated that he still had a lot to learn he may well ask you to go slowly with the feedback so that he could work on improving bits at a time and not get snowed under or depressed with too big a mountain of improvement to climb. He would powerfully manage the learning process.

We can imagine ourselves acting like this if we were to enrol in an expensive writing class. So getting the motivational climate right can certainly make a difference to the manner of participation of the students and the ability of students to regulate their learning.

What should teachers do to manage the motivation of their students?
So often we do not have the 'obvious' conversations with our students that we should have; conversations that will actually make all the difference to your relationship with them and their willingness to learn. Discussing with them what they think about schooling and learning is not all that common. There are three things that are worth discussing with your students:

1. Talk about why you think they should learn what you want them to learn; why it is important. Talk about it as passionately as you believe. Your job is to ensure that

your students do learn what adult society sees as critical for children to learn if they are going to grow up to be competent adults. All of it. You have to be committed to all of it, to see all of it as essential.

2. Then ask them what their motivations might be for learning it? Are they motivated, do they care? What might have to happen for them to become motivated? Do they need a 'taster' experience? Will they become motivated when they begin learning and experience the excitement of the new skill or understanding? Will they trust you, because of their past experience of you or of teachers generally, to engage fully with this new learning until intrinsic motivation kicks in? Talk with them about it and jointly figure out what to do next: whether to rip into it or gently explore it and see how it goes. For most kids, especially the younger ones, motivation is not a problem, and doesn't become so until we manage to turn them off with boredom. At five years of age, they are eager and accept readily that if we say it is important, it is important. All they expect is that we will provide them with safe and genuine learning conditions. They won't be anxious about learning new things unless they have prior experience of where this has made them feel bad. For example:

'I was anxious about golf coaching because my previous experiences in sports coaching at school were mostly bad – I would regularly be made by the coach to feel stupid, lazy and incompetent. I was expected to do things that I did not have the skill to do and could not work out by myself. I would have been motivated about golf coaching if my previous coaching had actually helped me as a learner and respected me as a person.'

3. Then talk with them about how you want to engage them with the learning. Tell them what the big goal is, and what you intend them to learn over the next lesson or unit. Tell them how you intend that they find out where they are at with their knowledge in the bigger picture, so that specific next steps can be planned that will be relevant to all of them.

Do these simple things and watch the motivation lift!

The barriers to achieving a learning-focused relationship

There are many potential barriers to teachers achieving a learning-focused relationship. We covered some of these earlier when we discussed the different types of relationships. Below are some additional barriers that can arise.

Inadvertently privileging passivity in learning

Traditionally, we have thought of much learning at school as the students receiving 'input' from the teacher, with students being 'vessels' to be filled by the teacher. Peter Elbow beautifully describes how this works when, in the context of talking about literacy, he says:

'People think of listening and reading — not talking and writing — as the core activities in school. (An old tradition has not fully disappeared: Talking is the crime, writing is the punishment.) If we stop to think about it, we will realise that students learn from output — talking and writing. But we don't naturally think of learning as talking and writing. Notice, for example, how many teachers consider assessment or testing as measuring input rather than output. Tests tend to ask, in effect, how well have you learned others' ideas?'

Elbow, 2004

He goes on to argue that even tests that suggest questions such as 'How well can students build new thoughts out of what they have studied?' are still a subtle test of input and that we need to think further than that and ask, 'What new ideas can the student come up with?' as a true indication of the extent to which students have really actively made learning their own.

It is not that we do not want students to learn about how others see the world, but that if this is as far as their learning goes, and the process for doing that learning is substantially passive, then the learning will be superficial. It will limit the extent to which the student can use the learning for school, work and life, and will lessen the extent to which the student can build capacity as an originator.

Inadvertently weakening student agency

Whenever a teacher *requires* students to comply in any way, the teacher is reducing the extent to which the entire relationship is co-constructed and consistent with the guiding principles, reducing the ability of students to exercise agency. It is not that requiring students to be quiet will destroy any possibility of building a successful learning-oriented relationship with the students. Not at all. But each time a teacher intervenes to cause students to do things that are not transparently a part of the co-constructed programme or transparently connected to the agreed learning, the ability of students to exercise agency is reduced, even if slightly, even if temporarily, even if only towards aspects of the relationship that are only tangential to the actual teaching/learning focus.

When the teacher unilaterally takes actions independent of co-construction there is a distancing of the student from the relationship. If such intervention is frequent and characteristic of the teacher's approach, then the students will not experience agency and will not experience the relationship as learning-focused. Such experiences will turn them away from learning.

Inadvertently creating a task focus

If the students experience decisions and actions by the teacher that they cannot connect with, the intended learning they will do will be one of two things. If they are strongly motivated to learn and are confident originators of action, they will query the teacher's decisions and actions. If they do not have the same confidence they will retreat into compliance with the request and disengagement from any deliberate acts of learning. The classroom will become a centre of activities rather than of learning. In these circum-stances, teacher feedback can be about anything because the students do not need it to learn (because they are not consciously learning) and may merely like it, if it is evaluative, because it shows whether they have complied or not. It is about task completion for both teacher and students.

'I have done my story, have you done the marking? We did lots of stuff at school today; I wrote lots, we worked hard. We have covered the curriculum, we have met the requirements for coverage.'

With an expectation to do things, the role of the teacher is to manage or organise the activities. Everything else follows from this. Feedback is not descriptive and critical about where the learning is at, but evaluative about how well the tasks have been done. Even when the task is 'to *learn* the times table or spelling list or . . .' there is still a task orientation rather than a learning orientation with an emphasis on how well it was learnt (success or failure) *rather than* on how well the learning is going.

The two orientations are differentiated

- by purpose: 'we are learning this because we can communicate more clearly if we can spell' versus 'we are learning this because the teacher told us to';
- by assessment type: 'use peer-assessment to work out the success of the learning and to pinpoint any words that seem difficult to learn (keep a record of how many you got right)' versus 'the spelling test is on Friday and we will mark them together to see who is the spelling champion';
- by type of feedback: 'which words are you having difficulty learning? You seem to find it difficult to remember how to spell words that begin with "ph"' versus 'you got 85 per cent of your words correct, good boy'.

Because task orientation is so much a part of our personal educational histories it is difficult to easily distinguish a task focus from a learning focus. Often we will mistake a learning focus for a task focus. At school, we expected to behave (or we expect teachers to expect us to behave), we expected to be praised or criticised, we expected to do things without deeply questioning them. Historically we don't have many problems with this because it has always been the role of children to do as they have been bid by adults. We don't expect school to be different. To do as we are told is relatively easy, and to check to see if we are doing as we were told is relatively easy and requires only superficial engagement with the tasks. When you are doing as you are told, you don't have to worry about why you are doing it, you don't have to enquire about it. That is for the teacher to worry about. Your job is to do, trusting that the teacher knows good reasons as to why. You often don't have to worry about how well you are doing something except in a superficial sort of way. If you are learning about magnetism, you have to listen, to read the bits in the book, to carry out the experiments, and to write up the experiments. Finally, you might have to sit a test. None of these things explicitly requires you to understand magnetism concepts. You might learn them, you might not. The main thing is task completion and the main feedback you look for is related to quality of task completion (50 per cent in the end of unit test is a pass), not adequacy of understanding of key concepts.

As teachers, we draw on our experience of our own schooling and this is always about obedience and task orientation. For us, as teachers, to shift to a learning focus is difficult and requires a lot of unlearning. We can use our students as guides and monitors by deliberately inviting them to check the quality of our co-construction of a classroom programme that supports their learning and builds their conception of themselves as originators.

Inadvertently making the learning inconsequential

There are so many ways in which a real focus on significant learning by both teacher and student can be lost. Think about these examples:

A good 11-year-old student is trying to become better at writing recount stories by using sparse, but powerful imagery, in the style of well-renowned authors like Janet Frame. The teacher, by way of feedback, suggests the use of more adjectives and adverbs. The student thanks the teacher (as you do) but finds the feedback confusing because it is suggesting that she try and use alternative literary devices to the ones she was wanting to improve her ability with.

Why would the teacher give feedback like this? Talking with the teacher later showed that the teacher was unaware of what the student was trying to do, was not particularly strong in her own understanding of sparse texts, and always tried to encourage students at this age to use a richer vocabulary. In effect her feedback was generated by a belief about what feedback students at this age need, rather than by a belief that feedback should be directly related to what the student is trying to learn.

A very common similar example is in cases where teachers 'mark' student work in terms of the grammatical and spelling errors, when the student has been expecting feedback in terms of the learning objectives. The students, over time, begin to realise that writing lessons are not about learning to improve their ability to communicate with a reader but to write grammatically and lexically correct sentences. Both teacher and student then begin to focus on improving the surface features of the writing. The student's motivation to learn to do this is low because it is not connected to a purpose that makes much sense to them (they recognise that it is superficial learning), so to the extent to which they engage in it they do so to comply, not to learn. The teacher also has motivation to engage in this type of teaching because it is a traditional activity of a teacher, not because it actually makes sense to them from a learning perspective. It is just what, as teachers, they expect to do. In effect both teacher and students carry assumptions around with them about what writing lessons are about that are not connected deeply with learning.

Neither of them have cause to question these assumptions, nor even to be really aware that they hold them, because there is nothing problematic about the lessons; they neither expect to enjoy them nor be motivated by them, it is just what you do during writing lessons. All of this changes radically when one of the parties (and let's face it, if the teacher doesn't do this, it's not likely to happen) begins to ask about what is to be learnt and the purpose behind the learning. Once both teacher and student have an explicit and shared understanding, it is more likely (but not guaranteed) that both the student and teacher will have a conversation about the extent to which the writing was successful in demonstrating the learning the student was aiming for, and what elements might be worth shaping further next time.

Inadvertently buying-in to students' expectations of passive learning

Many students do have a view that schools are places where you go to sit, to listen, and to learn, by absorption. If they listen hard, and are respectful towards the teacher, they will learn. To question, to debate, to assess their peers' work, is to violate their cultural norms around learning. Even if the students have the skills to question and critique, they do not see it as the right thing to do. Your role must be to reframe this construction for the students by reframing their view of the culture of the classroom and distinguishing it from the culture of their home. For example:

- At your home everyone removes their shoes before entering.
- In your home, younger members avert their eyes when talking with elders.
- These are the right things to do at your house — for everyone who comes to it.
- In this class you question.
- In this class you challenge the ideas and views of the teacher and of your peers about what we are learning about.
- These are the right things to do in this class — for everyone who comes to it. This is the right way to learn.

Inadvertently lessening the learning by 'needing' to control the classroom

Classroom management is an area where teachers have always seen it as appropriate for them to be in control, to maintain discipline, and to exercise their authority over what students do and do not do. This area is a major test for how broadly a learning-focused relationship can be defined. Is it reasonable or realistic for a teacher to 'allow' students equal agency around issues of classroom control? The answer lies in what it is that the students know and need to learn. If their motivation to learn is low, if their ability to exercise appropriate (learning-focused) agency is low, then the teacher has a major task to teach these things within the context of subject teaching.

Adult students within a tertiary institution who are strongly motivated to be there find it easy to respond to teacher requests to listen, to respond in turn, to shift to a different task, etc. There is no issue of 'classroom control' in these circumstances at all. All the students recognise the legitimate role responsibilities of the teacher in organising the learning environment. Equally, neither would the students find it difficult to suggest alternative arrangements for the environment that they thought might work better. With younger students within the compulsory schooling sector, the teacher has to manage and support both the student motivation and student learning about 'how to learn'.

It requires the teacher to be clear about what he or she wants to have happen by way of arrangements for learning, and to be able to teach those students who need to be taught, how to be appropriate within a learning environment. We don't want to underestimate the importance of this or, at times, the difficulty of achieving it. It requires very firm and clear teaching with good exemplars and modelling, and timely, appropriate feedback about learning attempts. If your classroom is 'out of control', this is the learning that needs to be focused on first. However, the tricky bit is that students will only learn to be appropriate if they can see that this makes sense in enabling them to learn relevant and important (curriculum) things. They need to be motivated to learn. They won't be motivated if your curriculum lessons are badly planned; if you are not clear with your students about what you want them to learn; if you are not able to explain the relevance of what you want them to learn; and if the learning activities do not lead to high levels of academic engagement.

Inadvertently reducing the agency of the student

When the teacher ignores elements of the context that are important to the student — maybe recognition and affirmation of their culture — it makes it harder for the student to feel respected and therefore to exercise agency. Students do need to feel respected for who they are as people, and to feel that their right to be in the class as equals with all others is fully recognised and celebrated.

Another common way of reducing student agency is through the deliberate or unintentional withholding of information that students need for their own legitimate learning-focused decision-making, or misrepresenting the information, and then making it impossible for students to discuss the information.

One of the most common and frequent examples with assessment, where the teacher's actual purpose of assessment — traditionally so often to grade and sort students and to make unilateral teaching decisions on the basis of the results — is misrepresented as being about learning in the subject being assessed. This is not to say that grading students is always a bad thing because assessment for qualification is essential in society. The issue is to do with misrepresentation of the purpose and the way in which this affects student agency. In these circumstances the teacher

- makes the decision about what and when to test (instead of it being a joint decision);
- administers the test;
- marks the test;
- makes a decision about what feedback the student gets, including whether he or she has 'passed' or 'failed' (instead of the nature of the feedback being decided jointly) — if the student has 'failed', the teacher may not want to make the student feel like a failure so uses their own judgement of failure to withhold this information.

In the same circumstances, the student

- does not have access to the teacher's thinking about why the test is appropriate in terms of assessing progress with the learning at that stage;
- is not able to provide input as to what aspects of the progress of learning they might be interested in assessing;
- is not able to engage in any real dialogue about what feedback would actually be useful or the usefulness of a pass/fail overall assessment — the student may still be under the misapprehension that they are unable to improve because they have no measure of where they are at in the first place.

In such a situation a genuine learning-focused relationship does not exist, and the most rational (and traditional) choice the student can make is to play their own game of 'what do I need to do in order to get a good grade?' In these circumstances neither teacher nor student are directly focused on learning, but neither admits this. The student recognises that the learning is in fact about learning what needs to be learnt in order to 'pass'. The student wants to comply or pass. Any real learning is a lucky by-product of doing whatever is necessary to pass the school game. The teacher can easily eliminate the information differential, and establish a learning-oriented relationship, by sharing all of the assessment decision-making with the students so they recognise that the assessment tells them as much as it will tell the teacher and that both teacher and students have a joint interest in determining what has been learnt. There are no legitimate reasons for not doing this, but traditionally this is not how it has been.

Traditional examinations — what students have learnt that has a predetermined percentage of students passing irrespective of the knowledge demonstrated in the assessment — are not directly connected with ongoing learning but with grading students into categories of ability. We all need certificates or degrees indicating that the accrediting institution deemed us to have reached a certain standard of capability, but we should not confuse this with having learnt anything.

Schools may also well wish to use some measure of current achievement to determine placing of students in class. Schools do need some rational way of deciding which students go with which teacher, so placement on the basis of what students know makes sense. It makes more sense if the students can be connected with this assessment in exactly the same way as above so that the results, once they are with their new teacher, can be used to begin learning immediately.

The difference between how you relate and how you think you relate

In most instances, people's actual principles, underlying beliefs and assumptions are quite different from the ones they think they hold and are quite different from the principles needed to really sustain a relationship for learning. Extensive research (Argyris & Schön, 1974) shows us that we are not aware that there is a big difference between what we think our principles are and what our actions show them to be. While this can be a shocking realisation, if it is the reality for everyone it might explain why our own teachers were so seldom able to provide really good learning-focused relationships for us in our own schooling.

The research actually says that without help it is highly unlikely that you can create those conditions yourself. And worse than that, you often don't know that there is a big gap between conditions you create and the conditions you think you create. You are not aware that you don't do what you think you do. How scary is that?

Checking the quality of your current relationships

If it is possible that the way we relate with our students is not as good as it could be, then it would be useful to have some simple ways of finding out how it could improve. There are a number of ways in which you can directly check the quality of your relationship with your students:

- You can ask the students — if you do this so that students have genuine opportunity to tell you what they really think — getting a colleague to use the quick test shown earlier is one way.
- Video your interactions with some students — negotiating learning intentions or giving feedback — and analyse it with a peer to see if all interactions are consistent

with the principles and strategies for a learning-focused relationship.

- Ask the students to discuss and work out a description of what a good teacher would be like and then ask them how you match up; if you are brave enough to do this you probably have a good learning-focused relationship or you will have a substantially better relationship by the time you have finished the discussion with them.

- Think about these things:
    - A learning-focused relationship is never lazy or taken for granted – it requires commitment – you are constantly thinking about, and checking with the students, how to help them take the next step in learning; you always know what that next step could be, but you worry about whether it adequately captures the deep learning that you want, the deep understanding and insights, the purpose for the learning.
    - A learning-focused relationship knows that learning is the thing – that all else is secondary and both the teacher and the student know this.
    - A learning-focused relationship is challenging, rewarding and exciting – for both the teacher and the student.
    - You see yourself as a coach as much as a teacher; working with individuals to tune their individual performances.
    - In a learning-focused relationship both teacher and student monitor each other's motivation for the relationship and provide encouragement to each other when motivation slips during times that are hard for the learning or for the teaching, and recognition and celebration when it has gone well.

Teaching students how to be partners in learning-focused relationships

Teaching students the capabilities they need to be good partners requires exactly the same teaching approaches as teaching any other concept or skill. What is different about teaching students how to learn is that it is 'learning about learning' which is like 'thinking about thinking'. We can do it, but it can be a little confusing at times.

A good starting strategy is to be upfront with the students and discuss with them exactly the type of relationship you want with them, see what they think of that, and then jointly work out what they will need to learn to do differently to attain it, and what you will also need to learn to do differently to attain it. Then see if you can agree on a methodology for helping each other learn these things that is consistent with the end relationship.

What students need to learn

Below is a simple description of what students need to learn about how to be a part of a learning-focused relationship. The complete set of six capabilities shown in Chapter 1 in the archway on page 24 should be shared with students. What is not here is a repeat of the earlier discussion of the importance of student self-esteem and ability to be originators, although this is implied.

Students need to

- confidently initiate discussions about their goals, strengths and weaknesses and next learning steps with their peers, teachers and parents;
- contribute to the content and the lesson process;
- use a checking routine to give guidance to the teacher about how their learning is going ('Does my teacher know how my learning is going?' 'Are there barriers to my learning that I have not told my teacher?' 'Does my teacher know how I am feeling about my learning?');
- expect to learn and know that the teacher expects all students to learn;
- know that the teacher is also a learner;
- have the skills to be honest with the teacher and trust that the teacher will respect that honesty in the service of learning.

Conclusion

Finally, what does all this add up to? What do we want to see?

We want to see every learner in every classroom highly motivated to be there, to deeply know that they are there to learn, and that they are learning for a high percentage of the time they are there. We want all learners to be able to say what they are learning, why they are learning it, and be able to describe how they are progressing and how they know they are progressing. We want them to be able to say that they are in charge of their learning, that they regulate their learning progress and path.

We want them to say that they see their teacher as a guide and mentor who provides them with excellent feedback, challenges and motivates them to do better, respects their capacity to learn, and who doesn't waste their time with distractions and irrelevancies.

Teachers have a significant responsibility to ensure that every learner experiences their learning in this way, and this cannot be done without first establishing a learning-focused relationship with each student and with the class as a whole.

The next chapters are about the assessment for learning approaches that will enable and nurture this relationship.

Chapter 4

BEING CLEAR ABOUT WHAT IS TO BE LEARNT

Why it is so important to be clear about what is to be learnt

If students are to truly have responsibility for their learning then it should go without saying that they must be as clear as they can be about what they are intending to learn. Paradoxically, clarity is not what we ever really start with but what we work towards. How can you really be clear about something you don't know about yet? The more you know about a subject the clearer you are about what that subject really is. The more the students learn, the clearer they get.

As the teacher you should be very clear about what you want them to know, but they don't know what they don't know. Our job, as teachers, is to stay focused on the process of clarification, to work with them to enable them to use what they currently know, to envisage something of what they might learn next.

Using clarification as a process also means that we need to not only spend time at the beginning of a lesson or unit of work clarifying what we want them to learn, why we want them to learn it, and how we intend that the learning should proceed, but we also need to come back to that intention over the course of the lesson. We need to repeatedly return to the big idea of the learning and check progress: 'Are we getting there?'

When we are clear, research shows that there are a number of important shifts for the students. Their motivation improves, they stay on-task, their behaviour improves, and they are more apt to engage in self-regulation. In other words, they take more responsibility for their learning.

Being clear about what is to be learnt

Good planning is essential to being clear. Doing the hard thinking that is required if you are really to know what you want your students to know is absolutely critical. There are no short cuts. And it is a necessary precursor to later co-construction. Chapter 9 describes the processes involved in effective planning. That said, there are two parts to supporting a learner to become clear about what is to be learnt: naming or identifying the learning (learning intentions), and describing the learning (models or exemplars and success criteria).

These are two parts to a whole and you must not lose sight of the whole. Naming and describing are two techniques to achieve the important overall goal of ensuring that students are clear about what they are learning. Use both parts flexibly and creatively so that you achieve your goal. Together they need to paint the best possible picture of what is to be learnt. For example, for some learning, for some students, words may not be the most sensible way to convey the intended learning. For very young children, for those with severe language deficits, words may be the most inefficient way of conveying intended learning and we might choose to use modelling or exemplars to carry the whole message.

Learning intentions

Learning intentions describe what it is we want students to learn or what it is that students want or need to learn.

What's in a name? — learning intentions, objectives, goals, aims . . .
It doesn't matter what term is used when you are being clear about what is to be learnt,

as long as you are as clear as you can be with your students. All of these terms have been used by different writers to mean very similar things.

In recent years the terminology to describe what we want students to learn has varied from learning objective or specific learning objective to learning intention or learning goal. There has been an increased recognition that the actual process of learning is not always as definite, linear and lock-step as suggested by 'specific learning objective' and the type of knowledge implied by learners who have learnt a long list of learning objectives. It is not always simply a matter of teaching students a large number of discrete specific learning objectives that would, in total, add up to the national curriculum. For example, we don't want doctors who make incisions, stitch lesions, and drain wounds successfully. We want doctors who can do all of that, but who can carry out a complete operation on a patient successfully and have a sense of the wholeness of their profession. What we want students to know is not necessarily made up of lots of discrete bits. Competence at language is certainly not. It is all a lot messier than that, and the path of learning is not linear, although there is often a 'common' sequence of learning and progression.

So it seems better to capture descriptions of what we are wanting students to learn at any one time as what we are 'intending' them to learn. 'Learning intentions' is perhaps the most commonly used term at the time of writing and it is the one that you will see most often in this book.

How Barbara-Anne explained the importance of learning intentions to her class

When introducing learning intentions to my class I realised I needed to do it in a way which made it simple and clear. I began by asking them to imagine a dark tunnel. We talked about what might happen if we tried to walk through the tunnel without a torch to light our way. The students shared ideas such as we might bang into the wall, or we could fall over, we could get lost or even start walking in the opposite direction without even realising it.

I then explained that there have been times in my teaching where I have sent them into a dark tunnel because I haven't made it clear to them what it is I intend them to learn. I introduced the term *learning intention* here and explained that this was going to be the torch in my teaching and their learning. It would help us to know we are heading in the right direction, taking away some of the confusion and unnecessary obstacles that could slow their progress and understanding down.

Together we broke down what a learning intention was. Students suggested words such as our goal, aim, or the learning we hoped would take place. We also looked into the dictionary and defined what *learning* was and what the word *intention* meant and put them together to gain a greater understanding of the term *learning intention*. I told them to tell me whenever they felt 'in the dark' about what they were meant to be learning.

We talked about our learning being like a journey through the tunnel. This was where I introduced success criteria and we likened them to signposts along the way through the tunnel because when we referred to them throughout the lesson we would ensure that we continued to travel in the right direction, not take any side tunnels, and work our way towards our intended learning destination.

Often a picture of a torch was placed beside the words *learning intention* and signposts beside the success criteria.

Success criteria — unpacking the learning

Success criteria help students to gain a better understanding of what successful learning might look like in ways that they can recognise from what they know now. They can either be constructed so that they make salient the most important features of what is to be learnt, or so that the learner can understand how successful learning might be assessed, or both. For example:

Learning intention: we are learning to write a short, exciting, narrative.

Success criteria:

- The narrative will have an introductory paragraph and a conclusion.
- The narrative will sequence events.
- The narrative will use the present tense to build a sense of immediacy and urgency.

These criteria make salient the important features of this type of narrative. They spell out in greater detail the learning intention. A short, exciting narrative of the type being studied has these features. By making them explicit, it focuses the learner on what their narratives need to contain, and makes explicit for both learner and teacher what both will look for and assess in a completed narrative.

It can be helpful to separate success criteria into two types. *Process criteria* unpack the important features of what is to be learnt or how we will go about the learning. *Product criteria* describe the way in which students will know at the end of the task that they have achieved the learning intention.

Depending on the learning intention, the important features might be of both types. Sometimes we will want students to learn how to do or make something (process criteria) and also attend to the qualities of the product (product criteria). For example, in the learning intention above we have only included product success criteria. We could have also included some criteria about how they might go about constructing the piece by suggesting the following:

- brainstorming of ideas and possible language features, beginning with a small group;
- individual crafting;
- proofreading.

In a science lesson where the intention is shaped around developing an understanding of electricity, we might well want to include some process investigative criteria, as well as criteria around electrical concepts. If we include both product and process criteria, we should also write the learning intention (or intentions) to make clear that the learning is intended to encompass both.

To construct criteria of the important features of the learning requires that you, as teacher, know the subject extremely well. What teachers usually find difficult, when they first start developing success criteria, is to decide what the critical features are that they want students to pay particular attention to as they work towards the learning. It could be that they are unsure of the features, or that deciding on the features that will be of most help to students tends to cause them to rethink what is most important. This is a difficult, but very useful, process in beginning to formulate teaching as a learning-focused endeavour. Engaging in this thinking with colleagues is perhaps the most powerful way to do it. It is an excellent opportunity for teachers to share and clarify their subject understandings. For example, a discussion which leads to a shared understanding of the important features of narrative writing will ensure that all teachers are clear about this and that all students have equal opportunity to learn.

If the learner does not know what the criteria mean, such as 'sequence events', then a new learning intention, with its own success criteria that describe the important characteristics of sequence, might be shaped. For example:

Learning intention: we are learning to recognise sequence and be able to write a series of events in order when it suits our purpose as writers.

Success criteria:
- Our writing will begin with the very first thing that happened.
- Our writing will have all the events in the middle in the correct order of when things happened.
- Our writing will end with the very last thing that happened.

Sometimes it is not possible to write success criteria that are in any way helpful. For example:

Learning intention: we are learning to recognise the present tense and to be able to write in the present tense consistently when it suits our purpose as writers.

Success criteria:
- Our writing will contain indicators of the present such as tense-related adverbs like 'today' or 'now'.
- Our writing will have all verbs in the present tense.
- All other grammatical features will agree with the verb tense.

How helpful are these criteria? It depends on how much the student already knows about language. But understanding the success criteria may well require as much knowledge as the learning intention itself. There is a good chance that if they can understand these success criteria, they will already be able to control tense. Defining some success criteria for this learning does not add much value, and it will be much more useful to the learner to provide multiple examples of 'present' tense and 'not present' tense, with the learning coming from repeated attempts of using present tense language correctly in the presence of, and with feedback from, an expert language user: the teacher.

The example above shows that not all types of learning are susceptible to clear criteria that will add value to the learners' understanding of what is to be learnt. Not all learning needs extensive criteria in order for students to come to understand the important features. Sometimes few people know how to articulate the important features. Describing a list of indicators of the present tense, for example, is not easy. And we do not typically learn tense through that approach. For some learnings — typically things such as language and motor skills — success criteria, no matter how they are written or described, add little as guides to learning. With these types of learning, success criteria might become a simple guide to how success could be assessed.

For example:

> **Learning intention:** to learn to use initial letter sounds as an aid to decoding unfamiliar words.
> **Success criteria:** we will know you are trying this when you make the beginning sound of words you don't know.

This criterion is worded in a much more child-friendly way than the learning intention (which also needs to be reworded into child-speak), and suggests a performance target of actually attempting to sound the beginning letters of words so that the child knows what they have to do in order to meet the teacher's expectation of engaging with the learning. There is some trust required from the child that this will make sense in time. Another example:

> **Learning intention:** we are learning to ride a bike.
> **Success criteria:** to ride in a straight line for 10 m without falling off.

This does not add much to 'learning to ride a bike' but again it does give a little performance target along the way. However, it is probably more meaningful to watch someone ride a bike: a model or exemplar.

A tertiary course in macro-economic theory will normally be accompanied by a textbook. Normally each chapter of such textbooks invariably summarises the significant learning objectives of the chapter. These are in effect the learning intentions *and* the success criteria. A test of the extent to which your understanding of the chapter matches against the success criteria comes from your ability to successfully complete the problems given at the end of the chapter! If you can do all of the problems, then you probably have a good understanding of the concepts described. Such a textbook contains both types of success criteria.

These examples should not be taken to imply that success criteria are not important in some circumstances. Quite the reverse. These examples show that in all learning you have to find ways, suitable to the nature of the learning, of articulating what features of the learning should be attended to as learning proceeds, and what success at that learning might finally look like.

What is to be learnt — exemplars of what it is and of what it is not

Perhaps the most powerful way of describing what is to be learnt is to provide an exemplar or example of it. Words cannot describe everything. As Sadler (1987) points out, it is difficult to express progress and quality in words alone. Words are needed to describe criteria and examples are needed to demonstrate quality. In *A Journey in Ladakh*, Andrew Harvey (1983) puts it another way:

'All words fall short of the shining of things, things exist that are unnameable, we need to be able to see through the word to the thing.'

If the learning is a process or skill then showing a *model* is an appropriate way of demonstrating the intended learning. (For example, showing someone riding a bike, delivering a speech, giving feedback to a teacher about a lesson, taking part in a group discussion.) If the learning results in a product then an exemplar might be more appropriate. (For example, showing a piece of narrative writing, handwriting, a fully worked mathematical algorithm, a painting in a particular style.)

Showing someone an exemplar of the learning (for example, riding a bike) not only clearly demonstrates what the learning is intended to result in, it also allows you to draw attention to particular aspects of how it is being done ('Notice how he pushes the bike forward to gain some momentum at the start. This helps him gain his balance.') — to describe or derive the success criteria with the students. These can then be written down if this will help the learner.

Figure 3: Poetic writing exemplar

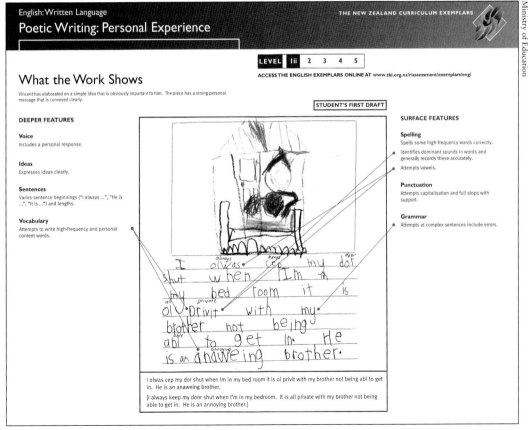

www.tki.org.nz/r/assessment/exemplars/eng/personal/wpp_1b_e.php

The exemplar should

- be relevant to the learning intention and exemplify the intended learning;
- exemplify the next steps of the learning rather than being several steps removed from the learning: if you want the student to really make meaning of the example, do not use an example that is so sophisticated that it is difficult for the student to understand how the features that are important to the work can at all connect with the level that they are at;
- allow in-depth discussion between teacher and student about the features of the example that the student should attend to so that success criteria can be co-constructed.

In well-organised teaching resources, where the learning requires an increasing level of sophistication in performance or understanding by the student, such as in written language or in use of the scientific method, exemplars are supplied for a series of levels of development along with a matrix of success criteria that apply to each level. The New Zealand National Curriculum Exemplars are an excellent example of one such resource.

Learning to recognise a concept can often be helped with exemplars of the concept and with exemplars of what the concept is not. For example, helping students to recognise and use metaphors in writing, you might give them some examples of metaphors, and some examples of other descriptive strategies that are not metaphors, and ask them to analyse the distinguishing features.

How to develop learning intentions and success criteria

How do you work out what you want your students to learn? There are two places to start in thinking about what we intend our students to learn. The first, in a learning-focused relationship is, of course, with the students, and what they know now. The second is with the curriculum.

What they know now

Any learner knows that the next learning step they take in any area must build on what they know or can do now. Unfortunately teachers have often not provided classroom conditions where this happens. A study of Year 7 and 8 New Zealand students showed that, prior to a unit on the Antarctic environment, they, on average, already knew 45 per cent of what the teachers wanted them to learn, with wide variation around that average (Nuthall & Alton-Lee, 1997). This means that many of the students risked becoming bored during the unit because they already knew what the teacher intended that they learn! Another study (Marsano, 2004) showed a strong correlation (0.66) between a student's prior knowledge of a topic and the extent to which that student learns new information on that topic. The more you know about a topic, the more easily you will learn more.

What these, somewhat contrasting, studies suggest is that it is absolutely critical to deter-mine, or assess, the prior knowledge that your students bring to the upcoming topic or unit to avoid either teaching what they already know or teaching them something that they cannot bring prior experience to bear on. There are a number of ways in which you can do this.

The most obvious way is through assessment. Traditional assessments are carried out *by* the teacher *on* the student. The student may be told the mark or grade but often that is the extent of their involvement. It makes more sense from our perspective if the assessment is collaborative and the student is fully involved in the selection of the assessment tool (where there is any choice), the administration, the marking, and especially the analysis. We spend more time on this in Chapter 5, but the analysis should result in both teacher and student having a deep understanding of what the student currently knows, and what would make sense to both of them for the student to learn next. It requires the student to engage in some speculation, or hypothesis making, as to what that next learning might look like. This process of speculation is hugely advantageous in actually engaging the student actively with the next learning, of keeping the learner in control of the learning. Peter Elbow puts it this way in reference to developing ability in reading:

> '. . . *students invariably read better if they write first — if they start by writing their own thoughts about a topic that the class will tackle in a text. Even if the topic is scientific, factual, or technical, and students know little or nothing about it, I tell them, "Write your hunches about this topic — even your fantasies. What do you wish were true?"*
>
> *'For example, before having students read an essay about dropping out of school, I might ask them to free write about whether they think the number of dropouts has gone up or down in recent decades — and speculate about the causes of dropping out. Before reading an analysis of environmental degradation and a proposal on how to deal with it, students might speculate about the causes and suggest solutions of their own. Before conducting an experiment that involves rolling balls of different weights down inclined planes, students might speculate about the results. Starting with writing rather than reading highlights how learning and thinking work best: as a process of hypothesis making and hypothesis adjustment in which the mind is active rather than passive.*
>
> *'After writing their hunches students are more attentive to what the author wrote — sometimes out of mere curiosity to see how well their ideas match the material . . . '*   Elbow, 2004

When a more formal type of assessment is not possible or desirable, a discussion can take place with students about what they know already about a possible learning intention. And you can ask them to speculate about what they think they might learn or what that learning might look like. This leads of course very easily into an examination of exemplars and an analysis of the features that characterise those exemplars.

If you have used this approach of having your students (*all* of your students) helping to tune your learning intentions to their needs they will be highly engaged and wanting to begin the learning. All you have to do is ensure that your intentions fit with the curriculum!

The curriculum

The New Zealand curriculum consists of a set of key competencies, eight essential learning areas, and underpinning values. It is the responsibility of each school and each teacher to adopt a planned approach to ensuring that every student has rich opportunities to learn what is in the curriculum before they complete Year 13, to the level that they are able at a pace that is suitable to them. Each teacher at each year level has a responsibility to ensure that all students build on what they learnt the previous year.

We don't need to read the curriculum every day, but we do need to know it very well and to have a professional commitment in ensuring that our children have opportunity to work towards its aims. For each learning area in the curriculum there is a one- or two-page 'essence statement' that describes what the subject is about, why we want children to study it, and how the curriculum is structured. You need to be very familiar with all of the statements that apply to your teaching and be able to paraphrase them for students at whatever level they are at so that they are also completely clear about why they are studying the subject in the first place.

The essence statement gives the highest and most general description of what we want students to learn. They are the most global of learning intentions. In fact they are more general than global: *universal* might be a better term. We never teach at such a high level but it is where we start our thinking and our planning about what students need to know and be able to do. And in fact we might choose to share these universal learning intentions with the students so that they can also keep the big picture of the learning in mind as they focus down on specifically what they will learn next. The focusing down may go through several different layers that lead directly from one layer to the next. For example, see Table 6 on the opposite page.

It might be useful to think of these differing layers as sort of making up a pyramid of learning intentions with the very few universal ones at the top and the specific at the bottom. A significant 'tool' for teachers is the breaking down of the learning into manageable 'chunks'. There is an almost infinite number of possible learning intentions at the specific layer because even small learnings such as 'full stops' may themselves require breaking down into even smaller learning steps for some students, such as 'we are learning to recognise full stops', even if it does not take them long to learn and the only success criteria that can be ascribed to them is that they can successfully point to full stops in a variety of sentences. We can then move on to more significant learning.

Once you have determined what the students want to learn next you can go to your subject-derived general or specific learning intentions and revise them as appropriate.

Being clear about why it is to be learnt – the relevance of the learning

Being clear and explicit about what is to be learnt is only a part of the job. Students also need to gain agency over the relevance and the process of the learning. Relevance is derived from two sources. The first aspect of relevance comes from relating the learning to more immediate demands of students' current life. One student was asked why learning to describe a character in detail was important. He offered the view that the relevance of learning was so that a good description of someone caught stealing could be given to the police. It might not be why you would learn it, but it made sense to this student and gave him the motivation to learn.

Teachers can, however, tie themselves up in knots trying to create real-life relevance for learning. For example, the learning of how to do quadratic equations is difficult to relate to real life, at least for most students. For this sort of learning, relevance is mostly related to the logic of the subject, which is the second aspect of relevance. Explaining why something should be learnt should be convincing and easy if you have constructed your learning intention top down from the essence of the subject as shown in Table 6 opposite.

TABLE 6: LAYERS OF LEARNING INTENTIONS

	Layer	Source	Learning intention	Success criteria
1.	Universal – essence	From the English essence statement.	By engaging with text-based activities, students become increasingly skilled speakers and writers . . .	Our speaking and writing match exemplars of adult speaking and writing.
2.	Universal– curriculum strand and level	From the English creating meaning strand, Level 2 achievement objective: Purpose and audiences.	Show a developing understanding of how to shape (written) texts for different audiences and purposes – through choice of content, language and text form, constructs texts that demonstrate a developing awareness of audience and purpose.	We can produce texts for different audiences that have all the qualities shown in the Level 2 English Writing Exemplars.
3.	Global	From prior assessment of students and the school English scheme.	'We are learning to write an argument which is convincing.'	Our argument • starts with a summary of the argument; • uses persuasive language; • uses logical sequence; • is written clearly for the reader (grammatical) so that they don't get distracted from the argument; • has a conclusion which appeals to the audience.
4.	General	From layer 3 success criteria.	'We are learning to sequence an argument.'	Each step in our sequence will • logically follow on from the previous one; • contain the main points of the sequence of the argument in a paragraph; • our teacher and our peers will agree there is a logical sequence.
5.	Specific	From layer 3 or 4 success criteria.	'We are learning what a paragraph is and when to start a new one.'	Our paragraph • usually starts with the main information; • follows with examples or ideas to support the main information; • stops when you have a new point to make.

For example, here is a learning intention in which the relevance is derived from two sources:

Learning intention: we are learning to write a short, exciting narrative.

Success criteria:

- The narrative will have an introduction and a conclusion.
- The narrative will sequence events.
- The narrative will use the present tense to build a sense of immediacy and urgency.

Relevance: so that we grow our ability to shape (written) texts for different audiences and purposes; so that we can write e-mails and texts to our friends that they want to read.

When teachers consider the relevance of the learning intention it will often challenge its quality. For example, learning to use capital letters and full stops as a learning intention is thin in quality, without the thinking around why and how punctuation is important. After that thinking, it may well be that the learning intention changes to become much richer; for example, we are learning to make our ideas clear to the reader. The capital letters and full stops then become the success criteria that evidence this learning.

The reason *you* think they should learn it should come both from your intellectual understanding of why it is important to children to learn what is in the curriculum, and your emotional commitment to their learning. If they don't accept your explanation, then there is something wrong with the way you have explained it. Maybe you don't really believe they should? Maybe you don't feel connected to that subject yourself and don't have either an emotional or intellectual commitment. That is your problem, you should solve it, and you should make certain that you don't make it the children's.

Being clear about how it is to be learnt — the learning process

Describing to the students how you have thought about the intended learning process (tasks and activities) is very important. Not that it is necessarily negotiable, any more than the curriculum is negotiable. Co-construction is not about giving up your power to the students, but ensuring that neither they nor you exercise any power in a way that is detrimental to the other's agency. However, sharing your intention and seeking acceptance or improvement is hugely important in providing students an opportunity to voice what they believe might not work for them and why. As in any co-constructed process, merely voicing a view is no more than that. If you accept it, you do so because you believe that the view has validity. If you reject it, you will give your reasons for the rejection and each of those reasons needs to be testable. Students who buy-in to the learning intention will seldom argue about how you intend they learn.

Points to watch out for

Being clear with your students about what is to be learnt sounds straightforward, but there are a number of things that it pays to consider every now and again.

Keeping the focus

Learning intentions need to form the reference point for the lesson, always keeping the big picture in mind, and be referred back to when teachers and students reflect on how their learning/teaching is going. This means that generally they should be displayed and there are a variety of ways of doing this, including 'mental display' where they are not written down at all but just referred to frequently by the teacher. This way of course carries some dangers from poor memories or latecomers because they are not available to the learner to refer back to.

Being open to emergent possibilities

No teacher likes the idea of being 'locked in' to a narrow, tightly specified curriculum that does not enable them to bring their own thinking, flair, energy and intelligence to the classroom. On the other hand, if everything that we teach is to be derived from the curriculum, how do we avoid it? The answer is that when you have a good grasp of the 'bigger picture' of what the curriculum is asking you to teach students — as described in the essence statements — you can see that there are a myriad different ways of having students develop those bigger understandings. This means that if, in the midst of a unit of work or a lesson, a new, timely context emerges, perhaps from the students themselves, that you believe will allow you to guide the students to learn even more effectively, then you can change tack because the overall big picture is still the same. If you do not have this big picture you do not know the overall direction you are meant to be heading in and you will feel stuck in a narrow teaching rut.

Alignment

It may seem obvious, but the success criteria and the exemplars need to illustrate the learning intention, and all three need to be closely related to the learning tasks. We often find that there is no alignment at all, or that it is so loose that it is confusing for the students. For example, in a recent lesson:

> **Learning intention:** to observe and record or write down the steps to making a sandwich.
> **Success criteria:** writing the recipe using action verbs (refers children to a list of action verbs).
> **Exemplar:** teacher models making a sandwich and describes the process they are going through, and the reasons they have selected each ingredient, with the expectation that the children will write down the procedure as they do so.
> **Relevance:** if you eat good food you will lessen the chances of getting diabetes (as the students reported it).

What messages can the students possibly take from this? Is the lesson about procedural writing, about health, about both? Who can be sure? Not surprisingly, in this lesson, 80 per cent of the students were off-task during the demonstration and all of those interviewed thought the lesson was about making a healthy sandwich. To make it more focused on the learning intention the teacher would need to scaffold the learning more clearly around the children writing down each step of the process as they went. They might talk about each step, discuss what might be written and why. They would not include distractors such as the nature of the ingredients. If it was an integrated English and Health unit, they would need to find some way of separating the two learning intentions so that the students did not get confused as to what the demonstration was about. Another example:

Learning intention: to learn to write a recount using a formal structure.

Success criteria: the recount will contain:

- an introduction that describes
    - where
    - what
    - why
    - when
- a sequence
- a conclusion

Learning task: highlight the verbs in the following recount.

In this example, the learning intention and the success criteria are fine but there is no alignment with the task, so how can the students be clear about what they are meant to be learning? These confusions happen because teachers themselves are not sufficiently clear at the planning stage, and the confusion continues when they do not really check with the students that they are clear. Students should be able to report that they see a clear alignment between tasks, intentions, criteria exemplars and relevance throughout the entire lesson or unit.

Using appropriate language

Shaping elegant learning intentions is of little use if they are not accessible and meaningful to the students. Depending on the age, cognitive and language levels of the student you may well have to reword your learning intention and elaborate on it so that it can become meaningful to the student and provide both of you with a shared vocabulary to describe what is to be learnt.

For example, to revisit a learning intention used earlier:

Learning intention: to learn to begin to use initial letter sounds as an aid to decoding unfamiliar words.

Reworded learning intention: what we want to learn is that if you can't read a word, a place to start is to say the beginning sound — this will help you then guess or find the word.

This might be supported by the teacher commenting:

'You are learning this because it's a useful way of trying to read new words. I will know you are trying this when you make the beginning sound of words you don't know.'

Another example:

Learning intention: to learn the role played by different parts of the digestive system.

Reworded learning intention: what you are learning to do is understand the journey of food from entry to exit using the names for each body part.

If specialised language needs to be learnt, and this is often the case, then that becomes another learning intention.

Is there an order to the use of learning intentions, exemplars and success criteria?

Most often teachers will plan a unit with the students — finalise the learning intentions, exemplars, models and success criteria — and then begin teaching. While this is a sequence that makes sense, it can be altered if it suits the learner and the learning best. For example, in a science lesson the teacher may decide to start with a demonstration of an experiment, followed by a discussion time about what might have happened and why, and then a collaborative shaping up of a learning intention.

This looks like a different sequence but in fact is a motivating way to determine what students' entry-level knowledge is and to invite them into being active learners through hypothesising about the demonstration. It is all shaped towards enabling the students to be clear about what the learning is.

The sequence is not important. Teachers of reading do a similar thing when they read a story to children, pause at a certain point, and ask the children what they think might happen next. It both provides the teacher (and the student) with information about the extent to which the children can do this, and engages the student actively in creating meaning for themselves.

How often do we need new learning intentions?

It is important to remember that the teacher does not need a new learning intention for every lesson every day of the week for every student. A new learning intention is only necessary when there is new learning to be done. Many teachers photocopy their short-term plan and put it on display. As part of their formative planning they adjust their planning, which as the week goes on becomes more and more messy as notes are added, but it is always visible for students to comment on and contribute to.

Confusions that often occur with learning intentions

'Learning' or 'doing'?

What is the difference between what you want students to learn and what you want them to do? This should be simple, but seems a difficult distinction to make sometimes. Asking people to abseil is quite different from asking them to learn to abseil. And they will not want the sequence to be in the wrong order. What often happens in school, however, is that students are asked to engage in activities — like writing a story — when it is not clear to the students that they are meant to be *learning* something about writing a story. Because they are not clear that the activity is about learning, they just get on and do it.

Here is a list of learning intentions:

- learning to abseil
- learning to write a story
- learning how to write a story
- learning to make a ruler
- learning to understand measurement

Here is a list of activities:
- abseiling
- writing a story
- describing how stories are structured so that they are interesting for the reader
- making a ruler
- measuring the length of a table

The difference is semantic, and therefore very important. The first list is explicit about everything on it being needed to be learnt. The second list is just stuff that needs to be done as activities that will aid the learning. Unless you are explicit with your students, they (and you in fact) will get confused.

You need to remember that what you write and what you say is all that your students see or hear. If you write your learning intention as 'we are writing recounts' they will not see it as 'we are learning to write recounts'. Neither will they see it as 'we are learning how to write recounts'. The 'how' is a very interesting little word and you need to be clear about what you mean by it. In some contexts it doesn't mean very much.

Learning how to abseil, and learning to abseil, are probably one and the same, but in other contexts it signals a big distinction. We generally do not want students just to know how to write, we want them to be able to actually write. In the overview at the beginning of the book, we made this distinction clear by showing that the 'how' is on the way to knowing and owning, not the other way around.

Quite often the best way to have students become skilled writers is to work with them to have them understand the 'how'; the structures and artificers of language that can be used to create particular effects. The 'how' can provide a framework for thinking about something that assists the doing of it. For example, knowing how to write a piece of persuasive writing suggests that the writer has in their head some bullet points (the success criteria if you like) which they can make mental reference to when writing a piece of persuasive writing. This comment from a student makes the point powerfully:

'We've been writing speeches for years, but we didn't ever know how to write one until now. From now on when we have to write one, we'll know how to do it.'

And again, from a principal:

'I remember clearly, in the 6th Form, being coached in how to read and answer exam questions – that impacted significantly on my exam successes right through my tertiary education – I wasn't taught to answer them – I was taught how to answer them – read the question, locate the key words, think about what I was being asked to do, think about what information I knew and how to reorganise it so that it answered the question . . . '

It is important to go beyond the 'how' to actually skilfully write the persuasive speech or exam answer. So, in phrasing learning intentions, we have to think very carefully about what exactly we do want students to learn.

Merit, significance, relevance?

When teachers start to avoid the language of activities and engage the language of learning, they often find themselves suddenly dissatisfied with their first attempts at formulating learning intentions, especially when they have to explain to their students why it is important to learn it. For example, with a learning intention of 'to learn to use adjectives in my recount story', the teacher can struggle to provide an explanation of relevance that is convincing to herself, let alone to the students.

A learning intention such as 'we are learning to write an argument which is convincing' produces the opposite problem. Here the learning intention is defined so globally that it is very easy to explain the relevance, but not so easy to actually teach until it is broken down into a number of much smaller learnings, which can sometimes be different for each student. The advantage of beginning with such a global learning intention is that it does keep the wider importance of the learning clear to the students, even when they start to burrow deep into the superficial aspects of punctuation and spelling. The students will easily see why they need to learn some of the mechanics of language in order to be competent at the bigger learning.

When good learning intentions go bad

Teachers find the idea of being clear with their students about what they are going to learn very appealing. It makes a lot of sense and is something they feel they can achieve with their students. Often they find that their kids do like this new idea too; and it seems easy enough to use the labels of learning intentions and success criteria. However, over the ensuing months it can often become very routine; both kids and then the teacher get a little bored with it. Especially if the teacher decided that they needed to write up learning intentions every day, and even more so if they decided to get the kids to write them into their books. Now it seems that this once-good idea has turned out to be just another teaching trick that in fact doesn't really do the trick at all, and they begin to wonder why they bothered re-labelling things as learning intentions. They have just become words to the kids. They can repeat them if necessary but they don't really understand them or how they are meant to help. What goes wrong?

A big problem with any label is that, over time, it can cease to really signify the underlying idea; like a webpage hyperlink that just returns a 'the page cannot be displayed' error message when it is clicked on.

What to do about this? For a start, be wary of using labels too much. This is why this chapter is called 'being clear about what is to be learnt' rather than 'learning intentions'. We wanted to use a longer, less poetic but clearer title to be certain that the concept underlying learning intentions would be obvious. We could have made it even longer to say something like 'making sure that both teacher and students are very clear about what is to be learnt, how it is to be learnt and why it is to be learnt'.

Often, the connection was never there in the first place. Take this example from a Year 1 class:

Learning intention: we are learning where to use capital letters and full stops.

Success criteria: you will have capital letters and full stops in the right places, for example, at the beginning of sentences, names, etc.

Relevance: the teacher did not explain why the children should learn these things. But the children would be likely to give an answer that applies generally to the whole curriculum and schooling experience — 'that you need to be able to write when you are bigger'. This becomes of little help in really understanding the learning intention.

There are a number of problems with framing learning intentions like this over and above the issue of relevance. The first is that there is very little difference between the learning intentions and the success criteria so that the success criteria are in fact of little help in giving the students a clearer idea of what the learning intention is about.

Secondly, the learning intention is framed in such a way that it is difficult to understand what the bigger idea or concept is that you want the students to learn. And it won't be clear to the students either. All the students can take out of this is that they are learning to use capitals and full stops and they will have learnt it successfully when they can use them! Too often the learning intentions are written as concrete, specific things to learn that do not have any self-evident bigger idea associated with them. What is the bigger idea? Why should we learn how to use capitals and full stops? We don't really know what this teacher had in mind, but it needs to be a reason that is a little more concrete and immediate than 'it will be useful when we are older', and something that captures the essence of 'sentenceness'. Something less mechanical than 'learn to use capitals and full stops'; something that indicates 'why'. It might be 'when we are communicating to others we want to separate our ideas to others so that they see each idea clearly: in little packets'. If this is the concept (the learning intention) and it is then backed up with illustrations and exemplars, then this is much more likely to be meaningful and might look like this:

Learning intention: when we are communicating to others we want to separate our ideas to others so that they see each idea clearly — in little packets.

Success criteria: we will have capital letters and full stops in the right places: for example, beginnings of sentences, names, etc.

Relevance: so that others can understand all of our ideas in our writing clearly.

It is hard to write learning intentions like this and even harder to write them in language accessible to young students. So much of our own learning history is not based on being clear about what to learn. When we were at school we just did the activities and over time learnt things. But we seldom really knew why. We did not have agency as learners and we now, as teachers, do not appreciate the importance of this if we want active learners. Why do we write in sentences? If we, as the teachers, are not really clear, then we cannot really tell students clearly what we want them to learn and why. As a result our learning intentions will be somewhat shallow and meaningless and often simple repeats of what we were taught in school. When this is the case it is not surprising that 'learning intentions' start to feel plastic and boring to ourselves and to the students. The students start to fail to know what they are intended to achieve. When students don't know what the intention is behind learning intentions then we have clearly lost it.

The big question for us is: how do you really understand when you have framed your learning intentions properly so that they are not just shallow and superficial? This is difficult, really difficult, and requires sustained pondering on what you are really wanting students to learn. As you ponder your original learning intentions, they begin to change as you re-conceptualise them into more adequate frames.

For example, Allan and Robyn planned as a team. They might start with:
'learning to use adjectives in our writing'
which then becomes:
'learning to carefully describe an event that builds a picture in the reader's mind'
which then finally becomes:
'learning some powerful language tools that help your writing connect with the reader'.

Having colleagues critique your learning intentions is one way; having your students do it too is another. Give them the power to really critique your learning intentions and see if they (the learning intentions) survive. It doesn't matter at all if they don't because better, more adequate ones will arise in their place. To retain the connection the connection needs to be continually tested.

We have also found that teachers find the idea of being clear intellectually appealing, and easy enough to understand at a level at which they believe they can implement learning intentions reasonably easily in the class. In fact, what happens is that this intellectual engagement does not go the next step, which is to also really intellectually engage the students with the same idea. What we tend to do is tell them about learning intentions but we do not really engage them, or ourselves, in thinking deeply about what they really mean, what the actual concepts are, why we should learn them, or what it might be like once we have learnt them. So we should do that. We should ask questions of ourselves and of the students about what you *really* want them to learn. What we find is that as we continue to teach assessment for learning principles to teachers we continue, year after year, to understand all of the concepts differently, and more deeply. What seemed obvious and clear one year suddenly becomes very shallow and unsatisfactory the next year. Our own thinking about learning intentions followed exactly this pattern.

'Learning intentions' don't work unless you are metacognitive about them as well. If we had laminated our approach to discussing learning intentions then we would likely never have gone deeper and discovered that we did not understand them as well as we thought. We do this, in part, by asking new team members to teach learning intentions to teachers. They do not understand how we have written about them as we understand. They ask naïve and really useful questions about the gap between what they think and what they see from us that causes us to also see gaps. Sharing your thinking with your students will result in the same spiral of learning.

If you don't model reflection about everything, such as learning intentions, then you won't be reflective and you won't deepen your understanding, and your approach to learning intentions will become automatic and shallow and feel recipe driven.

Sharing learning intentions

Shared agreement and understanding between teachers, students (and parents) about what is to be learnt and why, is critical because often students, particularly underachievers, don't know what they are supposed to be focusing on. This can mean that they expend effort on the wrong things, get disheartened because their efforts don't lead to success and 'retire hurt'. They attribute their success to luck and their failure to lack of ability (Dweck, 1999).

Conversely, helping students attribute their successes and failures to effort and strategy rather than luck or ability is one of the most important things teachers can do for their students because it impacts on their achievement and the way they approach their ongoing learning.

Shared agreement and understanding between teachers and students about what is to be learnt and why is also critical because often it's not that students can't learn, it's that they don't want to or can't see the point. The problem is motivational rather than cognitive. Helping students see why something is important is more likely to trigger their personal desire to learn and this desire is an incredibly powerful force that can carry learners through repeated disappointments and difficulties (Crooks, 2002).

So, how should we do it?

What students need to learn to contribute to being clear about the learning

If you are being successful at being clear with your students, your students should be able to tell any interested party, in their own words, the following:

- their global and specific learning intentions;
- what quality work looks like and the criteria for quality (success criteria);
- how they can use exemplars to assist them in knowing what they are aiming for;
- why what they are learning is relevant and important;
- their individual learning goals.

You will also want your students to know that they should know these things and to tell you clearly and assertively if they do not around any part of their learning.

If your students do not have an expectation that they will know these things you will have to teach them. Here is a learning intention and success criteria that you might use, written from the students' perspective:

Learning intention: we are learning to know how to be clear about what we are going to learn.

Success criteria: clarity is about being able to state

- our global and specific learning intentions;
- what quality work looks like and the criteria for quality (success criteria);
- how we can use exemplars to assist us in knowing what we are aiming for;
- why what we are learning is relevant and important;
- our individual learning goals.

   We do this by
   - telling our teacher that we do not understand or are not clear whenever we are not;
   - telling our teacher when we feel they are not constructing the learning intention with us or from what we know now.

Relevance: so that we grow our ability to always be in charge of our own learning.

If you used the 'Try This!' unit on 'what learning is about' in Chapter 1, pages 25–26 this will slot in with it nicely and really consolidate the sense your students have of genuinely having agency in your classroom.

Having a discussion with your class about what might be learnt next

Teacher: Our programme has creative writing on it for the next three weeks, so we need to talk about what you might learn about creative writing over that time. What I want to do now is discuss the ideas I have for this, give you an opportunity to think about how you might want to build your creative writing skills, and work out together what we might actually do. Sound good?

Teacher: *I* have done my thinking and I don't want to flood you with it until you have had a chance to do your own thinking, so what I would like you to do now is find the last piece of writing that you did, probably the last piece of creative writing, but it may be another genre. Have a look at it against the criteria that were set for it, and see what aspects of those criteria you feel you will want to improve further. If you choose the piece that was done for the Assessment Tools for Teaching and Learning (asTTle) assessment, have a look at the analysis of that and see what ideas it gives you. If you get stuck, ask me or one of your friends for help. Everyone understand? Thumbs up? Sideways? Down? Okay, ten minutes for this.

Teacher: Now, has everyone got something in their heads? Good. Now *you* and I have got something in our heads about what you might learn next. You all probably have different things. Let's 'think, pair, share' and see what you come up with. Let's see what is common, if anything.

The class carries out the exercise and generates a list of what the kids want to learn. There are some commonalities about impact on the reader.

Teacher: So it seems that a lot of you want to continue to find ways of more powerfully hooking in the reader. That is really interesting because that is what I had in my head too! I'm going to find some short pieces of writing that hook me in, you can do that too, and we will then bring them back, share them, and analyse how the writer has done it so that we can get our success criteria . . .

ASSESSMENT IS A GOOD THING

Chapter 5

Why assessment is a good thing

Learning is impossible without ongoing assessment by the learner. Assessment is an integral part of all learning, and somehow it often seems to be the most difficult bit in teaching. How can this be? Maybe because the learner is not in charge of the assessment often enough, even when we want them to be in charge of their learning.

In order to learn, you need information about what you want to be able to understand and do, and about what you currently understand and can do, so that any gap between the two can be made apparent. Learning is about attempts to reduce the gap. Assessment is the process of gaining information about the gap.

Learning is impossible without the learner engaging in at least tacit assessment of the nature of that gap.

Students and assessment

Assessment occurs with each attempt to reduce the gap. A learner who is actively engaged in learning is carrying out 'self-assessment' almost constantly in some way or another as a part of the problem-solving attempts to reduce the gap. The learner is repeatedly asking themselves 'what does this information tell me about how well I've learnt and what I need to do to close the gap?' The teacher has a number of roles to support student self-assessment. Teachers must nurture the motivation and capacity of the student to engage in that assessment, but they must also find ways of making the actual gap as apparent and as salient to the student as it actually is, so that the student's self-assessment becomes more accurate. In this process the student learns more about what they are trying to learn. To play these roles the teacher has to carry out their own assessments.

Teachers and assessment

Teachers, particularly in a class setting, are never privy to most of the assessment that students carry out for themselves, yet, for the teacher to be able to provide support and guidance for further learning they need access to timely assessment information about the current state of learning of all students. Without it they have no way of sensitively promoting further learning through support of self-assessment or prompting through scaffolding or feedback or discussion. Without it they have no way of seeing the patterns of learning progress throughout the class, of working out which groups of students need particular support for certain types of learning.

Teachers also have no way of thinking about a suitable future step in learning. With the information they get they are repeatedly asking themselves, 'What does this information tell me about how well my teaching is supporting learning and what I should do next?'

Everyone else and assessment

School managers, parents, school governors, and the Ministry of Education all need timely information about the extent to which students and groups of students are learning and are gaining the capabilities described in the curriculum. Without it these people who are charged, in various ways, with ensuring that the students, the teacher and the classroom are properly resourced to best support learning, cannot make evidence-based decisions about that resourcing. They need to be repeatedly asking themselves, 'What does this information tell me about how well my managing, or my parenting, or my governing, or my stewarding, is supporting teaching and learning?'

All of this information must come from the classroom. The teacher has a professional responsibility to gather it, and both the teacher and the students have a responsibility to ensure that it does provide a dependable picture of the standard of learning at the time of the data collection. But this information has to be obtained in a way that does not lessen the motivation or capacity of the students for learning, or unnecessarily disrupt the learning.

The trick for the teacher is to manage the entire assessment process so that *all* get the information that they need, when they need it. The teacher is the co-ordinator of information flows out of and into the classroom, ensuring the right information gets to the right person at the right time. And they have to teach. In order to do all this, the teacher needs to know a lot about assessment, and needs to ensure that students also know a lot about assessment.

What students need to know about assessment

Students need to be skilled assessors of their own learning and that of their peers and able to use or participate in a range of assessment approaches suited to subject, context and purpose, so that:

- They know that the purpose of any assessment is for learning and that for the assessment to be useful it needs to provide timely, valid and reliable information.
  'When we do a test as a class we need to do it properly otherwise it won't tell us what we really do know and need to know next; we also need to do it at the right time so we can use the information to help us with our next goals.'

- They are able to produce and describe the evidence of their learning.
  'I now know how to group numbers to get bigger numbers, I can check my answer through mental estimation.'

- They use success criteria astutely to compare with actual achievement and to identify next learning.
  'My story still hasn't got the impact I want.'

- They describe the result of that comparison and the reasons for it.
  'I haven't reached that success criteria because the audience didn't respond in the ways I hoped.'

- They know how their progress compares with school and national norms, where there are norms available.
  'I don't seem to learn as quickly as some kids, but I do learn and I am happy with that.'

- They expect that the teacher will help them with assessment if they need it so that they get timely information about their progress.
  'My teacher does another running record with me when we both think I have made progress or if I seem stuck; it is really useful to keep an eye on how I am going.'

- They expect whole-class or school-wide assessments to be explained by the teacher in terms of the explicit learning intentions of the lesson or the big ideas of the curriculum.

  'The teacher explains that when we do the same type of test across all the Year 4 to 8 students for reading it helps the teachers and the board to work out what bits of reading we are best at, and what we might need special support for as a school.'

- They expect that any information relating to their learning gathered from whole-class or school-wide assessment will be fed back to them promptly to inform their next steps in learning.

  'It is really annoying when you do these tests for the school and you don't find out anything at all about your own learning.'

- They understand the information that comes from assessments that the teacher carries out.

  'When we do an asTTle test the teacher helps us to understand any of the technical language that is in the report and helps us to analyse what we know and what we might learn next.'

- They see themselves as having value as a source of information to help their peers' learning.

  'Because we all assess against the success criteria we can help each other with this assessment because often I can see things for improvement in my friends' work that they can't and they can see things in mine.'

If you are being successful at enabling your students to maintain agency in assessment, your students should be able to give good answers to all of the bullet points listed above if they are posed as questions. Can they?

Teaching your students about assessment

As has been the case with developing learning-focused relationships and clarity about learning, if your students do not know these things about assessment, you will have to teach them. Here is a learning intention and success criteria that you might use, written from the students' perspective:

Learning intention: we are learning how to use assessment to help our learning.

Success criteria: we will be good at using assessment when we

- keep thinking about our success criteria and any exemplars as we go;
- help our classmates to also use the success criteria and exemplars;
- ask for reassessments when we think we need them;
- try and make sure that any assessment we do will tell us about where we have got to with our learning;
- tell our teacher and our peers in our own words what we think they have told us about how we can improve;
- tell our parents what we know and what we are going to learn next.

Relevance: so that we grow our ability to always be in charge of our own learning.

Once again, the 'Try This!' unit on 'what learning is about' in Chapter 1, pages 25–26, will slot in nicely here, giving your students a strong feeling of having consolidated their sense of agency in your classroom. Of course a single lesson or unit on self- and peer-assessment will not result in students who can always assess perfectly. And they won't do it at all if they are not motivated and clear about what they are trying to learn.

The younger the students, the more you have to scaffold their learning about self- and peer-assessment. But students can be taught to self-assess as a routine part of their learning process, right from the beginning of school, providing that the teacher spends time modelling the process with the students and giving them the language to use when talking about their learning. Often teacher modelling of self-assessment of their own 'learning' is a convenient way of doing this, or the teacher might use a student's work as an exemplar, and review what self-assessment of the work might look like against the success criteria.

Teaching self-assessment

Teacher: Today when we wrote our stories we were working on trying to spell words that we don't know all by ourselves by

- saying the word slowly;
- writing the letter sounds that we could hear.

. . . just like we did when we wrote the story together on the mat. We were also going to make sure that we were using these success criteria to guide what we were doing; to self-assess. Let's look at the way Thomas has tried to use the criteria. Can you tell us, Thomas, how you assessed yourself against each of these criteria?

Thomas: I don't know, Miss.

Teacher: I saw you trying to spell 'school' by yourself and by sounding out the word slowly. So that means he met how many of the success criteria? [asking the question of the class] Two? That's right, excellent. Then what did you do, Thomas?

Thomas: I wrote down the first sound I could hear like that . . . and then I wrote down the next and the next.

Teacher: That was very good, Thomas, so how many of the success criteria did you meet altogether?

Thomas: All three of them.

Teacher: You did too, well done! Good self-assessment! What do you think might be your next step in being a self-assessor, Thomas?

Thomas: I think I have to make sure I look back at the success criteria as I am working and think about how I am using all of them.

Teacher: I do too, so tomorrow we will do more work on that, shall we?

This might be followed by asking a student to independently talk through this process. For example, the teacher might say:

'Albert, today in your story you tried to write "home". That was a new word for you and you got most of it right; can you tell us what you did?'

The discussion refers back to clear learning intentions that the students understand and supports students to talk about the learning process they have attempted to implement; it keeps them focused on what they were trying to learn and how they went about it. Self-assessment requires them to consciously examine what they did against what they were trying to do.

Another approach might be to simply ask the students:

'What did you learn in mathematics today? What do you need to learn next?'

Or to say:

'Turn to the person sitting next to you and tell them what you learnt in mathematics today and what you still have to learn.'

Then follow with such questions as:

'How do you know you can do that?'

Each of these questions asks the children to reflect on what the intended learning was, how they went about it, and assess where they got to with the learning.

Students can learn to self-assess by first learning to assess the work of their peers. Taking someone else's work and analysing it to see if it meets the success criteria is easier than analysing your own at first.

'Pupils assessing one another: Pupil groups can mark each other's work, and thereby learn to think about the aim of a piece of work and to understand the criteria of quality. "One teacher's view of this was 'This makes me realise how much potential there is in a group work session for individuals to have that much-needed discussion about where they go wrong each time. Fifteen times more potential than if they wait for a one-to-one with me!"'

Black et al., 2002

Self- and peer-assessment needs teacher support

Think about the abseiling lesson from Chapter 2, page 28. The highly motivated students were repeatedly assessing their attempts to put on their gear against the model given by the instructor, and taking whatever action seemed appropriate to reduce any gap they detected. They were repeatedly asking themselves, 'How closely does my attempt at securing the harness seem to match what the instructor showed me; what should I do next?'

The problem for the abseiling students is that because one of the things they are learning is to be able to recognise when they have not secured the harness correctly, they cannot necessarily recognise this initially. The act of recognition is itself a skilled act of assessment. You cannot see what is wrong if you don't know what is right. The instructor recognises an incorrectly secured harness at a glance. The instructor can accurately assess the gap; the student may not be able to. In order to learn, the student needs firstly to 'see' the gap. If the student cannot 'see' the gap, they self-assess. A peer who is further ahead of the student may be able to give useful guidance from their assessment, but otherwise the student is stuck without further instructor input.

The choice the instructor has to make is about the best way to communicate to the student the results of the instructor's assessment. The easiest way is for the instructor to show the student what is wrong and how the student might correct it. If this demonstration is done so that the student is then clear about what was wrong then the student might be able to make a correction, and then practise correct securing now having a much better idea of what 'correct' looks like. But there are situations where the instructor or teacher might decide that there are more powerful ways in which the student can engage with 'gap detection'.

Take for example, Year 5 students learning to develop techniques to visually represent landscapes so that emotional connection with the landscape is apparent.

The teacher expressed this to the students as 'We are learning to paint landscapes that show how we feel about them'.

The teacher wanted them to develop their ability to

- know and try ways of using the elements of line, texture, colour and shape, and of creating depth by overlapping;
- use drawing techniques with felt pens and coloured pencils;
- make drawings in response to artists' works.

Students do self-assess when they can!

To give her students a sense of the way writing develops over time, one Year 3 teacher showed her students the national writing exemplars from Level 1 to Level 3. This was done in a casual way, and once the teacher had finished with the exemplars, she pegged them on a wire below the whiteboard, and there was no more discussion about them. A few days later, during the course of a writing lesson, one student put up his hand and told the teacher he was working at Level 2. Amazed by this, the teacher asked him and the rest of the class where they thought they were working and most of them indicated they assessed themselves to be at Level 2. Unknown to her, they had been comparing their stories to those on the exemplars and had measured their performance against them.

The teacher started by having them talk as a class about landscape and how some scenes can make you feel happy, others can make you nervous, others can feel threatening, others warm and secure. They then got the students to paint a landscape of the school playing field and grounds with their own homes behind it, asking them to think about the emotion they wanted to capture in their painting.

The teacher then showed the students a range of six paintings from (anonymous) students who had done this work the previous year, and asked them to work in groups of four to rank the paintings in terms of the extent to which they could see an emotional connection in the work. They needed to come to agreement about the ranking as a group. They were to put them in any order to begin with but then to discuss which they thought showed the strongest emotion, and which showed least, and the reasons for this. All groups were able to do this. Finally they were to discuss the techniques they thought might have been used by the artists; how did the artists do that? As a class they then discussed what the emotions were in each painting and how the artist had achieved this. The teacher then showed them some work by professional artists (Graham Sydney and Don Binney) whose landscape work powerfully portrays emotion and they discussed the techniques used by them. Finally they began a series of activities designed to give students opportunity to practise the use of these techniques for portraying emotion prior to a repainting of their original landscape. Once they had all finished their paintings they spent a final session reviewing the painting and the lessons. Firstly, in pairs, each student was told to tell their partner

- what they were trying to do;
- what techniques they were trying to employ;
- what they were happy with;
- what they want to improve on.

And then they asked their partner
- how *they* thought they did;
- what *they* thought they did well;
- what they might focus on next time.

They then did the same for their partner. Then, as a class, they reviewed
- what they were learning;
- what they had learnt;
- what had been difficult about the learning;
- how they had overcome the difficult bits;
- how they might further improve their landscapes were they to continue this learning.

These teaching processes, amongst other things, build the ability of the students to self-assess, without requiring assessment and direct feedback from the teacher, and to learn new insights about the learning from peer-assessment. The activities set up a series of rich comparisons for the students to make, each comparison in turn enabling the student to sharpen their understanding of what approaches might enable emotion to be captured in landscapes. The activities enabled the students to deeply engage with the intended learning by requiring them to 'have a go' themselves first, using whatever skills they had already.

The following group comparison exercise then required them to not only make their own assessment (to some extent in comparison with what they were able to produce themselves) of the anonymous paintings but to listen to and actively engage with the assessments of their peers. Whatever differences (or gaps) they themselves saw between the paintings were enriched by the assessments of their peers. The value of peer-assessment is often not whatever feedback might follow from that assessment but the new insights about how to understand the intended learning that comes from the different perspectives of peers.

In total, the activities also keep the responsibility for the learning with the students. They were the ones doing the assessment, the comparing, the deep thinking about what they are achieving, what others have achieved, and what might happen to reduce the gap. The teacher can consolidate this by enquiring of the student, once a gap has been established, as to how they might think of going about closing it: 'How do you think you might go about achieving that effect?' Whatever the student's answer, the teacher will assess it and decide on what needs to be done next to support 'next steps'.

All of this means that no matter how much students might be 'in control of their own learning' it is not possible for students to always usefully assess their own learning because they do not know what they do not know. Learning and teaching is a partnership in which the subject and pedagogical expertise of the teacher is vital.

Involving pupils in their tests

'Pupils usually see tests as the last judgement. By involving pupils in setting test questions, in inventing mark schemes, and in marking one another's answers, teachers helped pupils to achieve a different view . . . They feel that the pressure to succeed in tests is being replaced by the need to understand the work that has been covered and the test is just an assessment along the way of what needs more work and what seems to be fine.'

Black et al., 2002

Self- and peer-assessment in a new entrant classroom

Julie realised that if she were to get her young five-year-olds assessing and reflecting on their learning, then she needed to give them a language to use.

Julie thought about ways to help the students to self- and peer-assess, and came up with the idea of a card for the success criteria. This card had on it the symbols of the criteria the students were aiming to show in their writing. A big 'C' meant capital letter; a big '•' meant a full stop; a drawing of a rocket ship meant leave spaces between words; and an '&' meant making a compound sentence by using the word 'and'; finally 'M' meant 'does the story make sense?' She had many copies of this card, one for each student working on this learning intention, and she laminated these so that the students could write on them with whiteboard pens.

There are many stages to writing prior to writing a sentence or a story. But day by day, these five-year-olds became clearer about what to use in their writing and Julie met them every day at the end of their session to guide them through the self-assessment process. This grew into guiding them through the peer-assessment process too, especially regarding what sorts of things the students could say to each other about their work.

With a learning intention like 'We are learning how to write about our own ideas', Julie modelled for the students a way to see how well they had done and to set goals by themselves and with a buddy for what they would like to improve on next time. From this modelling, the students developed the language and the processes to make self- and peer-assessment a regular part of their writing programme. It has become a routine part of the writing process for them.

For example: Reuben assesses his story.

He looks at his self-assessment tick card, and looks at his story. Each time he says 'yes', he ticks the symbol on his laminated card.

- Capital letter? Yes.
- Have I got any full stops? Yes.
- Have I got spaces? Well, I have got a few.
- Does it make sense? Well, I have to read it . . . yes.
- Have I got an 'and'? Yes.
- I feel . . . Good (and places a tick beside the smiley face).

Reuben reads his story to his partner, Jordan, and then asks him, 'How do you feel about my story?'

Jordan says, 'I feel happy because you put an "and" in it, and you used a full stop and it's got a capital letter.'

Jordan reads his own story to Reuben.

Jordan guides the peer-assessment by asking, 'Does it have a capital letter?'

Reuben says 'yes', and Jordan ticks his card.

Jordan asks, 'Have I put a full stop?' And Reuben looks for it on the page and nods yes. Jordan ticks his card.

Jordan asks again, 'Have I put spaces?' and Reuben looks carefully at the work, pointing to each space between the words. So Jordan ticks his card.

Jordan asks, 'Does it make sense?' Reuben says, 'You'll have to read it to me.'

So Jordan reads his story to his partner again. He asks again if it makes sense and Reuben, who has listened carefully, says 'yes', so Jordan ticks his card.

He asks, 'Did I put an "and"?' Reuben carefully scans the text to find the use of 'and' in the story and puts his finger on it. Jordan ticks his card.

Jordan asks himself and his partner, 'Do I feel happy? Yes, because I put an "and"', and he ticks the smiley face.

Jordan asks Reuben: 'Thumbs up? Do you think I've done this well?'

Andre (three months at school) looks at his own story and at his laminated tick card containing the success criteria and he mutters to himself as he recognises the success criteria in his own work:

- 'Capital letters? Yes.' (Tick)
- 'Full stops? Yes.' (Tick)
- 'Spaces? Yes.' (Tick)
- 'Does it make sense?' He pauses and reads his story to himself and ticks the card.

He then asks his buddy Jessica, 'What do you think of my story?'

And Jessica says, 'Well, you have to read it to me, Andre.'

So he does. Andre reads, 'I saw a bat and an owl and a possum.'

Jessica says, 'Possum? . . . Possum?'

And Andre says, 'yes'.

And Andre asks her again, 'How do you feel about my story?'

Jessica says, 'Happy, tick the thumbs up.'

The thumbs up, down or sideways are the signs for how the buddy feels about the work.

For the self-assessment the students use smiley faces. Jessica asks Andre, 'And how do you feel, Andre?' and Andre ticks a sad face, the middle picture.

So Jessica (five years, six months) prompts Andre to explain why he feels this way about his writing this morning. 'Why did you tick the unhappy face, Andre?'

And Andre replies, 'Because I haven't done much writing.'

This prompts Jessica to take a more active role in the peer-assessment and she goes through the whole tick card again, checking for Andre, showing him how well he has done and even showing him that he had two 'ands' so he could put two ticks above 'and' on the card. While she was just checking if he had done all of them, she couldn't resist rewriting his full stop to make it clearer, even though it was Andre's book and Andre's full stop! Once they finish assessing the story they leave their laminated tick card with its ticks on it, inside their book and place their book in the basket for Julie to look at.

As her first group of new-entrant students move on into the Year 1 classroom, Julie is finding that this approach to self-assessment is being 'caught' by other students in the class. So she often finds students she hasn't taught to self-assess, talking about their learning and the evidence of the success criteria in their work, without her specific prompting. Julie finds it a self-sustaining process now and is excited about the rapid progress her students are making as a result of this clarity. Self-assessment proves to be a very powerful motivator for her students.

Checking in with your students

Keeping a check on what your students understand about what is happening is really important if you are going to sustain a learning-focused relationship. With the busyness of a classroom you need very simple but effective ways of doing it. There are a lot of tricks that you can use, and it is likely that you already have some of your own or you will develop new ones that are just for you and your class. Here are a couple of simple, non-verbal ways of checking whether you and your students are thinking the same way, or whether they understand what is going to happen next, if they feel clear that they know what the learning intention is . . .

'All those that feel confident that they understand what . . . show me your thumbs up. All those that don't understand show me your thumbs down. All those not sure . . . thumbs sideways.'

There are endless variations on this theme:
- smiley and sad faces
- traffic lights (green = speed up, orange = slow down, red = stop: need more help)
- clapping (one clap = understand, two claps = not sure, three claps: don't understand)
- pointing (pointing to the left means yes, to the right means no, up means not sure)
- ear pulling (pulling your left ear = easy, right ear = hard, pulling your nose = just right)

You can ask students to think of new ways that are simple, clear and effective that the class can use.

TRY THIS!

One way to help students to begin to self-assess is by getting them to focus on assessing whether their work is too easy or too hard.

First: Tell your students that you want them to learn to be able to tell if their work is too easy . . . discuss ways they can tell. Talk with them about the idea of being engaged with their learning, of what it means to be really learning and when they are not. A great start would be to talk with them about the idea of 'academic learning time' (ALT), where high levels of ALT mean that
1. they are working on important content;
2. they are 'on-task';
3. they are experiencing high levels of success with most (but not all) of the work.

Berliner, 1991

Discuss the difference between working hard 'doing stuff' and actually learning. Ask them to think of a time that they can remember really learning something. Shape some criteria with them around what that was like. Discuss what criteria might also look like for 'not learning'. Tell them you are going to spend a small amount of time discussing this every day for a couple of weeks (1–2 minutes) and that you want them to be thinking during the day about whether they are actually learning or not. At each discussion the teacher records student ideas and also adds their own thoughts. These lists of criteria are displayed in the room.

Second: Then ask your students how they know if their work is too hard . . . and repeat the above sequence.

Third: Then ask your students how they know if the work is 'just right'. Repeat the above sequence to the extent to which it is helpful. Help students work out that 'just right' should be between too hard and too easy, that it will feel like a bit of both. Help them to think about what self-assessment of 'just right' feels like and what they can do to keep their learning feeling like this. Then also help them to see how valuable self- and peer-assessment can be for judging other things about their learning too.

AND THIS!

All assessment, with the possible exception of assessment for qualification, should primarily be formative. Next time you have finished carrying out a reading running record assessment with a student (or any assessment for that matter), ponder on how many of these processes you engaged in.

Before the assessment:

- You started the process by telling the student that you thought it was time to reassess their reading and why. (You have asked me for a reassessment and I have agreed, this is the time for reassessment we agreed upon when the reading unit or programme was begun, it is school policy to reassess every . . . term, the class is halfway through the reading programme and it is time to take stock to see if expected progress against the intended learning focus has been made . . .)
- You asked the student if they agreed that reassessment was appropriate, and if not, why not. You also checked that the assessment tool was seen as appropriate.
- You asked the student if they thought they had progressed. ('Do you think you are reading better than last time we did this? Why do you think that?)

After the assessment:

- Explain the results to the student, mainly in terms of what they could actually do, and what they could do now that they couldn't do before, but also in terms of summative information about progress (reading level or age changes, etc). ('You certainly are better at working out what the next word might be by thinking about what word would make sense; you are now on Green 2, and that is a change of 3 levels from last time!')
- Ask the student about how this matches up with their own assessment of their performance, and their own prediction of their performance.
- Discuss possible areas for next steps, with target setting if appropriate.
- Agree on next steps and the processes for taking those steps.

So how many of these processes did you actually do with the student?

If you did none, then it is difficult to see how the student would experience the assessment as anything other than as something that was 'done to them' as a summative assessment. They are likely to feel judged by it and have no sense of its relevance to them and their learning.

If you did all of these, formally, extensively, you are likely to have bored them silly — unless it is the very first time you had assessed like this and then they might have been intrigued and both of you might have had a very interesting conversation.

If you are routinely formative with your students you will use the above prompts as a mental checklist to ensure that each student does know that the assessment is *for them*, not done *to them* for someone else. You know that you will have it right when the student is looking forward to the assessment or asks for a reassessment.

What teachers need to know about assessment
The role of the teacher in assessment is complex

Teachers are the assessment managers of the classroom
- They are the ones that must monitor the motivational climate of the classroom and ensure that students are themselves actively engaged in self-assessment and collegial peer-assessment.
- They also need to gather their own information about how their students are progressing, how they need support. They need to be skilled assessors, using a variety of assessment approaches, in partnership with the students.
- They are also the ones that need to check that every other person that needs valid and reliable information about learning gets it when they need it, and in a form that they need it; they have to understand the role of each person and their information needs, so that those people will be able to fulfil their role in supporting the teaching and learning in the classroom.

Students are not the only learners in education
Teachers, parents, senior staff, boards of trustees, and the Ministry of Education all play various roles in supporting the learning of students to achieve high standards. To the extent to which there are expectations about what good teaching, good managing, good governing and good stewardship looks like, all of these groups need information about how well they are actually playing these roles so that any gap is apparent and attempts to close the gap can be made.

Everyone needs information about student achievement
The quality with which teachers, parents, senior staff, boards of trustees, and the Ministry of Education fulfil their roles is judged, in part, on the standards of student achievement

achieved. Therefore, in order to learn about how to improve their role performance, all of them need student achievement information that is appropriate to their role.

The teacher must see the compatibility of assessment for learning, and the collection and use of assessment information for others

While senior staff, parents, boards of trustees, and the Ministry of Education do need information about student achievement, the gathering and supply of this needs to be compatible with teaching and learning. No data should be collected that is not also useful to the teaching and learning. This means that there should not be any assessment at all that is not also directly useful to the students and teachers in supporting learning. Schools with sound assessment practices and systems will not require any assessment for school-wide and external uses that is additional to sound classroom assessment practice.

The teacher is the one who has to gather and supply all the information

The teacher is the only one in a position to gather information. To do this effectively requires the senior management to be very clear about what is needed, how it is to be gathered, when, and in what form it needs to be recorded or presented. It helps the teacher to gather it correctly if the end use of the information is apparent to the teacher; of how it will be used to improve senior management or board or parent or Ministry of Education decision-making and learning.

What needs to be known

So, what do you need to know?

Curriculum understanding and informal assessment

You need sufficient depth of understanding of the specified curriculum, and the progressions of teaching and of learning in that curriculum, in order to be confident of informally assessing, for any student, where they are at now with their learning and their next learning step, by observing their work or attempts and talking with them. If you are not very experienced or not hugely knowledgeable about a particular curriculum area then you will need to get professional development, engage in reading, and seek support and guidance from your colleagues. Planning well and shaping clearly specified learning intentions and success criteria will help you gain a depth of understanding as well. But there are no short cuts to expertise.

You need to know how to observe learning

Observation of students engaged in learning is an act of assessment. You need to know how to observe, what to observe, in each curriculum area you teach in. Good observation requires detailed knowledge of what you expect a student to need to be able to do in order to make progress. You then observe whether they can do this or not. If not, what do they do and what are the implications for what you need to do next? Marie Clay (2005) gives this example:

'. . . a boy was quite confused about direction . . . during his first year at school. At the end of the first year he was equally satisfied with moving from right to left across print as he was moving from left to right. Visual learning about what to expect to see in print must be seriously disturbed if you do

111

not happen to scan English from left to right. By the end of the first year at school this boy had not established a consistent left-to-right visual survey of print. Organising to prevent reading failure depends a great deal on providing opportunities for observing what children are doing.'

If you don't know about the importance of establishing correct directionality in young readers, you are unlikely to observe accurately what a young reader is doing. Even if you do know this, you still need to give yourself the time to carry out the observational assessment. More than this, particularly for the student you are struggling to teach, you need to go beyond observing the expected, to struggle to understand, for that difficult student, what you have never understood before.

'Observation involves more than hearing the children read every day. It involves being a teacher who interacts with the child, who notices the child's responses to the story, its language and its meanings, and who takes the time to gather evidence of how the child is working on print. The teacher must be reflective and responsive to the negotiations of the child.'   Clay, 2005

Using your colleagues to help you with your assessment — professional learning communities

Earlier we described how the use of peer-assessment can help students to see qualities and features that they were blind to before. Similarly, teachers can use *their* peers to help them to evolve a better understanding of how they might help students they are struggling with. You can arrange for a colleague to observe in your classroom with particular emphasis on how you are supporting target children, or you can arrange to have a video taken of your work with these children for later joint analysis with your colleague or colleagues. When the focus is on 'how I can better support the learning of these children', it is highly likely that your colleagues will observe features of your interactions, and the ways in which the students are engaging with the learning, that you have not seen yourself and they will be able to suggest alternative teaching strategies. Establishing the conditions for this collegial support depends on exactly the same principles as for establishing learning-focused relationships with students. Helen Timperley and Judy Parr have produced an excellent book called *Using Evidence in Teaching Practice* (2004) about the whole process of using evidence to improve student learning.

Student self- and peer-assessment

As noted in the previous section, you need to know the value of student self- and peer-assessment and be able to coach students to use these approaches effectively.

Pervasive quality of assessment

You need to recognise that every observation or interaction with students contains an assessment component and that for this to be of most use to you and your students, you will need to be able to relate this to the learning intentions and success criteria of the lesson, but you will also have the expertise to realise when the student is engaged in some 'unintended' but valuable learning that also needs to be supported.

Keeping an eye on it all

You will be able to routinely assess, throughout the entire lesson, where individuals and groups are at with their learning and with your teaching. (How am I going? How are they going? Which bit are they finding to be the tricky bit? Is every student engaged? What can I do if one or more is not?) (See also Chapter 7.)

Quality management of assessment

You know that your whole class understands that a lot of people are interested in, and need information about, how the learning in the class is going apart from you and the students.

You and they know that it is very important that any information that is given to parents, senior management, board or Ministry is valid, reliable and accurate. You know that it is your job to ensure that the information is valid, reliable and accurate.

You make sure that any standardised assessment tools (such as the Reading Diagnostic Survey, Progressive Achievement Tests, asTTle, Numpa, STAR, Torch, PiPs, Yellis, Assessment Resource Bank tasks, etc) are administered, marked, and recorded in exactly the ways specified by the test manual so that the information from them is going to be useful. Note that these tools are mostly primarily designed as formative classroom tools but when used properly also provide quality summative information without requiring any additional time.

You make sure if you use other, non-standardised assessments — such as brief interactions with students in the course of moving or glancing around the class, quick tests you design yourself, assessment against the success criteria, or the New Zealand National Exemplars and matrices, Probe and PM Benchmark — that they are very cautiously used to report on standards or progress. Always try and avoid use of non-standardised tools for reporting purposes if there is a standardised tool available. Some of these resources are extremely valuable as a resource for supporting teaching and learning, but have not been designed for reporting purposes and the reliability of the results cannot be assured. Without good reliability, no conclusions can be drawn about standards and trends.

You make sure that all assessment results that are required for summative use are supplied accurately, and on time, to the school-wide aggregation, analysis and interpretation manager.

Collaborating with the students on assessment

Students must strongly buy in to the assessment. You will know how to use assessment tools with them to build buy-in, and then how to use the subsequent results to work with the students to check the quality of the results and then, if appropriate, identify next learning steps. No one assessment will always give an accurate indication of what the student can do. The results do need checking, and the best person to check the results is the student. For example, a teacher observes a student in numeracy doing an exercise on fractions and says, 'It seems like you are able to do fractions well'. The student says, 'Yeah, I think I can.' The teacher checks: 'Can you tell me how you arrived at that?' As a result of the ensuing conversation, both teacher and student recognise that the student does not yet have the required conceptual level.

Another example from more formal testing: A teacher found for one boy that his results on a reading test were much lower than expected from other informal assessments of him.

The teacher had a look at his test paper and found that he had not completed the last third of the questions. They asked him about it. Was it too hard for him? Was the test correct and his reading actually very poor? They found that he had lost interest in the test and couldn't be bothered completing it. He agreed to complete it and the subsequent re-marking changed the results completely, more in line with expectations. But as a result of this check the teacher now knew that the student was not motivated by the test and therefore was unlikely to be motivated by any subsequent target setting for his learning based on his original results. Without this investigation, based on his original test results alone, the boy would have been given remedial reading tuition; something he clearly did not need. The teacher now needed to further explore why his motivation for learning was down and what could be done about it.

The best assessment tool is one that can be tailored by the teacher and the student to validly and reliably assess what it is the students have been endeavouring to learn; the results can then be analysed by the students themselves to establish personalised next steps in learning, without the summative properties of the assessment being compromised. Of the new crop of excellent standardised assessment tools, asTTle has the edge in flexibility. It assesses students from Years 4 to 10 in Literacy and Numeracy in both English and Maori. It has been designed to allow some choice about the actual construction of the test. For example, the teacher can decide, with the students, what features of reading should be assessed and at what range of difficulty.

Once these choices have been arrived at through discussion with the class or with groups within the class, the asTTle software generates a unique test to meet these specifications. This test then becomes, in a very real sense, a test that the students themselves own which will tell them a great deal about what they know and what they might learn next. With your help they can analyse the results and work out what they know and what they will want to learn next.

Technical skill

You will understand and be able to explain to colleagues and parents basic assessment concepts such as validity, reliability and moderation, and basic statistical terms that you will find in the manuals of the assessment tools you use such as norm, mean, median, stanine, percentile rank, standard deviation, standard error of measurement.

You will be able to explain to students and to parents what the graphical or tabular reports from various tests mean for what students know, where they might go next with their learning, how what they know compares with what their peers know.

You will be able to examine all the reports on student achievement available for your school and determine which groups or individuals are most in need of additional support, what their particular learning needs are, and what targets for improvement for the coming year would make most sense to you.

You will know what the implications for your own teaching are from the school analysis and be able to translate these into your teaching programme, sharing these implications with the students.

Big picture of assessment

You will know which other stakeholders in the school community require assessment information, what they need, why they need it, and how those groups link with teachers in partnerships of learning. When you know this you will have greater ownership of the assessment processes and take the issues of dependability more seriously.

You will understand and use international (PISA, TIMSS), national (NEMP, ARBs, asTTle, PAT), local cluster, school, class and group achievement information to guide programme change decisions, as part of school reviews focused on improving learning.

Why assessment should be easy

Well-motivated learners who are clear about what they are learning and have good criteria by which they can assess their learning, do self-assess. If, as teachers, we celebrate this fact and bend our plans to nurture and support this then most of our assessment worries will disappear.

What we want to see

Teacher one: 'How do you know when to take another running record?'

Teacher two: 'My students tell me. They will tell me when they are sensing that they have made sufficient progress in their reading and want to see how much with a running record. Of course I keep an eye on it and if a child has not asked for one after six weeks (school guidelines) I will talk with him about what is going on with his learning and we may or may not do a running record.'

In a learning-focused relationship, assessment is for informing learning and for recording learning progress. Assessment is not difficult if you have established a strong learning-focused relationship and you and the students are very clear about what is to be learnt and how you will know it has been learnt. By this stage, all the hard work has been done because you will have also agreed on the assessment tool. It goes like one of these two conversations (with variation depending on the age of the student):

Conversation one

Teacher: 'Goodness, here we are at the end of the unit. That was quick. I wonder what you have all learnt? Where have you got to?'

Student: 'I think we have learnt heaps, Miss. I understand a lot more about how to write for impact on the reader. If we are at the end of the unit then we need to tell you where we have got to and how we know. I think I can now write at Level 3 because my story has all the qualities that that Level 3 exemplar has. I checked with my friend and he agrees. I know how to get more impact into my narrative writing by really putting myself into the role of the main character and imagining what was happening to me — how I felt, what I could see, hear, smell. All that stuff. I now have Level 4 in my sights but somehow

I think I have to build my vocab before I can get there so I have to read a lot more over the next year or so and think about the words that are being used in the stories.'

Teacher: 'That is all very astute of you. And I agree entirely with you. When I looked at your latest story I thought it had all those qualities too. And I agree about you now needing to build your vocabulary and try playing around with interesting words and descriptions you come across. I'm going to pop a nice, round "3" into my mark book next to your name. Sound good?'

Conversation two

Student: 'Formal Assessment time!!! Wheeee! Can we do it? Have we been fooling ourselves? Have we really learnt anything at all? Bring on that (asTTle) test and let's see. We know that we have focused on building our inference skills over the last term, but has it really helped us to understand at a higher level? Only one way to really find out. Let's go.'

Teacher: 'Yep. Once we have worked out where you have got to and where you will go next I can send the information about the scores and levels through for analysis by my syndicate and for school-wide aggregation.'

Student: 'Why would you want to do that?'

Teacher: 'So that as a team [of teachers] we can work out whether our teaching has helped all of you ok or if I need to find better ways of helping some of you.'

Student: 'So why wouldn't you ask us if you are stuck with helping some of our mates?'

Teacher: 'Good question and I do do that as well, but we teachers are meant to have expertise in helping students who are stuck with their learning so getting the wisdom of my colleagues is really helpful as well. If they come up with a good idea I share that with you and see what you think!'

Student: 'Choice!'

In fact, not much can be simpler. But you do have to know quite a lot.

Why assessment is often so difficult

- Assessment is difficult when we are not clear, either as teachers or a school, as to the purposes and relevance of assessment:

    We know that we are meant to assess but we have not thought through exactly why, what or how. Many schools are in this position. If the schools are in this position, then all the teachers within it are likely to be too. These schools are easily identified because they do not have clear guidelines about

- what is to be assessed across the curriculum;
- the primacy of formative assessment;
- when school-wide data is to be collected and how;
- how validity and reliability of school-wide data is to be protected in each assessment area;
- how school data is to be entered into a computerised data base;
- how the information in the data base will be analysed and reported to determine the standards of achievement and progress of individuals, groups and cohorts of students;
- how the analysed information will inform decision-making around programme improvement at parent partnership, board governance, management and classroom level.

- Assessment is difficult when we do it *to* students rather than *with* them:
    - Formal tests and examinations, where students sit still in trembling silence, take their pens up and put them down strictly according to teacher direction, and then wait to receive their ranking and grading are not about learning. They tend to create the motivation in students to either compete to demonstrate what they know, or to opt out, keep their heads down and wait for the tests to finish. Some students will be interested in the results and will enjoy the tests but others, particularly the slower-learning students, will not. Everyone finds the time stressful. Every student who is not engaged and motivated to do his or her best with any assessment actually threatens the validity of the results because they are not trying to show what they know. More than this, when a test is done to students, particularly under high stakes' conditions, it is less likely that the teacher will go back to the student to check discrepant results for fear of invalidating the test or exam conditions. This enhances the feeling of alienation of the student and can also cause the teacher to wonder about the use of it all when they know that some of the results are obviously wrong. Try asking the students how much use they think the assessment is in helping them learn and how it could be improved.

- Assessment is difficult when we assess for reporting rather than for informing learning:
    - When formal assessment takes place in the middle of the year and at the end, but not at the beginning, why are we doing it? Often the formal assessment which is capable of giving us the richest formative information is done primarily to inform parents and much of that richness does not find itself into the heart of the teaching/learning programme. This tends to make us feel stressed about the assessment itself because it does not have the value to us, as teachers, that we would want for something that is going to take so much time, and it adds little to student ownership of learning, tending to draw them towards 'getting a good mark' rather than learning.

- Assessment is difficult when there is no alignment between what is taught and what is assessed:
    - If assessment is for learning then any assessment needs to be carried out at a time when the results can be used to support further learning. If this is not the case because, for example, the 'testing week' is at a set time of the year unrelated to when the subject is being taught, teachers find it useless.

- Assessment is difficult when the results seem not to be used:
    - The 'results' go 'into the office' never to be seen again – or so far into the future we cannot use them at all for any classroom purpose.

- Assessment is difficult when the results seem to create confusion, or only to be done for the Education Review Office (ERO) or the Ministry of Education (MoE):
  - The school-wide results are displayed in such a confusing way that no sense can be made of them, and none is offered by senior management that we can follow. If we are expected then to sit and discuss the implications it compounds our alienation from the testing.
- Assessment is difficult when the school computerised data base doesn't give the teacher any useful information in a timely fashion.
- Assessment is difficult when we assess too much:
  - Some schools assess far too much, especially in literacy and numeracy. It is not uncommon to find schools using PAT, NSW Competition, Running Records (Probe, etc), asTTle, unit assessment against achievement objectives, and STAR, all for assessing literacy in Years 4 to 8. This is hugely redundant if the assessment is going to really inform learning and teaching. An assessment load like this takes up valuable learning time and is too much for teachers and students to really use.

PROMOTING FURTHER LEARNING

Chapter 6

Why the promotion of further learning is so important

Promoting further learning is about what happens, after assessment has taken place, to support the student with further learning. Providing appropriate support is a skilled act of teaching that must both leave students with responsibility and motivation for their learning and also help them to advance that learning. It is at the heart of effective teaching and is a capability that we never perfect.

We need to understand the essential characteristics of what we can do to promote further learning. *How* we prompt, *how* we scaffold, *how* we praise, *how* we discuss learning; these are all critical acts of teaching that must be done correctly if we are to honour our relationship for learning with the student. We need to develop a strong understanding of what is, for any given learner, the absolute best thing to do to help them learn further.

What teachers need to know about promoting further learning

For consistency with the research literature we sometimes use the term 'feedback' as a generic term that covers all the different ways in which further learning might be promoted, but we also accord it a specific role as a type of promoting that is different from the others. We hope the contexts support the different uses clearly.

The principles that guide effective feedback

In a learning-focused relationship, there are a number of guidelines that we can use to ensure that our feedback is effective. They cover the nature of the feedback, the role of the student, and the roles of those promoting further learning.

Good feedback depends on the quality and clarity of the learning intentions, success criteria and the availability of good examples. Without clarity around what is to be learnt it is very difficult to give feedback that will really support learning.

The principles of effective feedback
Learning-focused feedback
- affirms the learner's ownership of the learning. If we really believe that they own the learning then we need to give them feedback that respects that ownership and that they can use to learn; we know that we have given feedback that is respectful when they tell us that that is how they experienced it, that it was useful;
- focuses on the learning intentions and success criteria;
- is provided at the 'right' time; not so soon that the student doesn't have time to process it actively, not so much later that it is no longer possible for the student to use it to attempt improvement; for many situations, particularly discussion contexts, less than five seconds' wait-time is shown by research to hinder students' ability to problem-solve for themselves. In other contexts, such as oral reading, a shorter time of between two and five seconds is better because it is less interruptive of the flow of reading and the construction of meaning from the text;
- confirms what has been learnt and supports the next step;

- provides responsive, specific suggestions for improvement through techniques suitable to the nature of the learning: discussion, explanation, modelling, examples, reminders, scaffolding or reflection;
- does not swamp the learner with excessive or ill-directed prompts;
- allows repeated opportunity for the learner to act on the feedback by improving a piece of work, practising a skill set, deepening an understanding specific to the learning goals discussed.

The role of the student

When the student owns the learning, they will want feedback and must be able to influence

- the process of the feedback. For example: 'That is enough feedback for now thanks', or 'Can you tell me more about how you see the way I did . . . ', or 'I'm getting confused, can you explain this another way', or 'I'm trying to work out what some of these words mean but as soon as I make a mistake you come in with a question for me that distracts me; how can I get better at working out words if you try and help me so quickly?'
- the content of the feedback. For example: 'I'm sorry, but I don't want feedback about the neatness of my writing or a mark, I want to know if I have achieved the impact I wanted with the reader.'

They must be able to give us feedback on our feedback. Note that while these are not genuine classroom examples, they do describe what learners ought to be able to say in a relationship where they are able to exercise agency.

The role of the teacher, peer, or parent

When the teacher, peer or parent is giving feedback they must

- leave the ownership of the learning with the student: we help to do this when we give them time to assess their own performance, maybe to reflect on their own performance, maybe to correct their own performance, before we offer anything;
- be sensitive to whether the feedback is experienced as wanted, timely, and on-track ('Is this helping you? Is this relevant? Do you want this feedback now?'), and avoid giving comment that doesn't have these qualities;
- know that what needs to be said is helpful to learning, not what is interesting to you.

The overall role of the teacher is to monitor the extent to which both they and the students are acting consistently with their respective roles, and that any feedback is consistent with the principles. These roles are discussed in detail later in the chapter.

Strategies for promoting further learning

There are five fundamentally different strategies for promoting further learning. Which one to use depends on the context and the nature of the learning. Each one must be used so as to be consistent with the principles. These strategies are separated out so that you can identify those you use confidently, and those which you may not have considered and need to develop.

We explain the five strategies and then give some examples of feedback situations that suit each one.

1. Explanation

Explanation is where either a new explanation of a phenomenon or concept is given, or additional information is provided. It is perhaps the most important way of promoting further learning and tends to be overlooked as a very simple way of helping students to learn. Explanation is used whenever the student or class have not understood a concept, idea, or skill and the best way to help them move forward is to show, tell or explain again, maybe at a different pace or in a different way.

Good explanations require good subject knowledge and a lot of flexibility in the ways in which you can describe concepts. Look for alternative ways of explaining to the normal verbal methods. Try models, examples, comparisons (what it is like), and contrasts (what it is not like), a variety of explanations from books. Try enriched vocabulary to build in redundancy of meaning such as where you use three words in the same sentence that mean the same so that the chances of the student recognising one of them is increased.

Use others:

'I tried once to explain a concept to a student. I tried several different ways and just could not get it across. I tried examples, and other different ways of showing what I meant, all to no avail. But then I noticed that the girl sitting next to her who had been listening in, suddenly sparked up and I knew that she had got what I meant. So I asked her if she could explain to her friend what I was on about. She did so, using words and meanings that had never occurred to me, and they did the trick. What I learnt from that is that you do have to be really inventive in looking for different ways of making concepts understandable and that you should never view yourself as the sole source of wisdom.'

The teacher needs to be skilled at deciding when additional explanation or additional information (from teacher or peers) is needed and able to provide this in ways accessible to students.

Quick tip for deciding about additional explanation
* Ask the student if they need it!

---

2. Feedback

The purpose of feedback is to directly focus attention on aspects or features of the learning context, to increase the salience of those features, to indicate how the learner might act to reduce the gap between what they want to do and what they are doing. It is a strategy that is used at three different levels of support, which we call, after Shirley Clarke (2003), prompt types.

Reminder prompt (level 1)

A reminder prompt is given when you think that a student has almost achieved the learning and all they need is . . . a little reminder to use it; a reiteration of the learning intention or success criteria.

For example:
- 'Don't forget to look at the first letter.'
- 'Remember that the conclusion must link back to the topic in the opening paragraph.'
- 'Keep your eye on the ball!'
- 'Say more about . . .'

Scaffolding prompt (level 2)

A scaffolding prompt is the most difficult prompt to use skilfully because it is given when the learning is not consolidated and the student is still struggling significantly with the concepts or skills. The scaffold needs to be designed to recognise the learning that they have accomplished and provide them with the support needed to take the next step without spoon-feeding them and therefore reducing their own problem-solving attempts. The scaffold works by drawing attention to features of the learning context or environment that are important to the problem-solving so that the student starts to recognise the relative salience of the features. It guides them as to where to look or what to think about. Judging the right level of support requires experience and constant checking with the student to see if the scaffold has worked. If it has, they move on using the scaffold. If it hasn't, they get frustrated and their motivation for learning lowers.

Perhaps the simplest example of a scaffold prompt comes from oral reading where a student makes a mistake with a word and the teacher gives a semantic clue to support the student to use sentence *meaning* in aiding word recognition. For example:
- 'Start that sentence again, thinking about what word might make sense.' (Prompting the student to pay more attention to semantic cues.)
- 'Your introduction tells me who went to the zoo and when, but it doesn't say why.' (Prompting the student to think about including a description of purpose in explanatory writing.)
- 'Would the times you measured be the same if you repeated the tests?' (Prompting the student to focus on measurement error in science.)

Example prompt (level 3)

An example prompt is similar to giving an explanation. It is used when you feel the student still needs to clarify what they are attempting to learn. For example:

A student is learning how to build tension in their story. The first draft has been completed and you are having a conversation with them about where the story has built tension and where it has not. There is a passage where it becomes bland and descriptive.

You say to the student: 'Here you say "and then we found ourselves back on the beach". Up until now the reader has been in suspense and then you let them off the hook with a simple description of what happened. It lets all the air out of the story. Do you see what I mean?'

Student: 'No.'

You: 'Well, perhaps you could say instead, "Suddenly they felt sand under their feet. Was it the beach? Could it be the beach? Where was the sea?" or you could say, "Suddenly they were out of the trees, but now what!" What do you think? Could either of those examples help you keep the reader guessing, keep the tension up? Or you might have thought of how you might improve it yourself.'

Student: 'Yes, I see what you mean, keeping them wondering. I like that second example. I could try and use that.'

You: 'Good.'

One purpose of giving them two equivalent examples and allowing them to choose one is to encourage them to maintain ownership of how to solve the problem; of how to keep the tension. If you give them one, they have a simple choice of using it or not, and they don't have to think about whether it really fits or not. It becomes a matter of pleasing you. Choosing is itself an act of ownership.

Another purpose served by giving them two or more examples is to help them to see the underlying concept or idea. In the examples given to the student above, tension was kept by using questions to the reader as a particular technique. By giving two examples the student is better able to see the idea as well as the particulars of the two examples. The student may not necessarily choose or use one of these examples but understands the idea or concept enough to go away and rework the piece of writing.

Using an example prompt effectively is not always easy. Thinking of two or more examples can be difficult, especially on the spot. But it is an effective way of having a student begin to build an understanding of a new idea. For example:

A student is struggling to find a quick strategy to solve an addition problem: 32 + 59. The teacher demonstrates two ways this could be solved. 'You could add the tens and then the ones and then add the two together, e.g. 30 + 50 = 80, 2 + 9 = 11, 80 + 11 = 91. Or you could take 2 from 32 and add it 59, e.g. 30 + 61 = 91. In both these examples we are trying to create tidy numbers that are easier to add. You could use either of these or you may have thought of another strategy now.'

An example prompt is not the same as just giving the student more information. In oral reading, when a child makes a mistake over a word and you tell them the correct word, this is not an example prompt. It is simply telling them what the word is — which is a simple form of explanation. It gives the student a piece of information that they can then use to continue problem-solving the rest of the story. You might decide to use an example prompt in oral reading when the child stops at an unknown word in an early reading text. You could say, 'Good for stopping. Let's look at the picture to think what would make sense. It is something mum put in her shopping basket. It could be bananas, chocolate, or flour. Look at the word now to help you to decide.'

Feedback prompts can take several different forms depending on the context. They can be given as statements or as questions, verbal or non-verbal, and use modelling or exemplars.

You need to be able to flexibly use any of these three prompt types in giving feedback so that students experience rich, timely, focused information about their learning that extends their understanding of the intended learning, sustains their motivation for learning, and points towards their next learning steps. You might think that correctly choosing which of the three prompts to give to any particular student at any one time would be difficult.

What we find in practice is that you 'tune in' to where a student is at and you develop a sense of what type of prompt will work. You are not necessarily conscious of this decision-making at all but the incidental instinctive feedback you get from the student tells you what level of understanding they have and therefore what prompt type will work best.

The other strategy you need to use of course is checking. Give the prompt and make sure you see if it works. In the story-writing example above the student could easily have said 'no' when the teacher asked if she could see what was meant. If this had happened the teacher would have had to find other examples or ways of demonstrating 'holding tension in the reader'.

3. Learning conversation

A learning conversation between a teacher and a student, or between student and student, is where a learning-focused relationship exists and a concept or argument is examined through extended discussion. In this conversation both participants are equal, they

- accord each other mutual respect;
- look to maximise information;
- bring an attitude of inquiry to the conversation.

Further learning is promoted by the exploration of the concept or ideas under discussion. The student might give their understanding of a concept and the teacher (or peer) might talk about the parts of the explanation that they agree with, what parts they see differently and why, with illustration and example.

The student might then give their understanding of what the teacher had said and then also talk about any bits that were unclear or they had a different view of. Learning conversations can take time and so are not appropriate in many circumstances, but they are also hugely rewarding for both participants when a higher state of understanding is reached. They are an ideal vehicle for exploring the more profound concepts we want students to learn as opposed to giving direct feedback on learning intentions and success criteria where more direct strategies are applicable.

Learning conversations can also help teachers build confidence in giving other forms of formative feedback. If we focus on what has happened in the learning journey of individual students, focus on the progress they have made, then that leads us to a diagnostic/formative response to the student's work. This is exemplified through dialogue that hinges around supporting the student's own learning intention:

- Tell me about your picture/story . . .
- How are you going to . . . ?
- What are you going to look at to help you . . . ?
- I'm going to describe to you what I'm seeing in your work, you can let me know what I'm missing out on . . .

Practising these sentence stems can help to have the student see you as an active participant in the lesson. Here is another frame for thinking about learning conversations that might be useful in building conversational purpose:

- **Eliciting:** encouraging description, elaborating, collaborative problem-solving, etc.
- **Supporting:** supporting thinking by reminding about other similar problems or issues, providing background knowledge, demonstrating possible methods, asking people to explain a peer's thinking or method, etc.
- **Extending:** providing many options or solutions to promote reflection, encouraging the discussion of relationships among ideas, cultivating love of challenge, etc.

Student-to-student conversations are also very important and students need to be taught how to have them successfully.

4. Reinforcement of learning

All strategies for promoting further learning, in being effective, also build motivation. Reinforcement is something that occurs as a consequence of learning that rewards and consolidates that learning. Reinforcement can be either intrinsic (when the student views the learning as a reward in itself), or extrinsic (where there is tangible recognition from another, usually the teacher, of the learning).

The main thing to note about things such as praise, merits, gold stars, marks, edible rewards, prizes, team points . . . is that they do not constitute reinforcement unless they do improve learning and increase motivation for learning. It is critical that, to count as reinforcement, any extrinsic reward is given for learning, not for performance. For example, if students see rewards (given as marks, stars, etc) as ways of comparing themselves with others, or as a judgement or grading, then they will not see them as rewards for learning. Research (Black & Wiliam, 1998) shows that rewards of this type tend to focus students' attention on their 'ability' rather than on the importance of effort to learn, and damage the self-esteem of low attainers who tend not to get as many rewards for their (lower) performance.

All teachers do give praise. It is hard to imagine not doing so. We need to be conscious of what we are praising and ensure that it is learning, not performance, and not the student. The learning is the thing. It is easier to do this if we are always conscious of what we are wanting the students to learn and all of our incidental assessment is in terms of whether they are making progress with this or not.

Most reinforcements are short and immediate. A 'good boy, well done', or a gold star given does not take much time, but elaborate reinforcement systems are also common as ways of building motivation. One teacher set up an elaborate system of class and individual learning goals with her students. Students bought into the idea very strongly and she consolidated the motivation for it by establishing a reinforcement regime for goal attainment.

The students were absolutely delighted to 'earn' their lollipops or other negotiated rewards such as opportunity to spend time with a specialist teacher or in making biscuits in the staff room or 10 minutes' extra playtime. This was successful and does constitute a 'reinforcement' system in our terms because all reinforcement was contingent on learning, not performance. Students talked about what they were trying to learn, what struggles they were having with learning, and problem-solved with each other how they might learn more successfully and thereby gain their rewards.

All learners do want to know if their teacher sees them as making progress, if their problem-solving has been successful. We want affirmation and encouragement. We want to know that the affirmation and encouragement is soundly based. If we don't know why the teacher is praising our learning attempt, we might become suspicious that their praise is not about the learning. Frequent, incidental comment about what we have attained builds our motivation, builds a sense of competence as a learner.

Ask your students if they think you give them enough praise and encouragement for learning. Ask if they know what you are encouraging and affirming. Believe what they say.

5. Feedforward

'Feedforward' is where pointing to the next learning steps illuminates aspects of current performance. An important part of effectively promoting further learning is to make sure that the learner keeps one eye on where their learning is going. They can do this in two ways. One is from opportunities to periodically reflect with the teacher on the 'next steps'. This strategy is covered in Chapter 8. The other is from the way in which the teacher builds into the feedback a sense of future focus.

Feedforward is a strategy that keeps the student focused on the wider relevance — the 'bigger picture' — of the learning and gives them a sense of how their learning is progressing within this. The teacher uses this strategy when they want to help the student to build a sense of the bigger concepts they are just beginning to learn. Perhaps the easiest way of explaining this is through the use of a developmental matrix such as the National Writing Exemplars and the associated matrix that describes how writing features, such as sense of audience, structure and grammar, become more complex and sophisticated as the writing develops. Feedback occurs when the teacher gives the student a prompt about how their writing compares with a feature at their developmental level. Feedforward occurs when the teacher shows, perhaps through use of an exemplar, what even more sophisticated writing would look like.

Conversations about 'where to next' strongly build on current learning, build bigger patterns of meaning and understanding and enable the student to see the future of their learning.

Classroom example of powerful feedback strategies

What is important is the learning, and it doesn't matter where the feedback or support comes from. For example, in Barbara-Anne's class, other students gave feedback as often as she did, and they did it well. However, when either the learner or the peer got confused, they both knew that that was the time to go to Barbara-Anne for help. This is how it worked:

- Each student self-assessed a sample of their writing against the indicators in the National Writing Exemplar matrix. They highlighted the indicators that they felt best captured the characteristics evident in their work. BA monitored this but found that most children assessed themselves very accurately and she did not need to provide her own assessment.
- From this assessment they set an achievable goal (learning intention) for themselves for a new piece of writing.
- Children used the exemplars, discussion with the teacher and peers, to forge their new learning; small groups all around the room discussed what better qualities of writing looked like and how it could be achieved. If the conversation got stuck or confused, they called BA in.
- At any time, students could approach each other and invite them to read their piece and ask the child to read the story and tell them what they liked about it, and if there was anything that they should change, *particularly in relation to the learning intention.* Students used this technique to celebrate what they were pleased with and as an active mechanism for discussing and improving quality writing.
- After each writing session each child would write a small reflection in their draft writing books about how well they had advanced their understanding of what they were wanting to learn. They would also find evidence for their reflection in their writing and highlight it. If there were bits that they were stuck on they would asterisk them to indicate to the teacher that a conversation was needed about these bits. They also indicated the bits they wanted feedback on from the teacher.
- Once a week every child conferenced with BA who discussed and fed back to them about
  - their goal;
  - their evidence for their learning;
  - sticking, tricky bits;
  - where they needed to go next in terms of a new learning intention if the current one had been achieved.
- After the conference the child would re-craft the pieces of the story that were still problematic in terms of their learning.
- Few pieces were ever published because students had no interest in polishing material that was not directly related to what they were learning – they preferred to write a new story with new goals in mind.

Selecting different strategies for different learning intentions and contexts

Which strategy or combination of strategies you select depends on the learning intention and the context in which the learning will take place and the context of the feedback. The following five examples of different teaching contexts show how different strategies are used, and used in combination.

1. If you want to support a student with their oral reading, research tells us that 'Pause, Prompt, Praise (PPP)' is a very effective feedback sequence that demonstrably enables a student to improve their reading ability. The student reads, and when they make a mistake, you don't do anything at all for about 2 seconds (*pause*). This does give them time to assess their own reading and to detect an error. If they correct themselves you

let them know you agree with that correction (*praise*). If they don't, then you *prompt* them in some way — give them a clue, ask them a question. For example, you make the sound of the initial letter, or you tell them the meaning of the word . . . depending on how you have assessed their need. If they are able to make use of your prompt and correct themselves, you let them know that their new attempt was successful (praise). PPP meets all the criteria listed above for effective feedback. It also enables the one giving the feedback to tune in closely to the student's actual reading behaviour and know, because of the carefully researched basis of this programme, that if you follow the prescribed procedures closely your feedback will be wanted, timely and on-track. Although it might also pay to check from time to time too.

2. If you want to help a student with their swimming stroke (assuming you have the knowledge of what a good stroke is and how someone might progress towards it), you need to watch the stroke, assess the gap between a good stroke and their attempt, and then find a way of helping them reduce the gap between what they do and the ideal. More than this, you also want to find a way in which they can begin to assess the quality of their own stroke. One of the hardest things about a swimming stroke is to gain a sense of what a quality stroke *should* feel like. Typically this is done by giving them reference points about where their arm should be in relation to their body, etc. Then after some more practice strokes, you would want them to self-assess using those reference points (you wait while they do this), and give them further *feedback* about your assessment of their self-assessment, and also about the quality of their stroke. 'I agree, you did drop your head and shoulder on the down stroke. You might be able to stop that by concentrating on keeping your trunk rigid, like this, what do you think? Do you want to try and see if that will help you?' 'Yes, that's better.' (*reinforcement*).

3. If you want to support a group of students who have indicated that they have not really understood a concept you have just explained you might first ask them to give their best attempt to describe the concept (supporting them to engage actively with the concept, leaving ownership of the learning with them). Then you might find another way of *explaining* the concept again (never just repeat the first explanation) that better connects with whatever they did understand from the first explanation. Then you would ask them again (maybe in think, pair, share) their new under-standing of the concept (provides an opportunity for them to enrich their understanding after the second explanation).

4. If you want to give a Year 8 student feedback about an extended essay on 'the role of a learning conversation in promoting further learning', *wait time* is easy, because you are marking it on a Sunday morning at home. But the feedback comment you write on the essay will be about the quality of the ideas they have discussed in the essay; the gaps you see between your understanding of the theory and their understanding. The *feedback* will be in the form of a *commentary* on what concepts they seem to have mastered and which they have not or seem confused about. And you will want to write your comments in whatever way seems best in order to promote better understanding. You are likely to include affirmation (*reinforcement*)

of where their thinking matches your own. You are likely to provide incidental corrections to incorrect use of terminology, and you might suggest further readings (*feedforward*). You may give another *explanation* of a key concept that they seem to have misunderstood. You are less likely to give 'feedback' that is short and direct because that does not really capture characteristics of the intended learning all that well. You are unlikely to ask rhetorical questions because . . . they wouldn't seem helpful. Your comments are likely to be designed to provoke further reflection on the part of the learner; leave the learning with them. You won't write too much either; just enough to be really explicit about what their next learning should be. Unless you have little better to do, or you are somehow compulsive about spelling and grammar, you won't notice most spelling and grammatical infelicities because they are not what the student has agreed to learn about and they do not interfere with the meaning underlying the essay argument. You might well finally write that if they do not understand anything that you have written then they should feel free to discuss it with you. And you know that if the student had been sitting there with you as you marked, the two of you would have had an interesting *learning conversation* and you would have had to have written very little.

5. If you teach your students to assess the work of each other against the success criteria, an exemplar set and accompanying matrix of learning progression, then at any time students could approach each other and invite them to read their story, tell them what they liked about it and if there was anything that they should change (particularly in relation to the learning intention and success criteria). Students can use this technique to celebrate what they were pleased with and as an active mechanism for discussing and improving quality writing.

One powerful approach that promotes further learning

Barbara-Anne gets her kids to do the work in mathematics:

At the beginning of each new maths unit, I would give my class a school-developed pre-test containing all the learning intentions for both Level 2 and 3 of the strand we were studying. Each learning intention had some test questions.

Once we had marked this, I used — for each child — a checklist of the learning intentions to show what they already knew (highlighted) and what they still needed to learn (gaps).

I showed each child their learning path and explained that all the teaching and learning would be based on the needs identified in their pre-test. The consequence of this was huge student engagement and a desire to fill their gaps.

Students were grouped according to their needs.

When we had completed our unit, we post-tested.

Once tests were marked, students would come up to my desk, to fill in their achieved gaps on their checklist with a highlighter. My checklists never looked tidy but they showed the journey travelled by each student. I would share the improvement they had made overall (never the actual scores because that would focus on the wrong thing) and found the rest of the class would react to the improvement with claps and positive comments. My students chose to call all maths tests learning celebrations as they expected and saw progress and improvement in their own work and those of their peers.

If the strand was studied again during the year we would pick up the learning where it left off.

My class went from being a class who disliked maths to one where we would get so carried away by what we were learning, we would work beyond the time slot on our class timetable. Often when it came to marking work, my students would get into groups of three, checking their answers against each other's work. If there was a discrepancy between answers they would rework the problem until they agreed on the result or came to me to clarify a strategy.

The marking of their own work was not a planned activity; it came about because they wanted to work with one another in a deeper way. Students would go to one another when they had difficulty (often before they came to me), especially when I was busy on the mat with another group and they wanted to continue with their work.

Another powerful approach that promotes further learning

Marie Clay (2005) gives this wonderful example from a sequence of assisting a young child to write.

Procedure for eliciting a story:
At first the teacher creates the conversation. They
- ask genuine questions;
- elaborate on the child's ideas a little;
- make only minimal change to the child's ideas or use of words.

Then, at an appropriate point, the teacher asks the child to formulate the message to be written:
- 'What could you write about that?'
- Encourage him to tell you the message he would write.
- As you respond to his effort stay with his message, but encourage him to expand on his statement, 'say a little more', or 'tell what happened then'.
- One alteration from the teacher may be enough to throw the child so that he cannot recall what he composed. The process of composing is at a delicate stage of formation and is thrown by interference of this kind. Alter the sentence he gives you as little as possible.
- This is not a time to correct grammar. Use the correct grammar in your conversation to provide the appropriate model for him to hear. If you alter the child's sentence he is very likely to become confused and may not remember the alteration. Note down whatever bothers you so that you remember to work the alternative phrase into your conversation now and again. Be brief and clear and try not to confuse the young composer at this point.

Note the points she is making: she leaves responsibility for learning (composing) with the child, the teacher acts entirely as a skilled supporter, giving help but being careful not to overwhelm, recognising the fragility of the risky problem-solving the child is engaged in.

What students need to learn about promoting further learning

Students have to develop their own capability to manage the environment to best support their learning, to seek and use feedback to close the gap between the current state of learning and the desired goal. We want students to

- seek feedback from a range of sources: teachers, parents, peers;
- consciously manage and guide feedback so that it is linked directly to the learning intentions and has all the other qualities of effective feedback: timely, specific, affirming of learning that has occurred;
- politely critique or reject feedback that does not have the appropriate characteristics that will help them learn;
- act on the feedback in order to learn: manage the environment so that they have the time to learn from the feedback.

We will know when we have students that can do this!

TRY THIS!
How we should give feedback to students about their writing

A student wants feedback on their writing. This sequence shows how you might do it. The learning intention and success criteria are given first to set the scene.

Learning intention: we are learning how to hook the reader into our story (audience).
Success criteria: we know we have achieved this when we have used
- a punchy first sentence;
- language that describes the mood and feelings;
- the present tense to make it more alive.

1. Read the student's story bearing in mind the learning intention and success criteria.
2. Think about the specific feedback you might give.
3. Check that the writer is expecting some feedback and wants some. Don't give feedback if this is not the case; find out why or make another time. Most often feedback is a negotiated part of the lesson sequence and if you check too formally the student will think you are nuts. And if they have approached you for the feedback it would be silly to then ask them if they want some. But if you approach them, do check: 'Want some feedback on this story?'

4. If feedback is wanted, check the actual intention of the writer: 'What were you as the writer trying to tell the reader?' or 'What were you wanting to learn, or were you focusing on any particular success criteria?' or 'What were you wanting to achieve with your writing?' or 'I think that you were trying to really have the reader sense how terrified you were. Is that true?'

5. Check what the student's main intention was that they would like feedback on. Often there are a number of things the author was trying to do. Knowing what the priority was gives you a focus for your comments that will make them most relevant to the student.

6. Give one big suggestion about how well that main intention was achieved. Explain what your suggestion is and why. Discuss this with them and see if they agree with it.

7. Give your one big suggestion about how that main intention could be better met. This is where you also need to work out what sort of prompt type you will use to explain your suggestion.

8. If you start with a reminder prompt, check whether it is actually successful in helping the student make improvement. If it doesn't, try one of the others. If you need to go to an example prompt, make sure that they do choose one of the examples to try.

9. Check whether more feedback is needed. If that is enough, stop.

10. Discuss what the writer will do next to consolidate learning from the feedback: redraft the section of the story that you have given improvement prompts for, try a new story, or . . .

11. Exactly the same basic approach can be taken with giving written feedback. Indicate, perhaps by highlighting or circling the bits of the story where you can see the student has met the learning intention, and give brief reasons (related to the success criteria) as to why you think so. Indicate one or two bits where you think they could improve it further, and how they might do this using one of the three prompt types.

Teaching students about how to promote learning — the power of peers

The examples on pages 130–31 of Barbara-Anne's class show how strongly peers can be involved in promoting and supporting further learning when the class culture is focused on learning and the students have learnt the right strategies to use.

Teaching students how to assess the learning of their peers and of themselves was covered in Chapter 5. Teaching students how to promote further learning for each other simply takes that learning the next step. They need to start by following some simple rules for giving feedback against the success criteria. That might go like this.

Assessing the work:
- Only assess your classmate's work when they have asked you to or when the whole class is doing it.
- Make sure that your classmate wants you to assess the work and give feedback.

Then:
- Look at your friend's work.
- Compare the work with the success criteria.
- Look at each success criterion and see if you can see if your friend's work has met it.

If it has:

- Put a tick next to the criterion and highlight the piece of the work that shows you that the criterion has been met (highlight your evidence).

If the work hasn't met the criterion:

- Put a cross next to it, and remember what it was that made you assess the work as not meeting the criterion.
- Do the same for all the criteria.
- Think about what suggestions you might give your classmate about *one* of the criterion that has not been met.

Giving feedback:

- Show your assessment to your classmate.
- Go through each criterion and tell them what you decided and why (what your evidence was); for each criterion, ask them if they can see why you said it and if they agree with you. If they do, go on to the next one. If they don't, have a chat about it and see if you can reach agreement; if you can't, ask the teacher for some support.
- For one of the criteria that has not been met, ask if they would like a suggestion about how to improve the work to meet the criteria.
- If they say that they do want a suggestion, give it, using whatever explanation or examples you can; check to see if they have understood. If they have not, try once again; if you are still unsuccessful, ask the teacher for support.

The younger the student, the simpler you keep it. Five-year-olds can learn to do it very well, and it is impressive when you hear them doing it.

What is so difficult about promoting further learning?

The proper role of questioning

Up until now we have not specifically talked about questioning and you may be wondering why, because it is given a lot of space by many writers. Shirley Clarke has a chapter in *Unlocking Formative Assessment* (Clarke, Timperley & Hattie, 2003) devoted to it and others give it prominence.

Questioning is obviously a valid and important strategy

- for finding out something you don't know: for example, either as an assessment technique to find out what students' level of understanding is. For example, 'Who can tell me in their own words what photosynthesis is? What have you found difficult about that activity?';
- as a checking technique to ensure good communication. For example, 'Who feels that they are clear about what we are going to be learning and what you are going to do next? Have these problems been challenging enough or are they a bit easy?';
- to support reflection about the learning and the learning process. For example,

'How did you achieve that? What would you have to know in order to do that? I want to do that too. How successful do you think that task was in helping you to learn? What did you find difficult about this learning?'

Questioning is *not* a strategy for promoting further learning, but strategies and prompts can at times be posed as questions. To ask, 'From what you have read, what do you think might happen next in the story?' can support the student to reflect on the story and make a prediction about what might happen next. This could be achieved equally well by using a declarative statement such as, 'On the basis of what you have read so far, think about what is likely to happen next'. The two statements are different phrasings of the same scaffold prompt, one phrasing is interrogative, the other declarative. The purpose of both phrasings is to cause the student to use meaning cues to predict what happens next, not to seek information from the student. Both phrasings are identical, not in form, but in purpose and in outcome. Questions *can* invite students to think about what you want them to learn, invite a collaborative investigation of the topic under question, and help them to go deeper with their learning. But so can statements.

Feedback strategies are described by purpose, not by linguistic form such as 'questioning'. Purpose is paramount in guiding effective feedback. If we want students to go deeper with their thinking we can ask them an intriguing question.

This distinction is important because questioning is often misused in schools. Too often, questioning turns into interrogation, and the student begins to feel like a contestant on a game show trying to guess what is in the quizmaster's head. It might be entertaining for the rest of the class but it is not useful for the student's learning. As a teacher it is never useful to have any goal in your head except 'What do I need to *do* next to support student learning'. When this goal is there you will never find yourself asking game-show questions. You will be focused on promoting further learning, with good-quality prompts. Sometimes those prompts will turn out to be phrased as questions, but they will be felt by the student as prompts.

Burn all those lists you have gleaned from various places about 'effective questions you can ask'. If you use them your students will think you are an automaton.

When good feedback goes bad — feedback traps

There are a number of things that we teachers often do that makes feedback ineffective. You might even recognise some things you tend to do from this list. Becoming aware of how or when you make feedback go bad is a good start to changing what you do. Your students will know when you give useful feedback and when you don't. You could share this list with your students and ask them to tell you which you use, if any, and when. You could then also ask them to help you learn to give better feedback by signalling to you, respectfully, when you have fallen into 'old patterns' and given feedback that is not helpful.

Giving the learner insufficient time to assess and adjust their own performance

Teachers often find it difficult to give sufficient 'wait' time before they provide a prompt or ask a question. The tendency is to leap in quickly. Research shows that this makes the feedback ineffective; the students are too busy listening to the teacher to actually connect the teacher's comments into their learning, and they do not have the chance to assess and problem-solve their own performance. If we are really focused on supporting the learning, we give the student time to learn.

Not knowing enough about the subject

When we don't really know a lot about the subject or the learning progressions within it, when we don't actually know what the student needs in order to learn or to problem-solve the learning, we tend to do one of two things:

1. *either* we give general evaluative comment ('Well done', 'Good try', 'Excellent work', 'Maybe you should add some full stops, capital letters and adjectives', 'Try harder'); *or*
2. we tend to interrogate the students about what they think ('Can you think of anything more you could add?', 'What else might fit here?', 'Have you explored all the possibilities?').

The general evaluative comment has little information value in helping the student learn, apart perhaps from encouragement if the comment is positive. The interrogation has no value and can easily leave the student feeling bad about not being able to guess what is in the teacher's head. Too often questioning is used to guard against our own lack of confidence and knowledge of the subject; it requires the student to respond and allows the teacher not to disclose that they could not easily think of how to help with an improvement suggestion. The easiest thing to do is to give general praise and then ask the student to think of how they might improve. This can only be helpful if the student already has a clear picture of what they are trying to achieve (see Chapter 4 on learning intentions).

Good meaningful feedback is not easy to give. It requires you to really engage with what the student is trying to do and think deeply about what might need to happen for further learning to occur. It is not easy to do this, particularly on the spot, unless you do have some good curriculum knowledge. The much easier thing is to say, 'Can you think of how you might improve . . . ?' When they say 'no' you are in trouble. If you don't know, be transparent: say you don't know, that you will think about it and get back to them soon.

Talking too much so that the learner gets distracted from what they are trying to do

For example, this long-winded prompt:

'I really liked how you were noticing when you got here that it did not say "go to the shops" and you went back and fixed it up. You did some good problem-solving. On this page when you were trying to figure out "zoo keeper" I saw you checking the picture. Does it start right for "keeper"? Would you expect to see that "k" there?'

Rather than this somewhat more to-the-point-one:

'Good problem-solving! Show me "zoo". Now look at what letter comes next; the first letter of that new word!'

Rewarding performance rather than rewarding learning

There is a subtle but important difference between the motivation to learn and the motivation to perform. As teachers we need to be careful to make this distinction, especially when we might wish to use extrinsic reinforcement to build motivation.

'Learning refers to the information processing, sense making, and advances in comprehension or mastery that occur when one is acquiring knowledge or skill; performance refers to the demonstration of that knowledge or skill after it has been acquired. . . . stimulating students' motivation to learn includes encouraging them to use thoughtful information-processing and skill-building strategies when they are learning. This is quite different from merely offering them incentives for good performance later.'

Brophy, 2004

When we use praise, star charts, ticks for items correct, stickers, points, novelty items, etc, we need to be very careful about ensuring we are building motivation to learn, not merely motivation to perform.

Giving only evaluative comment

Missing out the really important bits like, how to do it better . . . 'Fantastic work, well done! Awesome, spectacular, you are a star.'

Supportive comments such as these are very important, but why do we so often neglect to go on and give prompts for doing it better? Perhaps it is because to give really constructive comments requires from you a much higher level of cognitive engagement with the learning process. With a full class, this is exhausting and we don't always have the energy.

Another reason is that we are not focused on the learning, not really clear about what we want the student to learn, so it is not obvious to us what feedback to actually give except for generalised encouragement.

Giving a summative grading

Evaluating how the student has achieved, especially in comparison with their peers, almost always de-motivates, certainly at least, at the bottom 50 per cent of the class and provides little information, if any, about how to improve. (For example: 53 per cent, C+, D-, you came 21st out of 29 in the class.) It does provide comparative performance information, but if this does not stimulate and motivate further learning you would not do it at all in a learning-focused relationship. Don't do it. It is anti-learning. If it is school policy, change the school policy.

Repeating the same explanation a number of times

If it didn't work the first time, why would it work the second? It might do, maybe they want to hear it again so that they can work it through, but let the student be the judge of that. Don't go on and on. Try an alternative way of explaining the concept. Don't persist; stop and work out something different. Use models, examples, enriched vocabulary where you use three words in the same sentence that mean the same so that the chances of the student recognising one of them is increased. Use comparisons and contrasts.

Giving prompts not related to the intended learning

Both student and teacher have to be clear about what is to be learnt before there is much point in giving any prompts. If you are not clear, don't give any feedback.

Asking questions that do not in fact support further learning

Teachers like asking questions. Research shows (Leven & Long, 1981) that teachers ask up to two questions a minute, up to 400 a day, with about a third of the teaching time devoted to them. Most of these questions (between 30 per cent and 60 per cent) are about classroom management or procedures ('Is your name on it?' or 'Have you finished yet?', or 'Can you all move quietly please?'). Only about 4 per cent are higher-order questions which invite students to think. Not surprisingly, more often than we would want to believe, students often don't like teachers asking them questions.

Remember the sequence you used to hear as a student:

'Miss, can I have some help please?'

'Certainly, where have you got to?'

'I seem to have got stuck on this . . . experiment, Miss.'

'All right, let me see. What have you done here? I see, what do you think might be a way to fix that? Can you think of one? Where do you think you might go next for help? What is it we do when we don't know what to do? Can you think about it a little more, and then if you are still stuck, try asking Mary. Okay?'

'Yes, Miss.'

Or:

'Can I have some help, Miss?'

'Certainly. Let me see. You should do this, and then what should you do? And then? And then? And then?'

At the end of it the student is exhausted with the extended interrogation and has got very little, if any, extra information from the teacher who has insisted on making them reflect and reflect and reflect, rather than just telling them what they wanted (in order to learn) and then being able to get on with it.

The student might be kept on track and be able to use each of the question prompts to problem-solve the learning, but if the student has asked you for help and all you have done is ask them to think more about it by asking them questions, you are not making them happy or keeping them efficiently focused on their learning! To do that would have required an efficient answer to their original question. Why do we do this? Why don't we just give the students the information they want?

There are two reasons. One is that we don't know the answer, and asking a question allows us to keep control of the conversation. The other is that we have this understanding that comes through the literature, that good teachers ask good questions. There are many books and articles on how to ask good, deep questions that will prompt students to learn deeper and better. What we have tended to do is take Bloom's or the SOLO Taxonomy and use them as a structured way of interrogating kids. In fact, both taxonomies were designed to enable teachers and instructional designers to ensure that what we intended students to learn had a desired level of cognitive depth, and did not either only focus on the shallow, nor plunge too swiftly into relational concepts ahead of student ability to comprehend.

If we have used good formal assessment tools (that have been designed, using the taxonomies, to probe student understanding across conceptual levels; for example, asTTle and Progressive Achievement Tests) correctly to inform our planning, and we are intending our students to learn the deep and meaningful, and we have aligned the learning tasks and activities around the intended learning, we will have no problems in promoting their learning of sophisticated concepts and, when it is appropriate, of asking them deep and meaningful questions as we help them to learn.

TRY THIS!

Have a colleague video 15 minutes of a lesson where you are giving a lot of feedback to students:

- Then, with two colleagues, review the video. Each of you should independently code every bit of feedback that they see in terms of the five strategies on pages 122–27.
- Then, share your codings. How much feedback about the intended learning was given? Which was the predominant strategy? Did the three of you agree in your codings?
- Then, discuss each piece of feedback. For each piece consider
  - what type it was;
  - how effective it was in meeting the principles for effective feedback — to what extent was it specific to the intended learning:
    - what the wait time was;
    - whether the student retained ownership of the learning;
    - whether it helped the student to take the next step;
    - whether the evidence showed that it was successful.
  - how much reinforcement was given? Sparingly or generously? Were any reprimands or put-downs given? What was the ratio of positive comments to negative?;
  - were any of the feedback traps fallen into? Which ones predominated?
- Then, sum it all up. How successful was the feedback? What might you want to change?

ACTIVE REFLECTION ABOUT LEARNING

Chapter 7

What is active reflection?

Teachers are, as a profession, very reflective. They do think about what did or did not work in a lesson: what they would have done differently and what they will do differently in future lessons. They make all kinds of decisions, based on this reflection, about class management, activities, individual students, how to change or renew resources, which colleagues to discuss issues with, and about what to do next.

Active reflection takes this process further so that it becomes goal-focused, evidence-based, and inclusive of the student. It applies to the teacher ('How do *I* think about this?'), to the student ('How do *I* think about this?'), and to both together ('How do *we* think about this?').

The better the information basis for the reflection, the more adequate it will be. Poor reflection is when you ask: 'Was that [lesson] okay?' and you affirm that it was, without further thought about what 'okay' might actually be, or further consideration about what information you would need to gather, to be able to reasonably objectively reach that decision.

Active reflection is fundamental to teachers and learners who are serious about producing and sustaining the conditions for effective learning. A learning-focused relationship — based on principles of openness, honesty and mutual respect — requires that both teacher and student spend time, individually and together, considering how they genuinely have experienced the learning process, assessing the effectiveness of the learning, and reflecting on the quality of the learning.

Active reflection is about monitoring every aspect of the teaching and learning process — planning, learning, teaching, assessing and student achievement — against a benchmark, standard, or quality indicator, so that connections can be made as to what has worked well and needs to be repeated. This enables adjustments to be made on areas that have not worked as well, to improve learning outcomes. It includes becoming aware of your own thinking processes, and being able to make those transparent to others. It is part of a process of regulation that occurs at the individual level (self-reflection); and at the class or collegial level where it is a co-constructive activity. Active reflection is conducted in such a manner that it permits the detection and change of ineffective ways of doing things; as well as ineffective assumptions or beliefs that may be held, for example, about the capacity of a student to learn some skill or understanding. Without skilled reflection, both teachers and learners can be blind to assumptions and values that they hold, that reduce their ability to generate effective conditions for learning.

Active reflection captures the idea that if a gap is found between how we would want teaching and learning to be and how it actually is, then something will be done to close that gap; it is not enough just to reflect or identify that there is a gap. In a way, 'active reflection' is the equivalent of combining the activities of assessment and promoting further learning at a meta-level. It enables a holistic approach, with planning and forward-looking characteristics, and reviewing and reflection characteristics.

Being actively reflective in a learning-focused relationship means that teachers and students
* make the practices and processes of teaching and learning conscious and overt, so any problems can be identified collaboratively;
* have the skills to do something to resolve any problems.

This chapter examines what it means to be actively reflective about learning and teaching, and provides guidance as to how teachers can become reflective practitioners: how they can reflect with their students on the teaching and learning process, and how they can teach their students to use reflective strategies to strengthen their own capacity to learn.

TRY THIS!

Gather evidence about how you finish a lesson; for example, on imaginative writing.
- Either ask a colleague to observe or video your teaching at the end of a lesson.
- Then use some of the questions on page 146 of this chapter to think about how you and your students reflect together about the learning process.

How did you go?

Why active reflection is so important

There can be no doubt that active reflection is a fundamental component of effective teaching and learning. There are four reasons why this is the case.

1. Research says so. The major OECD study into the attributes required to function effectively within democratic society identified reflection as the central attribute:

   'Reflectiveness — the heart of key competencies

   An underlying part of this framework is reflective thought and action. Thinking reflectively demands relatively complex mental processes and requires the subject of a thought process to become its object. For example, having applied themselves to mastering a particular mental technique, reflectiveness allows individuals to then think about this technique, assimilate it, relate it to other aspects of their experiences, and to change or adapt it. Individuals who are reflective also follow up such thought processes with practice or action.' (OECD, 2005)

   Additionally, the large literatures on self-regulation of learning (Zimmerman, 2001; Darr, 2005), metacognition (Borkowski et al., 1990; Jones & Idol, 1990) and reflective practice (Argyris & Schön, 1974) — which we see as contributing to a concept of reflection — substantiate the importance of reflective capability in supporting effective learning and improvement.

2. Active learning is pivotal to building a learning-focused relationship. If neither teacher nor student is effectively reflective, there is no mechanism for detecting, discussing, and resolving barriers to learning or relationships that one or the other might be experiencing.

3. Providing students with formal opportunities to reflect, and support for building their own reflective capabilities, also builds their sense of origin and self-efficacy and therefore their motivation to learn.

4. Active reflection provides opportunities to recognise and celebrate success in learning (and teaching).

There are two reasons why active reflection might be avoided. Often teachers can feel nervous or even afraid of genuine reflection, and particularly reflection that might be done with the students. They feel that if they really do enquire with the students as to how the teaching is going, the students might tell them things they don't want to hear. More than this, if they are then to take note of what is said, they may not be able to make the changes in a way that will improve anything.

Teachers who reflect

Reflective teachers establish informal and formal processes for constant evaluation of teaching, learning, and attempts to improve teaching and learning. They constantly ponder as to whether their students are learning as well as they might, and how they might adjust their teaching to support the learning even further. Sitting closely behind every teaching decision and action is a single, big evaluative query:

How is it going?

The power in such a 'large' question is that it can always sit in the back of your mind as a constant, always there, always probing how things are to see if they can be better. It provides a nagging driver to establish what 'good' looks like, so that evidence of 'what is' can be gathered and evaluated against it, and an understanding shaped of how it might be even better.

This query can also be posed with students and colleagues.

Reflection with students

Because teaching and learning is a joint enterprise that is mutually controlled and co-constructed, the stress in this reflective query is mostly on the 'we', as in:

How are we going with this teaching/learning?

The emphasis on 'we' drives how and when you gather information to inform and evaluate the queries — the direction of the teaching and learning, the pace, the level of challenge, the motivation for teaching and learning; these are all informed by this ongoing evaluation *with* the students.

Reflection with self and with colleagues

Reflection should also take place in terms of 'I', with respect to your responsibility and agency as a teacher. You query your effectiveness as a teacher not only with your students, but also by yourself, and with colleagues:

How am I going with this teaching/learning?

- What have my students learnt?
- Which students have made the progress I want; which ones haven't?
- What can I do to better help the students who haven't made the desired progress?

Both you and your students, and you and your colleagues, need to routinely reflect together on how all aspects of teaching and learning are going, taking in all five capabilities as shown below. We are not suggesting that everything that happens needs to be reflected on all the time. But we are suggesting that over a (longish) period of time all aspects of teaching and learning, as represented by the capabilities in the archway, will be reflected upon. At any one time, something might happen — a group of students may become disengaged, or 'learning intentions' may have begun to feel formulaic — where a more in-depth reflection of a particular aspect needs to be carried out.

The archway on page 146 shows the types of queries that you, your students and your colleagues can use to prompt reflection across the capabilities. Depending on who is actually doing the reflection, the actual voice of the question will vary.

Evidence to inform reflection

Unless good-quality evidence can be gathered about how things are now, and this evidence can be contrasted with some idea of how you would want things to be, then asking interesting questions about how the processes of teaching and learning are going is relatively ineffective, irrespective of the interest level of the questions. This book should give plenty of information about how teaching and learning should be, but what evidence should you gather about how it is going?

Reflecting with students

We can use some of the sets of reflective questions from the archway to examine this idea; for example, when you are with your students and you decide to think about this set of questions about learning-focused relationships:

- Is there a learning relationship in this class?
- Do we feel one?
- Is there genuine co-construction of the learning experience?
- What would further improvement look like?

What information is needed to provide a reasonable evidence base on which to answer these questions? How would you gather the evidence?

Reflection with the students about this should be done, most of the time, in an easy, simple way, with a minimum of formality apart from agreeing to devote some time to it. The 'evidence' will, in the first instance, come from how you and the students feel about the sense of partnership. It is not enough to just ask the students though, because they will make their judgements on the basis of how they understand partnerships to exist. You will first need to shape with them some criteria, which they understand, for what a learning-focused relationship *should* look like (see Chapters 2 and 3). This provides goal-focus for the conversation, but also the basis on which evidence can be gathered. If you have been using success criteria in your subject teaching, and students have learnt to self-assess and peer-assess, then it will be relatively easy for them to make judgements about the quality of the actual relationship, based on their experience matched against the criteria of what one should look like.

Figure 4: Active reflection across the archway

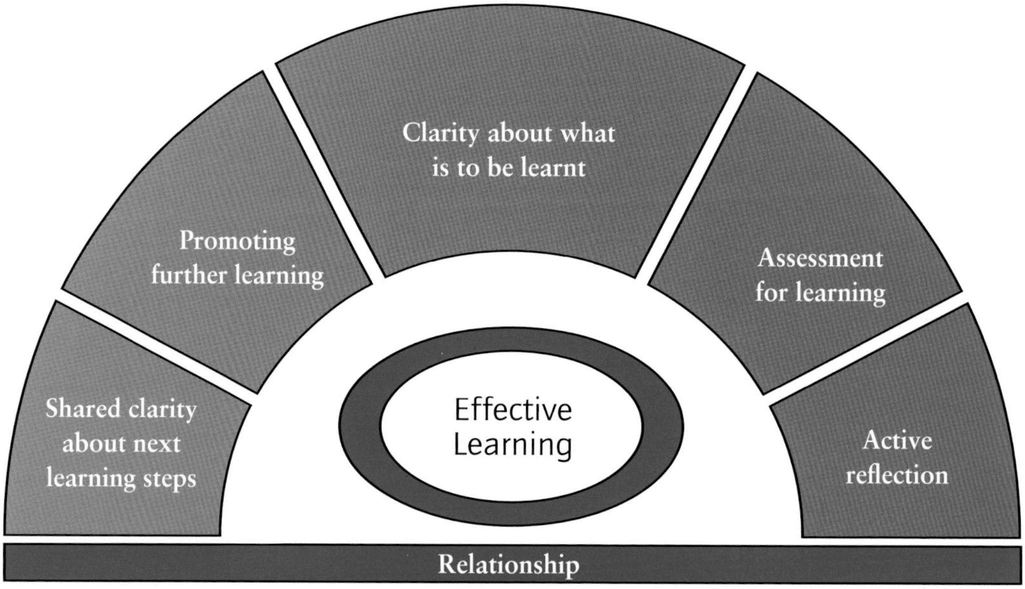

Clarity about what
is to be learnt

Promoting
further learning

Assessment
for learning

Shared clarity
about next
learning steps

Effective
Learning

Active
reflection

Relationship

Relationship
- What is my contribution to what we are learning and how we are learning it?
- What could I do to make the learning more engaging and enjoyable?
- What are the important messages about learning?

Clarity
- What were we learning today and why?
- How did the learning go? Who needs more help, and what needs to be re-taught?
- What new learning can we celebrate?
- What helped the learning to happen?

Assessment
- What helps us know where we are in the learning?
- What assessments are most helpful?
- How could we improve the way we assess?
- How does self- and peer-assessment help us improve?
- How do I make sure assessments give an accurate picture of learning?
- How well do I understand the results of assessments?

Promoting further learning
- What am I most pleased with about the learning?
- What opportunities are there for feedback?
- What are the different kinds of feedback that I give and receive?
- What kind of help moves the learning forward?

Active reflection
- What deep thinking happened when we were learning?
- What opportunities are there to reflect about what and how we are learning?
- How could we make reflection time more helpful?
- Do I think about how I am going often; not just when we are reflecting as a class?

Next steps
- Am I clear about the progressions of learning in this subject? How could I find out?
- Are the next steps achievable and at the right level?
- How can we measure where we are at?
- What is my contribution to what happens next?

Perhaps the simplest way to gather information is to ask the students these questions directly once you do have some reasonable agreement about what the criteria are. Ask them to think individually of their own answers, and then to also think of what evidence they have for those answers. You will, of course, need to do the same thing yourself. If you allow something like 3–5 minutes for this, then ask them to use their thumbs to indicate their answers to the first three questions to the class as a whole. (Thumbs up for 'yes', down for 'no', thumbs sideways for 'not sure'.)

Depending on the pattern of answers, you might decide to explore more, or to move on to the last one. If you think you should move on you might say, 'Looks like almost everyone feels that there is a good relationship here, so let's now see if there are ways we could make it even better. Do you agree, or do you want to talk a bit more about what the partnership feels like at different times, or do you want to do something else?'

Reflecting with colleagues

Reflecting with colleagues is essentially about how well students are achieving and about how well the teaching and learning is going. The principles of gathering and using evidence to guide reflection are the same for both, but the nature of the evidence differs.

If you are to reflect with your colleagues on how strongly the assessment for learning capabilities are evident in your practice, what information is needed to provide reasonable evidence on which to answer this question? How would you gather the evidence?

For your colleagues to be able to usefully reflect with you, you will all need to

- have *either* established agreed understandings about what effective use of assessment for learning strategies looks like in practice, *or* to individually have your own ideas that you are prepared to explain, or exemplify or model;
- have some evidence of current practice. (A video of actual teaching practice provides the easiest way of gathering objective information for later discussion.)

These two sources of information then allow all of you to discuss any differences that might exist between what should be and what is. As the discussion proceeds, it is highly likely that there will be clarification and further development of the understandings of what assessment for learning should look like in practice as well.

If you are to reflect with your colleagues about the standard of student attainment as in, for example, 'How well are the five boys learning who started the year with the lowest attainment?' then you need to know both their expected performance and their actual performance.

Information around expected performance should be based on the beginning-of-the-year performance, with some estimate of expected progress since that time. (If it is not possible to make an estimate, then it is not sensible to set this as a reflective question; it might be better to examine evidence of engagement with their learning.)

Information on current performance should of course partially come from the most recent assessment.

The additional piece of information needed before really examining any gap between expected and actual attainment is the joint view of yourself and the students, that both assessments did accurately capture the level of attainment at that time. Without this assurance, reflection about gaps and progress is fraught.

Teaching students to reflect

To really engage in joint reflection with you, students also need to have reflective ability of their own. Highly effective self-regulating learners query their effectiveness as learners, with you and their peers, and independently. They constantly assess every aspect of their learning environment. They assess whether the learning environment they are in is conducive to their learning, whether the teacher is good at facilitating that learning (and if not, they will have their own strategies for deciding what to do about it). They assess where they are with their learning, which bits they understand and which bits they are stuck on. They assess the extent to which what they are learning is motivating and relevant. As a result of these assessments, they evaluate the options for what to do next. All students do this to some extent ('It's too hard', 'It's too boring', 'She's useless'), but reflective students take it to the next step and ask what they could do about it. Students who reflect like this are highly effective learners. One of your roles as a teacher is to maximise the number of students who reflect in this way.

For students to learn to be truly reflective, they have to understand the bigger picture of why it is relevant to them. They need to know that reflection about their current learning will help them in future learning situations, where they will be able to apply insights from how they have learnt in this situation to how they might be able to learn in the future. They have to know that reflection often works best when they can check how they are thinking about their learning with others. They also need to know that reflection is not always easy and improving the ability to reflect is ongoing.

Steps to teach students to reflect

1. Planning

Being deliberate about introducing the idea of reflection requires as much planning as any other concept you want students to learn. The set of steps provided here is intended to give you some ways of beginning your own planning. Let's start with a learning intention:

Learning intention: we are learning how to reflect — or maybe: make decisions about how our learning is going — and be able to talk about it with our peers.

Possible success criteria: (to be developed with the students)
- We will be able to describe what we are learning and why we're learning it.
- We will be able to describe the learning process (how we've gone about our learning).
- We will identify the parts of the learning process that are going really well or not quite right (all capabilities in the archway).
- We will take action to change things when parts of the learning process are not quite right (for example, ask the student next to me to be quiet, raise the issue at a class plenary [see page 153], discuss with a teacher).

Relevance: it is important to be able to be reflective because it helps you to manage — or have more control of — your learning and to learn more effectively.

While reflection is described as a generic capability, it is only really ever known or experienced in the context of other specific learning (such as learning to read, or understanding the nature of groups in society, or counting in twos) and so it also needs to be taught using subject learning as the context.

2. Introducing reflection to students

You might like to begin by talking with the students about the idea of reflecting on their learning, and how important it is. The most concrete way to do this is to start by reviewing the learning intention, so that this is clear in their minds. Then ask them to engage in a little self-assessment against that, and *then* to think about how that worked, for example:

> *'Think about what you did learn to do this morning. Turn and tell your neighbour. Ask your neighbour what they learnt this morning . . . Now think about how you learnt it. What helped you learn? See if you can think of that. Share that with your neighbour. See how you go.'*

Or you might want them to reflect on other aspects of the reflection archway shown on page 146, for example:

> *'Think about what it is like to learn things in this class. When we were learning to . . . this morning, did you find the class a good place to learn or was it too noisy, (or) did your neighbours help you when you got stuck, (or) . . .'*

Some students will find these reflective queries very easy, others will find them difficult. Make sure every student has a chance to think, and is supported to reflect. Capture all their ideas on the whiteboard, to show that they have been heard and to refer back to later. You will find that you have to support them in different ways, depending on how well they can reflect already.

3. Developing success criteria

Once they have understood what you want them to learn and why, you will want to talk with them about what success criteria for learning to reflect might look like. To do this, you could use the method we outlined in Chapter 5, to help students assess the difficulty level of their work. Discuss the difference between when learning is going well and when it is going badly. Ask them to think of a time they can remember really learning something. Shape some criteria with them around what that was like. Discuss what criteria might also look like for 'not learning well'. Tell them you are going to spend a small amount of time discussing this every day for a couple of weeks (1–2 minutes), and that you want them to be thinking during the day about whether they are actually learning or not. At each discussion the teacher records student ideas and also adds their own thoughts. These lists of criteria are displayed in the room.

4. Using exemplars and modelling

You might then decide to model what this thinking might be like for them. It helps students realise that they *can* think about their thinking when the teacher actually models this. You can do this easily by engaging in 'self-talk' or 'think aloud' where you are very explicitly talking about the sorts of things a student might be thinking about their learning.

'Think aloud'

As you check in with students' learning you can encourage them to reflect on and talk about the thinking process they use. This is often called 'think aloud' (Palinscar & Brown, 1984). As some students find the articulation of their thinking hard, you may need to model this by doing your own 'think aloud'. For example, at the beginning of a junior class group guided reading session, the teacher might model the thinking she goes through to problem-solve how to read new words. She might say:

> *'When I get stuck and I know that the word I tried looks a little bit like the word in the book, but it doesn't make sense, I read back to the beginning of the line and think about what else would fit in the story that looks like that.'*

After the students had read the text and the teacher has checked in with their processing, she might model the thinking again and ask students to think about times when they had gone through the same process and identified how they got there.

> *'I want you to find a quiet place in your mind, to think about the question I'm going to ask you. I don't want you to answer it straight away . . . but I do want you all to think about it. You may find you think better if you shut your eyes or look at a spot on the floor. The main thing is that you aren't interrupted or that you don't interrupt somebody else. When I've given you 30 seconds to think about your answer, I'll tell you the 30 seconds are up. That's when I want you all to look at me without talking. To start off with, for a few times, I'll model some answers that will share how I think about the questions. Then, when some of you feel ready to give your answers, we'll listen carefully to what you have to share. What we will be doing is sharing about how we think in our heads. I'll start by sharing how I think in my head. For these types of questions there are no wrong answers. Every answer will give each of us a chance to add to our own ways of thinking.*
> *'I want you to think about what you are most pleased about in building a sense of tension in your writing [the current learning intention] . . . There you are, think about that.'*

The teacher then models an answer to a question that relates to the learning intention.

> *'Now you may or may not have anything in your heads so I'll give you some ideas. Just sit there quietly and think about whether any of these things apply to you. Okay?*
> *'Now, you might have been thinking that you were pleased to know what you were learning . . . thumbs up if that was what you were thinking . . . Okay, thumbs down. Maybe you were pleased with the examples we had of pieces of writing that really made the reader tense . . . thumbs up*

if that applies to you. Quite a few of you. Okay. Maybe you were pleased that you could build tension using one of the techniques we discussed earlier . . . any thumbs for that? Good.'

The teacher decides when the students are comfortable enough with this process to move into offering their own responses.

Teacher: *'Now, some of you might have been thinking some other things. Anyone able to share what they were thinking?'*

Student: *'I was thinking that we worked well in our groups and shared ideas really well.'*

Teacher: *'Thank you, Beth, anyone else think that too?'*

Some more sharing and then the teacher needs to make sure that the 'so what' is built in to the reflection. Otherwise, the whole reflection becomes merely a nice chat without any real focus on learning and reflection about how to improve the learning, for example:

Teacher: *'So now that we have shared about what we were pleased about, what is important about all of this? What should we do tomorrow when we think about all that has been said?'*

Student: *'I think we need to all make sure that we know what our learning intention is before we start learning . . . '*

5. Using student reflection
When you are doing this reflection with students, you have to be ready to understand and respond positively to the thinking that they do share, some of which will surprise you. Often they will come up with an idea that makes sense to them from their perspective, but is not appropriate. You have to be able to explain very clearly to them why their idea is not good in terms of designing an appropriate next learning step. For example, one of them might suggest that they want to enrich the language of their writing to really get the audience on board, but if they don't have sequence yet, then your role is to convince them that they need to get reasonable sequence before they tackle audience involvement. Your expertise needs to be voiced in the discussion and heard. A reflective session is an excellent place for such a discussion; but you have to be prepared to both advocate well for your position (so that the students can see your point) and also ensure that the students still feel heard, ensuring next time they are asked they will feel it is worth their while giving their opinion. A discussion about next steps must never detract from the expertise of the teacher, or the agency of the student.

6. Promoting further learning
If, at any time, the students don't give reflective answers that relate to the learning, you will need to go back to modelling and bring them back on track. As they become more used to reflecting, you can move from modelling to other types of prompts available.

You might use example prompts with students who do not need direct modelling but still find it difficult to describe how they are thinking. For example, they might say, 'When I watched you working I wondered if you were thinking like this . . . or perhaps you were thinking like this . . . .' Which one of these is closest to how you were thinking? This is an *example* prompt. See also 'Think aloud' (see page 150) in this chapter for another way of exemplifying the thinking and learning process.

You might use a *scaffold* prompt to support them into thinking, by beginning with a low-order question, such as 'What did you find interesting about . . . ?' and following it with a higher-order question 'Why did you find that interesting?' or 'What did you think/feel when you read that? Why?'

For students who are skilled at reflection you might just use a *reminder* such as 'Tell me your thinking from our last lesson'. Students who already know how to reflect might need a gentle reminder to use what they know on a similar task, or on a new task if appropriate. The teacher might say, 'Yesterday we thought about how . . . , is that helping you?' or 'See if it still works'. An even gentler prompt might be, 'Remember to spend a little time reflecting about how . . . before you start'.

7. Assessing the learning about reflection

At some stage you will want to assess, with your students, how well they think they can reflect; how well they have achieved the learning intention. This can be done incidentally with individual students, or with the whole class. From this assessment you will, jointly, plan the next steps.

Using reflection in the classroom

Having taught your students how to reflect, you then need to make sure that you jointly make the most of reflection to aid learning. So when should you reflect?

Incidental reflection

If 'How are we going with this teaching/learning?' is the large reflective question that always sits in the back of your mind, then it should spring into action whenever it senses that it has a role to inform and improve things; it should be true for your students too. Here are some ways of thinking about it that might be useful in promoting the use of incidental reflection.

A powerful thing about a learning-focused relationship is that it requires both teacher and student to keep the other informed of what is going on for them, and to check that the other is aware of this. It is this checking that is a constant and pervasive feature of the relationship. If you are being reflective about the relationship, you will be checking the quality of it with the students as the teaching and learning proceeds. In particular, you will be checking that both you and the students are bringing the full archway of capabilities to support the learning. You know what this should look like if the students are engaged, you know what it should feel like if you are engaged. Keep checking whenever you detect any deviation from what should be for either you or for the students.

This does not need to lead to interrogations. It is not a big deal. It does not take significant time, but is extremely useful in helping you detect early when things are going wrong. A simple reflection at the right time can help you or the student get unstuck or modify what you are doing to make it more effective. For example, if a student is disengaged from an activity you have a choice. You can *either* say:

> 'You seem to be not engaged with your . . . investigation, writing, geometry exploration, handwriting practice, virtual fieldtrip analysis . . . Am I right? Are you finding something tricky? How can I help you? What needs to happen for you to get back on track?'

or:

> 'I'm not sure that my last explanation was of much help to you. Did it help you move forward? Can you explain that concept to me now?'

Both of these queries are legitimately reflective, and are easily asked incidentally, as they spontaneously arise from organic classroom interaction. They will both get good reflective answers when there is an effective, learning-focused relationship in existence.

Structured reflection

Making reflection a consistent feature of classroom life is a must if the value of reflection demonstrated by the research is to be realised. Capturing the moment for incidental reflection with students is important, but there is also value in building in structured approaches as well.

There are two main ways in which reflection takes place within a classroom: reflection between the teacher and a group of students, usually referred to as a 'plenary', and reflection between the teacher and an individual student, normally referred to as a 'conference'. Peer-to-peer reflection also can play an important part.

Plenary

A plenary is a planned, formal reflection time of 5 to 15 minutes at some stage of a lesson for the whole group or class. It is an opportunity to reflect on what has been achieved, and to look forward. Here are some simple decision steps to guide you successfully through plenaries.

1. **When?**

   The end of the lesson, or a chunk of learning, is a good starting place for introducing students to the idea of plenaries; however, once everyone is comfortable with them they can be used anytime that suits the particular need. Some teachers hold them at the beginning of a new lesson to help with the recap of the previous one. At other times it makes sense, particularly if you think that something is going wrong (everyone appears to be off-task, for example), to hold a plenary in the middle of a lesson and to reflect on what is happening and get it sorted.

   Many teachers comment that the plenary has become one of the most exciting parts of their teaching process, as they build a close relationship with their students to support their learning.

2. **What?**

Predominantly, a plenary is used to focus on what was intended to be learnt and the extent to which the learning processes have helped or hindered learning for all of the students. However, anything that is of value or importance to you or the students (any part of the reflection archway) can form the focus for the plenary. Much of the time you will want it to be about the learning itself.

3 **How?**

- Setting up: Gather the class or group and tell them what you want to reflect on. If you decide to go with a review of the learning, then recap the learning intention and success criteria.
- Self-assessment: Ask them to briefly assess how well they thought the learning had gone against the learning intention and success criteria, or how they are finding the learning relationship, or how the test has gone . . . This enables each student to do their own personal 'stock-take' about how things actually are and provides a basis for reflection about how they 'should be'.
- Reflection: Then ask one or two of the reflective questions from the archway (page 146), so that students reflect at a deeper level. These questions, or a subset of them, are usually displayed in the room so that students become familiar with them and expect them to be asked. Students are given up to 30 seconds, thinking time before any responses are sought. This sets an expectation that all students are engaged in thinking and should be able to respond. It also gives those quiet thinkers a chance to reflect, without the time being hijacked by the quick responders. Students are then given the opportunity to respond either in pairs or individually. When the teacher and students get a feel for how the reflection topic has gone, they can discuss and determine the 'where to next?'

The plenary session takes the idea of self-assessment further. Rather than identifying what was tricky or easy, it engages the students in identifying *why* the learning was tricky and how that could be overcome; or what was especially thought-provoking or interesting and where that might lead us in our learning; or what new learning happened in that lesson that should be celebrated.

A plenary at the beginning of a 'chunk of learning' or lesson

Reflection can be used at the beginning of a chunk of learning, when this is linked to the previous learning. Many teachers find the placement of reflection at the beginning of a lesson an ideal reorientation time for the students as well as themselves. Teachers might say:

'Yesterday we were learning . . . how did you go with that? Can you remember what our success criteria were? Good, so who managed to complete . . . There seems to have been a bit of a problem with . . . Can someone explain which part of that seems tricky? Okay, you seem to all be

having the same problem. Would it be helpful to you if I teach you how to do that part before we carry on with this?'

Immediately all students get the message of what we are learning today, that it is a continuation of yesterday's learning, and that the teacher is going to teach something new before we actually get on with our own tasks. Teachers have used parts of this process for many years with success. In the complexity of the busy school day, students and teachers find a reflective session at the beginning of a lesson extremely beneficial for re-focusing their attention on the learning intention and the finer points of the learning process.

'I find that I run out of time to hold a reflective session at the end of a science class, so I begin the lesson with it the next day. First of all I have a quiz with the class on what we learned in the previous lesson. Then, as we mark the quiz, I find out which bits are still causing them difficulty and I use the chance to re-teach before getting into the day's lesson. This has had a tremendous effect on the students, who are now keen to see how well they've done, what they've understood or remembered, and who are confident in the knowledge that I will help them with their learning before we move on to anything new.'

Conferences
Conferences with individual students or small groups follow exactly the same process as the plenary. Like the plenary, they might happen incidentally or in a more structured way. Some teachers arrange formal conferences with each student that take place, either at a set time, or when the student believes they have finished some agreed learning.

Conferencing with a dice
Dave put each of six reflective questions on the side of a dice. At individual conference time, the dice was flipped twice and the student responded to each of the questions that came up. In listening to the students talk about their reflections, Dave could elicit whether desired understandings had been matched. This process of discussion and reflection helped Dave to decide whether the student actually needed more practice or more explanation.

Dave found this to be a fun and interesting way to have students really think about their learning and, over time, build their language for reflection. However, like any other fun approach, remember to always keep checking that it serves the purpose of learning. With the dice, don't get stuck with the luck of the dice; always make sure that the questions are sensible in relation to what you want the student to think about.

Individual conferencing
Teacher: 'Do you know what your learning intention is in writing?'

Student: 'To take risks in my writing.'

Teacher: 'What does taking risks in your writing mean?'

Student: 'Using amazing words.'

Teacher: 'So, have you used amazing words in your writing? [The teacher reads what the student has written: "The suspicious jaguar creeps on his unsuspecting prey."] That is wonderful language, I think you are taking risks and using amazing words in your writing. Is there anything tricky about taking risks for you?'

Student: 'I took a long time to get that down.' [The rest of the class have written about half a page or more.]

Teacher: 'Yes, it can take a lot of thinking sometimes to come up with amazing words, and sometimes it needs time to do that thinking. What do you think you need help with?'

Student: 'I want to get my ideas down quickly.'

And the teacher then has a conversation with the student about how they could try that.

Peer reflection
Two other ways of structurally building reflection into the culture of your classroom are to use reciprocal teaching and co-operative learning approaches. Both of these strategies are highly effective at giving students control of their learning and enabling them to learn cognitive and meta-cognitive strategies to guide learning.

Pair reading — a simple co-operative learning technique
Pairs of students work together on this exercise. First, both students read the same section from text or instructor-provided materials. One student explains a single paragraph, or short section of the text, to his or her partner. The partner listens and then asks questions if he or she does not understand the explanation. The listener then rephrases the explanation. The students alternate roles of explainer and listener until they complete all the material. When the entire class has completed the exercise, groups of students are asked at random to explain the material to the whole class. This serves as a check to make sure the students do indeed understand the material they are reading. (http://www.tki.org.nz/r/esol/esolonline/classroom/teach_strats/coop_read)

Reciprocal teaching
Reciprocal teaching refers to an instructional activity that takes place in the form of a dialogue between teachers and students regarding segments of text. The dialogue is structured by the use of four strategies: summarising, question generating, clarifying, and predicting. The teacher and students take turns assuming the role of teacher in leading this dialogue. The purpose is to facilitate a group effort between teacher and students, as well as among students, in the task of bringing meaning to the text (Palincsar, 1986).

Ways to present reflective questions

1. Have one reflective question (from the archway on page 146) in a large font per page in a spiral-bound booklet (pages could be laminated to be self-supporting). They can sit on the whiteboard ledge or in a convenient place ready for the plenary session.

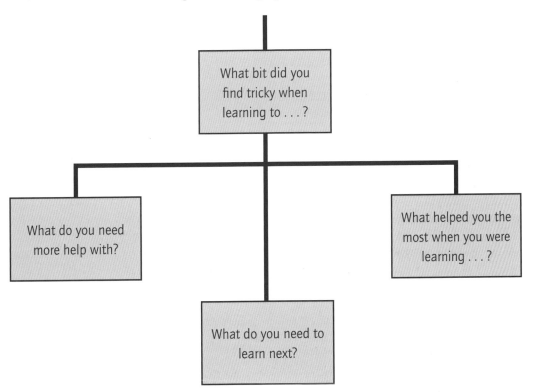

2. Have each question on a poster or wall display, so that they can be pointed out during a plenary session.

   Reflect on your learning:
   – What could I do to make the learning more engaging and enjoyable?
   – How did the learning go? What were the tricky bits?
   – What helps us know where we are in our learning?
   – What kinds of help best move my learning forward? What do you need more help with?
   – How could we make a reflection time more helpful to the learning?
   – What should we learn next?

3. Have a mobile with the questions hanging on different-coloured, laminated cards.

What bit did you find tricky when learning to . . . ?

What do you need more help with?

What helped you the most when you were learning . . . ?

What do you need to learn next?

4. Write one question on each face of a dice. Students can throw it to select the questions during the plenary session as they reflect on their learning.

5. Have a circle divided into sectors with a reflective question on each sector, and a spinner in the middle. Students spin the arrow to decide on the reflective question to discuss.

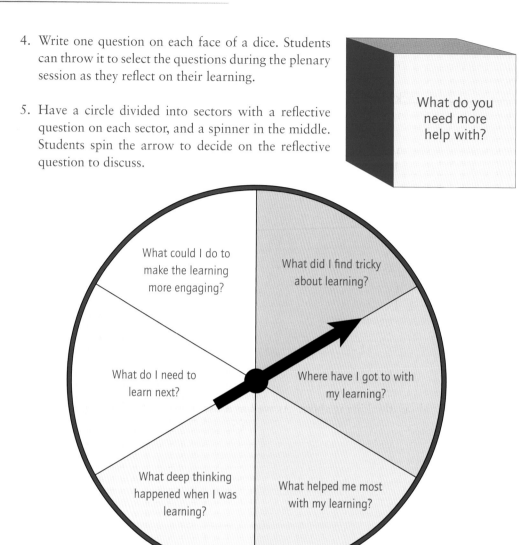

What do you need more help with?

What could I do to make the learning more engaging?

What did I find tricky about learning?

What do I need to learn next?

Where have I got to with my learning?

What deep thinking happened when I was learning?

What helped me most with my learning?

Building your capability to actively reflect on your own practice

Do we need to learn how to become reflective? Are we like our students? Or can we just do it? It is probably more a matter of finding ways of improving our ability to reflect, rather than learning anything really new. To be effectively reflective, we do need to be able to make conscious our own thinking about what is happening in the classroom, so that we can describe that thinking to our students or colleagues. We need to be able to use formal processes for gathering information and evaluating what actually happens in the teaching and learning.

Actively reflecting with colleagues or by yourself
**Increasing our awareness of how we think: how do you think
about how you think?**
Here is one little trick you could try with your colleagues for checking your collective ability
to make your thinking transparent.

Place an unusual word, such as 'fissiparous', that you think your colleagues will not know,
or be able to spell, on the whiteboard and tell your colleagues to try and remember it so they
can spell it correctly 15 minutes later.

- Remove the word from the whiteboard and ask them to write down how they went about remembering how to spell it: what learning strategies they had used.
- Then ask them to share about the strategies they used.
- You are likely to find that they all use different strategies. Some will have broken the word into syllables; others will have looked at beginnings and endings. The meaning and the root word will have been significant hooks for some, as mnemonics or the shape of the word will have been for others.
- What they all learned was to become conscious of their thinking processes and to articulate what they did when they tried to remember how to spell a new word. As a result of this discussion, the teachers appreciate that their students would also use a variety of strategies to learn to spell words, or to learn anything for that matter. The final step of the process was to get them thinking about sharing their thinking processes with their pupils. This enables the students to 'see an example' of what thinking about thinking is about. As well as a useful exercise in helping teachers to become more aware of how they think, this is also one way you can make a start in engaging your students in reflective conversations about 'thinking about thinking'.

Increasing our ability to make our reflection evidence-based
What should you consider when you want to reflect on your own practice? What information should you collect about that practice? The relevant information comes from two sources — information about student achievement, and information about teaching and learning.

Student achievement
Achievement is about the extent to which students have learnt to the level reasonably expected. This must be established before you can do any meaningful reflection, even about the quality of your teaching. We have much evidence from our work with schools that shows what looks like good teaching can often have a miserable impact on achievement, unless that teaching is definitely focused on moving the students on. Establishing what 'expected progress' looks like is never easy, and needs to be considered in the context of each student in each subject for which progress is expected. In subjects where there are not good assessment tools, you may have to rely on professional experience to make the judgement. As long as you do this with colleagues, there is nothing wrong with this. In subjects where there are good normative assessments available (literacy and numeracy), you can set good expectations at the individual, class and school level. From these expectations, it is then a matter of collecting the evidence of actual achievement and reflecting on the gap.

Teaching and learning

How well do you teach? How do you know? The capability archway described in this book (see page 24) provides one way of defining what 'good teaching' looks like. All you need to do is gather some information about your actual teaching, and then establish a situation where you can compare the two. There are two ready sources of information: your classroom and your students.

Videoing your practice

One way of gathering evidence about how you teach is to video your own teaching. A gentle lead-in to this practice is done by setting a video camera up in one corner of the classroom to capture the part of a lesson you want to focus on. The next step is to watch the video on your own and self-reflect. Some of the questions you can ask yourself are:

- How well did I teach?
- Did we discuss the learning intentions?
- Did I give the students a chance to co-operatively plan the success criteria?
- Did I give the students an opportunity to signal they were understanding the learning they were wanting to learn?
- Did I give them an opportunity to share their understandings with each other?
- Did I give them an opportunity to share their understandings with me?
- Did we leave the lesson with a clear understanding about the next steps in learning?

For an even better opportunity to reflect, you can choose a specific part of a lesson you are aiming to improve; for example, taking a plenary with the students. Asking a colleague to video a specified part of a lesson, viewing it together, and discussing the opportunities for improving that part, initially takes courage. However, if you are serious about improving children's learning and you have a colleague you trust who will be reflective about your teaching with you, you have an opportunity that is too good to ignore.

Student interviews

Students do have great insights into how well we teach them. Under the right conditions, they are quite happy to share those insights. If you are being explicit with them about how you want teaching and learning to be in your classroom, and invite them to contribute their thinking to this as well, then periodic plenary discussions about the extent to which you and they are jointly achieving this, will give you great information on which to reflect. If you are not quite sure that you are up to this, then you might ask a colleague to interview your students on your behalf and ask them questions about how they experience all aspects of the archway.

When to reflect

Quality learning circles

One of the ways that teachers can reflect together about their practice is to set up quality learning circles in small teams or syndicates. Stewart and Prebble (1993) saw quality learning circles as a way of responding to the difficult challenge facing every school: that of improving the quality of classroom teaching. They suggest that real value could be had in teachers observing each other's practice on a regular basis, with a focus on a narrow range of classroom behaviour, and discussing this in a supportive way. It is not problem-centred. It is about perceiving the teacher we observe as the demonstrator from whom we can all learn. The teacher is not only a person we can learn from but the observation of his/her teaching acts as a catalyst for reflective discussion.

Setting the ground rules

The establishment of a climate of trust is vital for members of quality learning circles. It is especially important for the teacher whose teaching is played for the group as a focus for discussion. Agreement reached about the discussion will help to nurture a culture of trust. Some points to consider with regard to this are:

- That the tone of discussion during quality learning circle meetings mirrors good assessment for learning practice. This means the teacher demonstrator may show the video footage and engage in reflective self-assessment, or they might introduce the video by setting out what they were trying to do and ask their colleagues to engage in peer-assessment about whether they achieved that or not. These collegial interactions are a wonderful opportunity for teachers to practise giving quality feedback.
- That the topic for discussion is the teaching of the demonstrator; it is not the person doing the teaching.
- That confidentiality is discussed. The group may agree that while the principles of excellent teaching practice may be shared outside the group, the teachers remain anonymous, or they may agree that no discussion takes place outside the group. This is particularly important in the third phase which involves feedback, discussion and reflection about observed teaching practice.

In practice

A suggested three-phase sequence:

1. Following the introduction of the selected theme, teachers talk about their interpretation of that theme as it relates to their classroom teaching and reflect on their students' achievements.
2. Input of theoretical information as it relates to classroom teaching in the form of professional readings.
3. Observation of video material of a teacher demonstrating their interpretation of the theme in their classroom practice, and discussion/reflection on what teachers have observed, what they know about their own and their colleagues' teaching.

One way to focus on student achievement is for teachers to look collaboratively at student work samples. Samples of student work give teachers concrete demonstrations of what is known and what is not known. In a practical sense, this could be as simple as regularly collecting samples of three or so target students' work and collating them over time. This authentic insight into students' learning can focus teachers on the consequences of their teaching and how the methods and techniques of assessment for learning can aid student improvement. Directed discussions, notably quality learning circles, can give structures for these conversations.

Timperley & Parr (2004) write about the importance of professional learning communities, where groups of teachers and literacy leaders meet regularly to share ideas and support one another with a focus on raising student achievement. They also talk about the importance of teachers having powerful 'learning conversations' at each of the three stages: 'collecting evidence and mining it for information; deciding what benchmarks to use; and interpreting the evidence.'

Barriers to active reflection

In the classroom

For some teachers, valuing formal reflection enough to put time aside for it with their students is difficult. Many teachers that we work with find that building time for a plenary or conference means changing their habits. So many tell us that they mean to but the time gets away on them and the bell goes before they have managed to get to it. To describe the problem as finding time to 'fit in' a time for reflection shows that the reflection is being thought about as an 'add-on', not as an essential part of the lesson. Anything that is essential gets done, by definition. To break the habits of a lifetime, begin the next lesson with a plenary that reviews where the learning got to last time and warms the students up to what might be done next. You will find it just as effective. Then try doing it at the end of the lesson. Make it the last 10 minutes and really give students a good chance to properly reflect on an aspect of their learning.

Following a stylised 'recipe' or format for reflection can kill it dead; for example, requiring every student to make some verbal contribution to a plenary so that it takes forever, or requiring students to keep 'reflective diaries' day after day so that they get bored. Always be prepared to review your reflective practices to ensure they do serve learning.

Sometimes, as teachers are learning about reflection they come to think that it is really about finding the 'right' questions to ask students about their learning. So they start a hunt for lists of 'really good' questions that will intrigue and interest the students. This is a mistake. Reflection is about questioning what is happening, but it is not about the question. The best teachers we see are the ones who are always thinking about what is going on and checking their understanding. As you watch them working with their students you can see the reflective look on their faces as they think through everything that they are doing. They frequently check their understanding of how things are going with the students, and adjust things as the students respond. They never worry about what questions to ask because those come to them as they continually ponder 'How is it going?' The students learn great reflection from this powerful modelling.

With colleagues

Arranging time to reflect with colleagues can sometimes be a barrier. Meetings are always meetings in that they take time and detract from your ability to do other things. When formal reflections with colleagues are well run, and are addressing issues of genuine significance to you and your colleagues, they become highly valued and treasured; other previously competing activities fall by the wayside. If your reflective sessions do not have this quality, reflect on why they are not working and solve that problem before you go back to considering problems of practice.

Sometimes schools decide to establish quality learning circles because it is fashionable or it is part of the professional development process they are currently undertaking. If teachers do not find them professionally valuable and cannot generate their own commitment to them, it is better to stop them than to continue. We know that when they go well, the enthusiasm and commitment is great. In these circumstances, the role of senior management is to ensure that they do all that is necessary to keep that commitment for professional learning. Management must be very careful not to impose formats or requirements on the quality learning circles that are counterproductive, such as requiring 'meeting minutes' to show the Education Review Office (ERO).

A teacher shares some positive feedback from students

I'm buzzing so I have to share this wee moment of celebration with you! I just did a reflection with a class I teach for Maths (not my own). They pair-shared and then I chose five children to share what went well for them in the learning today (we had already heard the things that didn't and what we can do about these tomorrow). These were the comments:

1. I got new learning.
2. I knew what I had to do.
3. I could see when I did the task that I really had got it [the new learning].
4. You explained it really well in the modelling [yay for me].
5. It was exciting to see where this learning fits in real life [I showed them their class's Box and Whisker graph results for writing as this group was doing Box and Whiskers].

They were in fluid needs-based learning groups too! All exciting — can't wait to tell you more.

WHERE TO GO NEXT WITH LEARNING

Chapter 8

What do we mean by 'next steps'?

Put simply, 'next steps' is about

- the direction or the plan that the teacher needs to have about where the learning is headed;
- what the teacher needs to do in order to effectively communicate the direction to the students; it addresses the question, 'After we have learnt this, what do we learn next?';
- what the students need to be able to do to play their part in ensuring that the teaching and learning has direction for them.

This may all sound very similar to what has been already covered in other chapters in this book; in fact it is very difficult to separate the concepts in this chapter from understandings of assessment and promoting further learning. This chapter examines teachers' understanding of the whole curriculum, the progressions within it that students need, and it looks at how to share all this with students.

A next steps capability for teachers and students has been included because teaching and learning is a dynamic process. Learning is always moving forward. Teachers and students who are really focused on learning do have a sense of direction, of what better learning will look like. This sense of direction informs their decision-making at every point of the learning, it gives them the direction for the next step, ensures that that next step is purposeful and an integrated part of the learning journey. To maintain a sense of focus and direction requires both teacher and student to have certain skills and attributes.

Next steps is not directly about the capabilities required for the promotion of further learning that we covered in Chapter 6. While the strategies and techniques are linked, the next steps capability is more about the broader knowledge and understandings that are needed in order to engage in focused support for further learning.

What teachers need to know

Adequately portraying to students the 'next steps' requires you to have the clearest possible sense of where the next steps are leading. To take the next step sensibly, and with confidence, requires that you know where you want to end up. If you have a learning-focused relationship, then both you and your students need to have a joint understanding of the destination before you can consider what the next step might be.

Starting with the end in mind

Good planning is the essential precursor to good teaching. As a teacher you gain a sense of direction from some combination of personal knowledge of subject matter, common progressions and pace of learning, and teaching approaches and materials. All of these things give you a sense of where the learning should end up and of the broader subject context within which that learning sits. Being clear about what you want the students to understand and to own by the end of the lesson or unit, the global learning intentions, is critical. Equally critical is your ability to paint this for the students and to keep it in clear view as the lesson or unit progresses.

The better you understand the big picture, the more you understand what the 'end' is, then the more you are able to support students to move in the right direction, both as a class and for each individual student. A clear intention in mind allows you to know what strategy to use to promote further learning to move towards that intention, to ignore distractions, while still being responsive to rich learning opportunities that arise along the way.

The more you know about a subject the better you will be able to signal to students what the destination of the learning is. Students need to know where their learning is heading and it is not enough merely to tell them at the beginning. The destination needs to be kept in lights before them so that they can see it always shining in the distance, and so that they too can make judgements about whether their own learning attempts are taking them in the right direction or not. Keeping the destination in front of them gives them focus and direction to taking the next steps with some assurance.

During a teacher observation session in our work with teachers, a facilitator observed the teacher at the beginning of the lesson talking extensively about the technology programme for the term. The teacher had mapped out the learning for the term and had it clearly displayed. Although it was week four, she went back and discussed where the students had come from, how much they had learnt already and where they were heading. 'Most of you will be about here,' she said, pointing at the planner for the term, 'but some of you still need to finish your overall design of the set, whereas others of you are ready to build detail.' By continually checking with the students where they were at, and confirming they knew where they were going, each student could then carry on with their work with a clear idea of the big picture as well as a detailed idea of what they were achieving in that lesson. After the lesson, the facilitator talked to some students, all of whom had a very clear idea of what they were trying to achieve by the end of the term and what they had already covered. Their enthusiasm and ability to talk so clearly about their learning was infectious. The discussion with the teacher was equally enthusiastic. 'How often do you go over the big-picture stuff?' the facilitator asked. 'Every lesson, of course. You can't expect the students to hold all that stuff in their heads and it focuses them on the big picture right at the beginning of the lesson.'

Subject knowledge

Central to teaching is subject or discipline knowledge. Your ability to really teach a subject is limited by your ability to really understand the subject. To be an expert teacher is to continually seek a deeper understanding of the essence of a subject, to increasingly grasp its wisdom. That understanding is key to a teacher's role in planning the way forward with students, knowing the next steps to being able to take them to deeper levels of understanding. It is difficult to imagine someone becoming a great teacher without persistent attention to their own understanding of the subject(s) they teach. The better the subject knowledge of the teacher, the more able they are to assist students to take the next step in learning.

A subject novice might, in some subjects, get by with teaching students what they themselves have learnt the night before by reading the textbook. But in fact, the best that happens in this circumstance, is that the students either listen to a good teller of tales and are engaged in the tale, or they engage with the novice in problem-solving the new knowledge alongside the novice; they work it out together. This situation is better than nothing if skilled teachers are in short supply, but it does not match the support and guidance of a teacher who is expert in their subject.

What is understood about the world, and how we understand the world, changes constantly. School curriculums also change over time to reflect this. Subject expertise also needs to be continually refreshed in order to keep up to date with these changes. This could include reviewing recent research, new technologies and new ideas in the subject.

Subject knowledge is key regardless of approaches to curriculum, such as inquiry learning, discovery learning and negotiated curriculum. These have enormous value in building student motivation, agency and engagement by supporting them to investigate problems or issues that genuinely intrigue them. All of these approaches essentially use generic problem-solving sequences (for example: 1. task definition, 2. information-seeking strategies, 3. location and access, 4. use of information, 5. synthesis, 6. evaluation) that places the teacher in the role of coach to help the students move through the sequence. No subject-specific expertise is required of the teacher. As the students are to engage in research themselves to shape answers to the questions they have generated about the topic, the teacher organises for colleagues or members of the community to be available if specific expertise that they do not have is needed. Alternatively, if specific expertise is required and the teacher does not have it, then they too can engage in their own inquiry and find out, modelling the process for the students.

The danger for teachers using such approaches is that the excitement and energy often produced by a generic problem-solving approach can effectively work as a misleading proxy for genuine subject-specific investigation and knowledge building. If teachers can generate such energy from children deemed to be engaged in 'research' then it is easy to overlook the fact that the students never find themselves investigating anything using techniques and approaches used by real biologists, historians or geographers. And it is easy to overlook the fact that the teachers might not know how either. If this is always the case then both teacher and students get locked into a belief that their general inquiry and problem-solving approach is in fact building good scientific or historical or geographical skills and knowledge. The subject knowledge of the teacher will determine the integrity of the inquiry and depth of learning.

The implication for teachers therefore is that, at a minimum, they must have sufficient depth of knowledge of the curriculum that they can work with any student in the class and be confident of being able to help identify his/her individual next learning step.

In designing units of work this should be recognised through an ability to capture the main concepts (essence statements, achievement aims and achievement objectives) of the curriculum in student-accessible language that can be shared with students. It is not a matter of rewriting the achievement objectives in 'student language' but of ensuring that you deeply understand the concepts and are then able to describe them in your *own* language.

Units planned collaboratively with students will show multi-level learning experiences (and learning intentions) to meet the multi-level diverse needs of the students.

Extending students' sense of 'subject' identity

The learning of a subject or a discipline is enhanced if the student can have some sense of identity with the subject, a sense of self as a 'writer' or 'biologist' or 'historian', even if this is limited to imagining the *possibility* of seeing oneself as a 'writer', 'biologist' or 'historian' (Gilbert, 2001). To see the subject from the perspective of a writer, mathematician, musician or historian changes one's relationship with the subject and contrasts sharply with seeing it as a non-writer, non-mathematician, non-musician, non-historian. To learn the language of mathematics makes more sense if you have at least a putative sense of self-as-mathematician than if you see yourself as a non-mathematician with a dislike and distrust of your ability with 'numbers'.

Shaping this identity builds motivation to learn ('I want to improve my writing because I am a beginning writer') but requires the teacher to establish conditions of learning that are relevant to the learning needs of novice subject specialists. The only way to build the sense of 'self-as-writer' of students is to have them craft their writing as writers do. The only way to build a sense of 'self-as-historian' is by having students do historical research in the same way that historians do. The only way for students to build a sense of 'self-as-mathematician' is by having students approaching mathematics as mathematicians do.

To do this places a considerable responsibility on teachers. The deeper you understand the essence of the subject the more you will be able to engage students in experiences that build identity with the subject. If you have no identity yourself with a subject, it is unlikely to occur to you to try and build this in your students; in which case, your students are likely to take on your sense of the subject as being something that is 'not you' and needs to be engaged with only under sufferance. How many subjects that you are contracted to teach do you know are 'not you'? To meet this responsibility, teachers need to not only develop their understanding of the subject but also become positive and passionate about the subject if the students are to engage with it.

Subject learning progressions

Not only do you need to know the subject but you need to know, or have access to, descriptions of the possible learning progressions of the concepts and understandings in the curriculum (often provided in curriculum resources such as textbooks or increasingly online from the multitude of education websites). As your skill in teaching builds, you come to understand common learning paths that students take in building their own proficiency, you get to know the concepts that students find difficult, you get to know the common misunderstandings, and you extend your teaching and explanatory strategies so that the students get multiple different opportunities to engage with and learn that concept.

Examples of available resources to assist with learning progression

Additional resources are available to support the visibility of progression in the New Zealand curriculum.

The New Zealand curriculum exemplars make apparent the key features of many of the achievement objectives. An exemplar is a sample of authentic student work annotated to illustrate learning, achievement, and quality in relation to levels in the New Zealand Curriculum. The exemplars relate to strands of the curriculum, to a range of achievement objectives, and to a variety of contexts. The purposes of the exemplars are to

- illustrate key features of learning, achievement, and quality at different stages of student development;
- help students and teachers to identify the next learning steps;
- guide teachers in their interpretation of curriculum levels.

Figure 5: An art exemplar

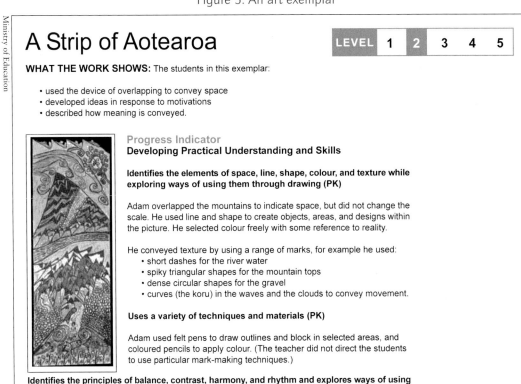

Ministry of Education

www.tki.org.nz/r/assessment/exemplars/arts/visarts/va_2a_e.php

To support these exemplars are matrices that contain descriptions (progress indicators) of the key elements of learning shown by the exemplars for each curriculum level. Teachers use these exemplars and matrices to make explicit and visible to students not only where they might locate their current achievement, but also the type of learning that they might now undertake: what the next steps of development might look like.

Exemplars are also being used to deepen teachers' understanding of quality work and possible paths to next steps. A common practice to help teachers develop shared understanding of progress and quality is for staff to plan a school- or department-wide unit or assessment task with their students. Each teacher then brings to a whole-staff meeting six samples (at low, mid, and high range) of their students' work on the unit or task. In turn, each teacher lays their samples out across the staff-room floor to show a continuum or progression from the lowest to highest curriculum levels. The teachers then group the samples of work. They annotate these grouped samples and record features of the work that they think are important. The teachers then compare their school samples and annotations to the relevant national exemplars and indicators.

Activities such as these help teachers in two main ways:

1. To develop common and consistent understandings within a curriculum area.
2. To deepen the teachers' understanding of progression and next steps within that curriculum.

Teachers have also been using exemplars with their students to help them better understand and judge the quality of their work. They have found that asking students to think about and reflect on their own and others' work prompts thinking by students, such as:

- How did they do that?
- What would I have to know in order to do that?
- That gives me an idea . . .
- So that's what good work looks like . . .
- I want to do that too. How can I learn that skill?
- Who could I ask to help me do that?

This approach allows students to see and discuss desirable qualities in real examples of work and enables them to realise that there are many ways to achieve their goals.

Exemplars are very powerful tools for teachers to use. Chapter 5 (see page 104) contained an anecdote about a student locating where he was with his writing on the progression of poetic writing exemplars that the teacher had put up along one wall. When students engage in self-assessment with this type of resource it becomes a relatively simple matter for them to then identify what they might learn next.

Exemplars can also be badly used. While we don't want to stress how not to use them, one example might in fact clarify how they should be used. Each exemplar not only contains an authentic sample of student work but also provides a fairly full description of the teaching context under which it was produced and samples of the conversation that the teacher might have with the student about where the learning might next go. The whole exemplar is designed to give teachers insights as to the characteristics of curriculum concepts at the given level and also, in association with the other exemplars in the set, of learning progression.

Each exemplar is a snapshot of learning at a level. The science exemplars exemplify broad scientific concepts and achievement aims illustrated through very specific teaching contexts. The teacher needs to see through the context to the concepts. Unfortunately some teachers have mistakenly thought that the context is the exemplar and that they would be doing the right thing by teaching the context itself. When this happens the students do not have any way of knowing what the next steps might be because the teachers themselves do not know, conversations about next steps cannot take place, and students cannot gain any clarity at all about where their learning is heading. All they are doing is completing a piece of decontextualised learning of very limited relevance. And an excellent teaching resource is ruined. Do not use them like this.

Well-designed formal assessment tools can also be used to make next steps visible to students. The most effective tool currently available for this is the computer-based 'assessment tool for teaching and learning' (asTTle) which allows teachers and students to design literacy and numeracy tests in English and Maori from Year 4 to Year 10.

Each test is 'designed' by choosing the curriculum level spread (up to three consecutive levels) that the test items should be drawn from (Levels 2 to 6), the proportion of items that should come from each level, and the curriculum functions that should be sampled by the test. Students should be involved in the design.

In schools where the tests are well used, students are clear that the purpose of the test is to help them work out what they know, and what they need to learn next.

Some teachers hand out test papers, group students and ask them to identify where the questions started to get hard. Students then look at what kind of questions the hard ones were and anything in common about them. They label what the groups of questions are about and use this discussion as a starting point for setting their next learning goals with the teacher.

Other teachers give the group learning pathway results to students to talk about. In each class the students are helped to understand the labels used for the reading functions, such as 'inference' or 'finding information', to further develop their language of learning. They are also helped to see how they could relate the reading functions analysis back to the actual test items. The teachers then ask the students to group and discuss what they thought the results meant about their current patterns of reading knowledge and what they thought they needed

Figure 6: asTTle console report for reading

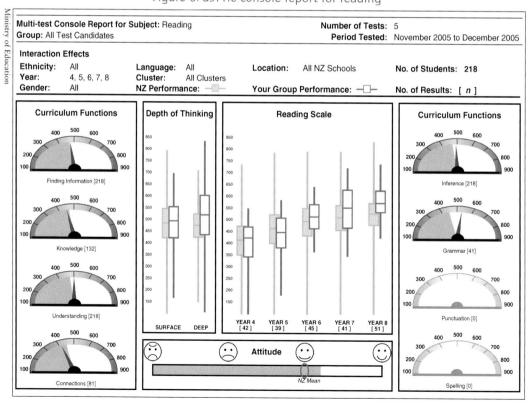

to learn next. The students come up with a detailed analysis of the reports and are highly motivated about what they want to learn next and how they want to learn it!

The teachers then build on this base by conferencing with each student about their own individual report and supporting each student to focus the group goals down to their own individual learning needs. This further increases motivation — especially when some of the students inevitably and spontaneously take the individual reports home to discuss their learning with their parents.

These are examples of using assessment tools that intensify peer support, create environments where 'getting it wrong' is simply useful, and make next steps very clear.

What students need to know

If students have the capabilities described in the first seven chapters of this book and are learning with teachers who have the ability to keep the big picture in front of them, then they need to do little else to be able to move forward with their learning. At most, all they need to be mindful of and to check is that

- they do know the big picture or global learning intention for their learning;
- they have a sense of the progression of next steps in their learning;
- the apparent next step is tangibly connected, or can be shown by the teacher to be tangibly connected, to that global learning intention;
- the apparent next step makes sense to them in terms of where they know their learning is at;
- they are able to initiate conversations with the teacher about what they need to learn next;
- they can normally identify their next learning step from their own self-assessment and through examination of material that shows progressions of learning such as a matrix, exemplar set, assessment analysis or textbook;
- they work with their teacher, where appropriate, to plan the next unit of learning.

PLANNING FOR LEARNING

About planning

Planning for learning is mostly about the thinking that is undertaken by teachers to ensure that all students have the best opportunities to learn those things that are most important.

TRY THIS!

A test of good planning is to find out whether your students are able to describe what they are learning, and how they have been part of the planning.

Try this little test with your students:
Take a small group of them (or ask a colleague to do so) to a quiet space and discuss with them the lesson just finished. Ask them what it was about, what they were learning, how they might know if they were learning, and how the decision to learn this was made. If they cannot describe what they are learning (they can always tell you what they are doing), then your planning could improve. And this chapter might help you.

Here is what some children said when the lessons were co-constructed with them:
'We are learning how to write about characterisation. We decided this when our teacher asked us what we knew about how to make characters come alive and we decided we wanted to get better at it.'

What do your children say?

'Thinking' is fundamental to planning: writing only comes after the thinking — the hardest part — has been done. Planning is about the hard thinking teachers need to do in order to design quality opportunities for student learning. Once the thinking has been done, it needs to be captured concisely and effectively in writing. This written plan can then be used as a memory prompt and reference to ensure scaffolding, continuity and consolidation in the teaching/learning enterprise. It can also be a valuable resource and reference to share with your colleagues. Good planning requires clear thinking, captured in a well-constructed, precise written plan and is a prerequisite to the art of effective teaching.

In this chapter we outline guidelines designed to support teachers who are committed to building on their ability to create a strong classroom learning environment based on assessment for learning principles. These guidelines encapsulate how we think about planning, and the examples show how we document this thinking. It provides teachers with an effective and practical guide to 'working smart' when planning.

Good planning

Good planning enables teachers to
• be very clear about which aspects of the curriculum they want students to learn at any one time;

- know how these aspects will be relevant to all students;
- know how they will approach teaching these aspects, and gather resources to help the learning;
- know how they will help students achieve the intended learning in ways that maximise the learning for all students;
- know how they will determine what students have learnt;
- know the possible pathways (progressions) for future learning;
- make the intended learning and the learning experiences sufficiently flexible and open-ended to be able to be co-constructed with the learner to meet the needs of the learner.

Good planning helps students to feel
- valued and respected by their teacher;
- that they have a role in designing their learning pathway;
- that what they are learning is relevant, important and progressive;
- committed and motivated to learn.

The planning cycle

Schools have the responsibility of ensuring that all students have the opportunity to access the full national curriculum, to be taught well, and to achieve to the highest possible standard. The complexities involved in meeting these responsibilities require careful planning of teaching programmes, combined with systematic monitoring and evaluation of programme effectiveness, with the results then feeding back into the next planning cycle.

Generally this planning and monitoring takes place at three levels of the school:
1. school-wide
2. syndicate or teaching team
3. individual teacher

Typically each level also requires a different time frame for its planning and evaluation cycle. School-wide is often referred to as long term or annual, syndicate level is medium term, and teacher level is both medium and short term. These levels are interrelated in that each both informs and depends on the other.

Long-term planning for the school

There are many factors that a school must take into consideration and plan for to ensure effective teaching and high standards of student achievement.

At the school level, teachers need guidance on how the school will interpret the national curriculum, how appropriate balance and coverage will be achieved, and how syndicates and teachers should accommodate the differing learning needs of students.

Decisions for effective long-term planning

Interpretation

The curriculum can be interpreted and delivered in a number of ways, so each school needs to make some basic decisions about interpretation. For example, the curriculum can be seen as:

1. A collection of discrete disciplines or subjects (English, technology, science, etc). From this perspective the matrix aspects of the curriculum (the key competencies, and the values) tend to be either treated as an implicit part of all school activities or as separate aspects of learning that are explicitly integrated into the teaching planned for each subject. In this option schools have often designed planning templates that include the competencies and values that are meant to be ticked or highlighted if they are seen by the teacher as being part of what is to be learnt in that unit of work. Seldom are specific learning objectives or related activities specified beyond this identification, so students would never know if they had learning experiences that had enabled them to improve their honesty, their thinking or their self-management competency. Some schools attempt to reverse this approach and concentrate on the competencies. However, this reverse approach does raise a number of issues: for example, competencies don't, indeed can't, exist without a context.

2. A set of learning experiences based around a common theme that enables discrete subjects to be linked or 'integrated' together. Often this integrated approach will take a science or social studies theme context (e.g. understanding the ecology of insects, or dinosaurs, or the Treaty of Waitangi) and have students shape their understanding of a number of subject concepts (curriculum aims and objectives) in relation to this context. Key competencies and values usually get the same treatment as in the first option.

3. An open-ended, often problem-focused, approach to learning that starts with questions that students have about the world. Teacher guidance then enables them to research answers to these questions and shape necessary curriculum understandings as they go along. If anything, compliance with the legislated curriculum tends to be retrospective, although the approach does guarantee that students have the opportunity to experience a broad and balanced curriculum over the course of the year.

A school does not have to choose amongst these options. It can allow all three to operate at once, dependent on teacher enthusiasm for each. But it does need to have a simple system for showing that all students have had the opportunities to advance their understanding, skills and attitudes in relation to important outcomes described in the curriculum.

Coverage

Schools have a legal obligation to offer an education that covers the curriculum. The concept of coverage has been interpreted in very different ways by schools. How a school thinks about coverage affects how the teachers in the school will plan.

Think about this. To 'cover' the science curriculum, we must plan to provide learning experiences drawn from the four context strands and the over-arching, unifying strand 'the nature of science'. What else is required? How should we think about it? Many schools interpret the rest of the science curriculum as requiring teachers to teach to the Achievement Objectives (AOs) and the seemingly discrete concepts represented by each. This leads to a very prescriptive and stress-inducing approach (an approach which is not in fact recommended within the curriculum document) that has usually meant that each teacher has decided on a defined set of AOs to teach to a whole class. This results in students who do not have a conceptual understanding appropriate to that particular AO not having their learning needs met. For example, if a student understands science concepts only at Level 1 of the curriculum, then it is highly unlikely that learning experiences focused at Level 3 will meet their learning needs.

An alternative approach, which is much more open-ended and recognises that students learn at different rates and in different ways, is to plan to cover all of the achievement aims (or the 'big ideas' that are contained in the essence statements) in each context strand each year. Achievement aims set the goals for each learning strand and provide the themes that link the achievement objectives of one level with those of adjacent levels. This means that for any one strand, there are only a small number of big ideas that we would want students to understand.

This interpretation of the curriculum makes 'coverage' a responsible educational notion because it guarantees that each year each student, irrespective of their rate of learning, will engage with key science concepts and develop their understanding of them.

Balance
Science, however, is only one subject in the curriculum. As all subjects have essence statements that encapsulate the big ideas, as well as achievement aims that tease the big ideas out a little more, it is possible to follow this same approach over the full range of subjects. It is necessary for schools to provide guidance to staff about how 'big' each subject is in relation to the amount of time available for teaching and learning. If a school has decided on utilising a negotiated curriculum or an integrated approach, the balance will be different than if they adopt a discrete curriculum approach. Regardless of the approach taken, however, guidance will still need to be given.

The following list has some useful additional guidelines.
- Check whether the Ministry has issued any new guidelines. For example, in October 2004 the Minister of Education announced a minimum time that schools were required to ensure that children engaged in meaningful and high-quality physical activity each week from 2006 onwards. That means there will be one less hour a week for something else.
- The Ministry has a national goal to 'raise achievement, reduce disparity' with the focus on literacy and numeracy. There is a message here. If you happen to decide that your Year 6 students need little direct time devoted to developing reading ability, you'll need to have your evidence ready.

- What does your own school data tell you about where the greatest learning need is? Writing? Mathematics? Music? Relating to others? Self-management? This data should inform your achievement standards and target-setting exercise underpinning your strategic planning. It should also guide your curriculum balance thinking.

The results of all this hard thinking are described in a document such as a curriculum plan, a scheme or an education plan.

Medium-term planning for the teaching syndicate or teacher

Planning at this level is not as difficult as it often seems if it is thought through in the right way. Following is a set of thinking points and actions that you might like to use as a guide when you are planning your next unit. Planning units as a team using this set of thinking points is a good way of getting the team to think deeply about what you want the students to learn and to be creative in the design of the learning experiences.

Whether you use the sequence we have used here or not will depend on
- how your school approaches the curriculum;
- how you want to collaborate with the students on the planning;
- how you go about assessing what students bring to the unit themselves;
- how you go about thinking through how you want to teach the unit, and provide rich opportunities for students to learn.

Firstly, we show you how you might use these thinking points in English; then we give an example science unit plan. Also included are case studies from a couple of teachers who have developed and successfully used variations on this approach. Hopefully these examples will help to make your medium-term planning relatively straightforward. Often the hardest part is gaining or arranging the content knowledge that you need in order to be able to design clear learning goals and effective learning experiences for your students. Don't forget that TKI and English Online have a lot of very well-developed unit plans that can provide much of the content for you and save you resource development time (if not thinking time). So remember to use these facilities when you feel the need or when you are stuck for inspiration.

Decisions for effective medium-term planning

See the flowchart on pages 182–83 for links corresponding to the following highlighted *text.*
- Consult the school scheme to decide what aspect of the curriculum needs to be taught next (let's take English[1]/narrative writing[2]), and for how long.
- Consult the scheme for which *strand(s)* and achievement aims[3] from the curriculum to focus on. If the scheme gives no guidance, get it reviewed and improved, and use the National Curriculum and National Exemplars.

- Write the Strand(s) and Achievement Aims on to your planning sheet somewhere near the top of the page.
- Decide if you know what the aims are really suggesting that your students need to know. Can you restate them in your own words so that you could explain them well to your students as **global learning intentions**[4]? (See Chapter 4, Table 6, page 85.)
- Decide when you will begin to involve your students in the planning. Will it be at this stage, at the next or the next? Don't leave it longer than that or you will give them no way in which they can feel they are active participants in the construction of their learning pathways. Co-construction is critical if you want them to take a good measure of responsibility for their learning and acquire their own assessment for learning capabilities at a high level.
- Decide how you will determine what your students already know in this area. You may have some assessment results already or you and your students may decide that some further assessment is needed.
- An easy way to determine how well students are able to write now is to carry out an asTTle Narrative assessment with them. This diagnostic test will not only help you and your students understand current writing skills, but also will allow you to formulate your plan for taking them to the next stage.
- When you examine class patterns of ability (using the Group Learning Pathways asTTle report) you might decide to focus on the richness of the *language features* in their writing. You might look at the asTTle Narrative Writing matrix and decide that the focus for the majority of the class is around the Level 2 aspects of the Language Resources feature:
  - evidence of attempts to add interest and detail through the use of descriptors (for example, adverbials, adjectives);
  - may attempt to use dialogue to add to story;
  - many simple sentences correct;
  - some complex sentences evident;
  - attempts to vary sentence types.
- These Level 2 indicators in this feature alone cover a lot of learning and it is unlikely you would want *all* students to focus on *all* aspects of them. So you need to determine what you intend the **specific learning**[5] to be. It would also be wise to leave empty bullet points for any related learning intentions that evolve during the unit.
- You should engage your students in this analysis of their writing needs. Each student will then have a slightly different focus — certainly this will be true for the students who are working at different levels. Together you will be able to identify where they need to go next in their learning.
- You might decide that your students need to learn to focus on more detailed and elaborate language in describing people or animals in their writing. You could do this by having them study a range of adult and student exemplars that you locate and have them decide on their own **success criteria**[6]. All this needs to be well thought through, so it can be very useful to summarise your understanding of the learning you want to invite students to engage with on the planning sheet.
- You now need to decide *how* you are going to assist your students to really engage with this learning. Not only will you use assessment for learning strategies richly, but you can also design some specific experiences or **activities**[7] that will enable them to delve deeply into the intended learning.

- Allow enough time to make sure that the whole unit is well resourced[8] and that you have thought through how you are going to ensure that the students understand the relevance of the learning and are motivated to engage in the learning.
- Note the formative emphasis for assessment. If you have established good success criteria and the whole school assessment[9] system is coherent and well planned then you will find that the assessment aspect is not difficult.

---

1. English
(Weeks 1–4, Term 2, 5 hours per week)

2. Narrative Writing

3. Achievement Aims or 'Big Ideas' from the essence statements
(By engaging with text-based activities, students become increasingly skilled and sophisticated speakers and writers.)

4. Global Learning Intentions
(To learn how to make our writing more interesting for others to read.)

5. Specific Learning Intentions
(To learn how to describe in writing what people or animals are like so that the reader knows what they are really like.)

6. Success Criteria
(To be decided by the students after studying some exemplars.)

7. Learning Activities

- Conference with the class about why you have chosen this focus for SLIs. Seek their buy-in, and be prepared to modify.
- Have students individually read samples of descriptions that are suited to their level.
- In groups (decided by level they are working within), discuss and decide what makes it possible for the reader to 'know' the person or animal being described. Have the students list the success criteria and put them in a place that will be a good source of reference for them.
- Have them write five descriptive paragraphs, with peer conferencing after each one. Provide the motivation for each paragraph. Conference to involve both discussing where criteria have

---

been met and how they could be further improved, with feedback using suitable prompts.
- Finish each session with a whole-class plenary.
- Finish whole unit with plenary and discuss how to display their improved descriptions.

8. Resources

Find a selection of paragraphs from authors that you like, and from student writing within the school at levels above that of the students (i.e. Level 3 writing is best for a Level 2 student), and National Exemplars

9. Assessment
(ongoing and/or end of unit)

- Have the students peer-assess against the success criteria, using ticks for criteria met, and other symbols for the three feedback prompts.
- Have the students conference with you to discuss the peer assessment and next steps.

9. Assessment
(end of term, unit, or according to school assessment timetable)

- Repeat the asTTle test — again conference individually or in groups with the students about what the results mean for where they have got to, and for next steps.

Short-term or daily planning for the teacher
Decisions for effective short-term planning

Once you have worked through all of the medium-term issues you will have a very useable unit plan that will meet all requirements. You should then also add 'brief formative notes' to your daily work plan as you work with students, engage with them and become aware of emerging needs that will require modification to the planned sequence. These 'notes' should include any information about the learning progress that will be useful for later reference.

This planning then becomes more than a list of the week's or day's activities. It is a record of what is actually delivered to the students, and is modified daily in accordance with the feedback from the day's lessons. Thus a weekly programme is started in advance, and the day's conversations and decisions from plenaries and conferences will then be included in the next day's programme. (It is advisable to include reference codes back to the unit plan so the links are obvious.)

As in unit planning it is best to leave spaces ready for next steps in learning that evolve during the learning process. Lin's short-term planning shown on pages 184–85 is very detailed for the week. She would also modify it with additional notes as the week progressed.

	Monday	Tuesday	Wednesday
TABLE 7: AN EXAMPLE OF			

Reading

Monday	Tuesday	Wednesday
Group 2 L.I: We are learning to put information together (synthesise). Read 'Special Effects': Discuss information under various sections. Explore how a film director would put info together.	Group 1: Follow up graphic organiser work — discuss the story's plot and identify intro/problem/resolution. Importance of characters — sociogram.	Group 3: Review tension words — emotional charges in Willie at beginning of story, middle and end — make-up of a narrative. Intro terms, problem, resolution.
Group 3. L.I: We are developing an understanding of narratives. Read 'Intruders' 3:3.99 Discuss introduction of tension. Note words/phrases that communicate tension.	Group 2: Finish 'Special Effects'. Practise putting info together with explanations for prepared scenarios — beautiful girl in a car crash.	Group 1: Report back on sociogram. Identify major, minor characters. Positive and negative relationships between them.
Group 1. Read 'Get out of my hair' 2.4:00 Reciprocal Rdg L.I. We are developing an understanding of narratives. Use a graphic organiser to classify parts of story introduction/problem/resolution.	Group 3: Finish reading 'Intruders' — write phrases that show tension and emotion (show don't tell).	Group 2: Write scenarios for special effects.

Written language

Monday	Tuesday	Wednesday
L.I: We are learning how to write explanations. Give exemplars to instructional groups. Children individually underline/highlight what makes them 'good explanations'.	In groups — share underlined, highlighted parts — success criteria of good explanations — a matrix for L2, L3, L4 qualities (add my own from L.T.P). Include audience, structure, time, relationships, topic, appropriate language, sentence beginnings.	Brainstorm lists of topics for explanation writing, e.g. the importance of newspaper ads, making an umu. Choose a topic, model writing an open statement (to engage the reader) — practise writing opening statements.

Centre of interest

Monday	Tuesday	Wednesday
'Fair Go' (consumer rights). Watch excerpts from video of 'Fair Go'. Who are the disputes between? (Customers/consumers and providers of goods/services.)	Identify who forms the consumer chain. In groups give students an item, e.g. can of peaches. Students make charts of people responsible for peaches from factory to consumer. Report back — develop a class chart.	Set up groups representing consumer chain, e.g. manufacturer (quality control), retail, consumer, monitoring agency (Consumer Magazine, Dept of Consumer Affairs). In groups discuss and list what their rights and responsibilities might be.
Introduction L.I: We are developing an understanding of the rights and responsibilities of people involved in the consumer chain.		

SHORT-TERM PLAN

Thursday	Friday	Weekend/Notes

What do I need to re-teach?

Thursday

Group 2. Read together scenarios. Critique them against info given in book, poor feedback — improve work.

Group 3. Review graphic organisers. Examine characters. Look at words author uses to get this reader to form opinion of character (show don't tell).

Group 1. Read between the lines. How do we know that Tamsin's family is stressed? Refer to sociogram phrases in story, relationships to narrative structure.

Friday

Group 1. Planning — review understanding of narrative — impact of characters. Input of title to convey story's message. Plan a story called 'Get Lost'.

Group 2. Review/planning: How did we get on with taking info apart and putting it together? What are you most pleased with? What parts were tricky?

Group 3. Complete graphic organiser using emotional descriptors in various phases of narratives.

Paired feedback about openings — referring to success criteria. Choose some to review/critique as a class.

Planning — What are we doing well? What do we need more practice with in writing openings?

Re-teach. 'Gaps' from yesterday's planning. Move on to 'body' of explanations — model writing.

Define 'ethical' code of practice for the people in the consumer chain. Then explore how they do their job — e.g. quality control. Honest advertising — Consumer Magazine. Who can help us with this information?

Identify the stages of fair testing. Fax children's questions to Dick Hubbard 'How does he manage with advertising?' What are the procedures/practices that protect the consumer?

Planning templates

It may be that you want to put the planning decisions and actions into a convenient format or template that you can apply across all subjects. One of the problems with most templates is that they endeavour to do all of your thinking for you and to enable you to have planning to show others (e.g. ERO) that they meet their idea of what planning should be. Templates should provide a guide for your own thinking about how to best deliver the next steps in learning to your students. Following is a template (below and continued overleaf) that could be used that has been completed for a science unit. What do you think?

TABLE 8: MICHAEL'S SCIENCE PLAN		
Unit plan		
Class: Room 6, Year 4	**Teacher:** MA	**Length of unit** (weeks, hours): Wks 3-6, 3 hrs/wk
Subject: Science	**Strand(s):** Living World & Nature of Science	**Context/topic:** Fish

Living world:

Achievement aims

Life processes: Students will understand the processes of life and appreciate the diversity of living things. **Ecology:** Students will understand the interactions of living things with each other and with the non-living environment.

Nature of science:

Achievement aims

Investigating in science: Students will carry out science investigations using a variety of approaches: classifying and identifying; pattern seeking; exploring; investigating models; fair testing; making things or developing systems.

Global learning intentions:

1. to learn more about how different living things can be grouped according to what they look like;
2. to learn more about how some special features of fish can help them to stay alive;
3. to learn more about how fish change over the course of their lives;
4. to learn more about what happens to fish when their environment changes;
5. to get better at investigation.

Summary of content area (what are the big ideas that you want students to know about)

Fish are living things that have very visible adaptations for living in water. Examining the characteristics of fish will also allow students to contrast these characteristics with those of land-based animals. (See more on p. 43 of *Developing Science Programmes*, MOE 1995.)

Notes about entry level of students

Discussions with the students showed that most of them knew little about fish except those from the pet shop. Focus Levels 1 and 2 of the curriculum for these aims. They know basic parts of a fish but not what functions the parts play apart from the eyes. Jamie, Rhonda, Ulesse and Elspeth are the biologists — Level 3 and 4.

Specific learning intentions	Success criteria *(where appropriate include success criteria for the different groups within the class)*	Activities/resources *(including Exemplars to be used)*
		Discuss unit with students, use a motivational device, use individual/small group/whole class discussion sequence to determine what they know already about fish.
To be able to identify between 6–12 parts of a fish from external inspection (depending on how much you knew beforehand).	Correctly label a picture of a fish.	Small group exercise to examine a dead fish and discuss/research and name parts of the fish – p. 43 of *Develop Science*. Sketch of a fish on paper for children to label.
To learn how each part of the fish helps the fish to survive.	Write a description of the function of each labelled part of the fish as above. Describe why each part of the fish needs to be that particular shape, size and make-up in order for it to work properly – p. 48.	Examine both digestion and movement Use focus questions of: how do fish eat? What do they do with the food? . . . and I dissect a fish with the class, probably focused on where the food goes – discussing as we go, exploring in from the mouth. Observe the fish in the aquarium eating: what do they seem to eat, not eat? How do their mouths work? What contrasts with ours . . . Observe goldfish swimming: what moves, what seems to be most important/why? Shape fair tests for ideas – p. 47.
To learn what happens to fish as they get older.	To be able to describe the main changes to fish as they move through their life cycle.	Resources on fish life cycle. Students discuss and reflect on info with reference to class goldfish and their life cycle.
To learn that the right environment is very important for the health of the fish.	List at least 3 features the environment must have if a goldfish is going to remain healthy in a fish bowl.	Examine the effects of light, temperature, 24-hr cycles and nutrients on behaviour – note ethical considerations.
To get better at observation and fair testing.	Make some shift in the investigation matrix that shows I am becoming good at scientific investigation.	

Groups (based on diagnostic assessment prior to unit):
Jamie, Rhonda, Ulesse and Elspeth can work on activities together, with the rest of the class grouped by student choice.

Assessment approach

Before the unit	After the unit
• 'Before views' discussion with class to gain sense of level and establish investigative questions. • Individuals identify where they feel they are on the investigation matrix.	• Children use self- and peer-assessment against the success criteria. • Evaluate the unit through class plenary. • Each child self-assesses again against the investigation matrix. I enter my assessment of their level on that matrix and a best-fit level for the context strand into the student data base.

Formative notes	
2/6	*'Before views' discussion — learning gap identified for many students about the difference between a fish and a mammal — need to add an extra learning intention to unit.*
11/6	*Eight students find it hard to write a description of body parts/functions — small group with teacher aide tomorrow.*
12/6	*Fish swimming activity — for this lesson students did not get a good enough look at the fish swimming and did not know much about fins being used to change directions.*
	Need a video for next time with a different fish swimming for students to see. 'Pause' & 'Slow' functions needed on TV from Audio-visual room.
18/6	*Five students want to compare environments of different fish in different parts of the world — Melissa, Albert, Mathew, Sione & Jack. Need to plan an investigation with them — TKI?? School librarian?*

Dave's view: A slightly different approach
How Dave thinks about his planning for learning

For me the issues around written planning are the answers to the questions a teacher should be asking themselves on a lesson-by-lesson, day-by-day basis.

1. What do I want them to learn? And what do they need to learn?
(Curriculums, Schemes, Overviews, etc, to be broken down into measurable and achievable learning steps, which are then negotiated with the students as co-constructed learning intentions.) What assessment tool will I use to find out what they need to learn?

2. How will I (or they) measure their success at learning this?
(A discussion with students about how to recognise when the learning has been achieved, and what successful learning will 'look like'.)

3. What learning activities can I, or the students, create that will help the students achieve this learning?
(These are not activities that fill in time, but activities that have been carefully chosen to contribute to the intended learning and success criteria. Fun is 'good', but is not always 'learning'.)

4. How will I monitor their learning and success?
(The activities themselves may allow the teacher to assess the students' achievement levels. Sometimes assessment activities need to be set up. Self- or peer-assessment activities may need to be organised.)

5. What is the next step (or steps) in learning associated with this programme?
(Some students will need extending, some will finish early, some will get stuck. The teacher needs to communicate that learning is a journey. There is always a next step. The teacher is better equipped to individualise the programme if they are familiar with the next steps, and can move the students towards that next step, at a moment's notice.)

6. What resources and equipment do I need?
(Decisions about learning rubrics, books, kits, photocopying, etc need to be made.)

Dave's algebra plan

Following is Dave's thinking/recording for his algebra unit. A lesson plan for this unit can be found on pages 192–93. He makes the following points to make the plan easier to understand:

- *The learning intentions page is displayed on the wall and in my planning.*
- *The stepping stones sheet (see page 191) graphically organises the learning; each student has an A4-sized photocopy.*
- *The activities match the learning intentions, number for number. If the pre-test shows they have a skill already, they colour it in; then as they work on the others, and show success, they colour these in too, in a different colour. The stepping stones then graphically demonstrate progress made (in levels of achievement) and make a useful entry in pupil portfolios.*
- *Before moving from one learning intention to another, each student conferences with me, answering at least two plenary-type questions in order for us to co-ascertain to what extent the intended learning has been achieved.*
- *As the students move from one learning intention to another, they place their individual names next to the particular learning intention they are working on; this gives me instant recognition of the progress being made by each student.*

Algebra learning intentions

The algebra learning intentions below could be for individual or group work while you are working with a group for instruction. 'Stepping Stones', on page 191, is also a useful tool to use with your students for them to map out their own learning intentions. In addition to these resources, you can see further resources on www.nzmaths.co.nz/numeracy/PlanLinks/AlgPlannerAA-AM.pdf.

TABLE 9: ALGEBRA LEARNING INTENTIONS

Step no.	Learning intentions — we are learning how to:	Practice work
Level 3		
1.	describe in words, rules for continuing number and spatial patterns	NCM 3.1, pp. 258–263 Ex 1 & 2
2.	make up and use a rule to create a sequential pattern	NCM 3.1, pp. 280–285 Ex 1 & 2
3.	state the general rule for a set of similar practical problems	NCM 3.2, pp. 280–287 Ex 1 & 2
4.	use graphs to represent number, or informal, relations	NCM 3.1, pp. 278–279 Ex 3
5.	use graphs to represent number, or informal, relations	NCM 3.2, pp. 312–313 Ex 3

TABLE 9 continued:		
Step no.	Learning intentions — we are learning how to:	Practice work
6.	solve problems like a + 15 = 39	NCM 3.1, pp. 268-269 Ex 4
7.	solve problems like a –15 = 39	NCM 3.2, pp. 297-299 Ex 5
8.	Level 3 Algebra Review	NCM 3.2, pp. 317-322
Level 4		
9.	find a rule to describe any member of a number sequence, express it in words, and make predictions	NCM 4.1, pp. 304-306 Ex 21:5
10.	find a rule to describe any member of a number sequence, express it in words, and make predictions	NCM 4.2, pp. 278-284 Ex 20:2, 20:3
11.	sketch and interpret graphs on whole number grids which represent simple everyday situations	NCM 4.1, pp. 320-321 Ex 22:9
12.	sketch and interpret graphs on whole number grids which represent simple everyday situations	NCM 4.2, pp. 306-310 Ex 21:7
13.	find and justify a word formula which represents a given practical situation	NCM 4.1 pp. 322-326 Ex 23:3
14.	solve equations like 2a + 4 = 16	NCM 4.2, pp. 271-273 Ex 19:7
15.	Level 4 Algebra Review	NCM 4.2, pp. 324-328
Level 5		
16.	generate patterns from a structured situation, find a rule for a general term, and express it in words and symbols	NCM 5.1, pp. 530-534 Ex 22:2
17.	sketch and interpret graphs which represent everyday situations, graph linear rules, and interpret the slope intercepts on an integer co-ordinate system	NCM 5.1, pp. 390-410 Ex 15:2, 15:6, 15:7.
18.	solve linear equations	NCM 5.1, pp. 310-321 Ex 11:5, 11:7, 11:10, 11:13.
19.	combine like terms in algebraic expressions	NCM 5.1, pp. 280-290 Ex 10:3, 10:5, 10:7, 10:9
20.	use equations to represent practical situations	NCM 5.1, pp. 306-309 Ex 11:4

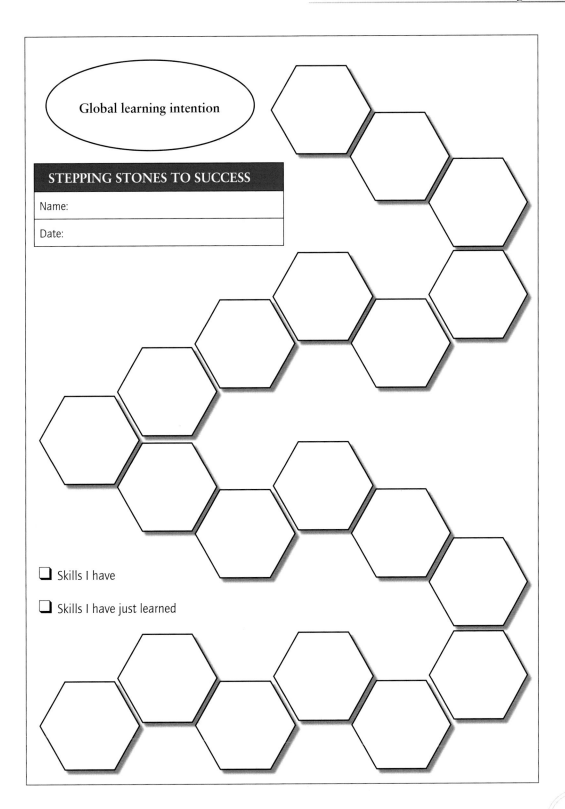

Global learning intention

STEPPING STONES TO SUCCESS

Name:

Date:

❑ Skills I have

❑ Skills I have just learned

TABLE 10: DAVE'S ALG

Lesson/unit plan: Algebra

Curriculum: Maths

Teacher: Dave Bradley

Room: 1

Achievement objective: The achievement objectives for L3, L4, and L5 algebra can be found on page 189–9

Intentions:	Success criteria:	Teaching and learning activities:
What do I intend them to learn?	How will they know they are successful?	What will I do to help them achieve this?

Global learning intentions: W.A.L. The skills of algebra. **Minor learning intentions**	Students will mark their own work, for immediate feedback regarding their progress. In the conferencing with the teacher, each student will demonstrate his/her learning on each individual learning intention.	Each student will • be given a pre-test to determine the work they alrea and what they need to learn, from Levels 3, 4, and 5 • be given a Stepping Stone Organiser (see page 216) outlining the learning involved in the unit; • colour in on the flow chart any skills the pre-test sho already have; • identify the skills yet to be learned from the sections uncoloured. These become their first individual piece learning in class time; • complete the activity outlined on the flow chart, atte the work independently, seeking help from the text, computers, dictionaries, or other students; • seek help from the teacher if necessary; • mark their own finished work; • sign on for a conference with the teacher in order to demonstrate that they have mastered the particular and understand the learning involved; • colour in the appropriate stepping stone, and move the next task, if the teacher is convinced they have m the identified learning; • move through all tasks identifying new learning on successive days, in this model; • move a name label along a wall-size version of the fl chart to indicate to the teacher, and class, where the currently working.

Catering for a range of abilities

Formative notes

N PLAN

Date: Term 3

Level: 3, 4, 5

¬ent activities:	Assessment for learning:	Resources:
I assess the Success Criteria?	What happens next?	

marking (80%+)
ugh the conference.
-test will provide summative feedback
vels.

This ongoing process will provide direct
learning feedback to students. If they aren't
ready to move on they will receive learning
support and extra opportunities to practise
their skills.

aluation

ヽ's learnings:

teachings:

TABLE 11: DAVE'S DEB

Lesson/unit plan: Debating   **Teacher:** Dave Bradley

Curriculum: English   **Room:** 1

Achievement objective: Level 4

Language features:
1. Uses a range of language features appropriately, showing an understanding and appreciation of their effect.
2. Uses an increasing personal vocabulary to create precise meaning.
3. Uses a range of oral, written and visual features to create meaning, impact and sustain interest.
4. Uses a range of text conventions appropriately, effectively, and with increasing accuracy.

Intentions:	Success criteria:	Teaching and learning activities:
What do I intend them to learn?	How will they know they are successful?	What will I do to help them achieve this?

Global learning intention: We are learning how to debate an issue.	**Students will**
	 • Participate in a debate using correct debating procedures
	   – persuasively
	   – informatively
		• Work through the instructional OHPs, discussing getting them to record their learning in their lite books.
		 • Organise class into groups of three to become debating teams.
		 • Facilitate brainstorming in order for them to sele to debate.
		 • Identify which groups are 'affirmative' and 'nega
		 • Allow class session times for teams to develop tc each member's debate speech. Edit these togeth a team effort.

Specific learning intentions: W.A.L. the elements of a debate. W.A.L. to write a persuasive argument in support of an opinion. W.A.L. to rebut the point of view of others.	**Students will** • describe the members of a debating team; • describe the speaking roster in a debate; • explain the role of the judge; • explain the meaning of 'persuasive'; • write a persuasive argument; • form a rebuttal during the debate.	• Work as a team to predict the content of the opp argument. Try to prepare a bullet-point list of ret arguments, in advance. • Allocate sufficient time for students to listen to ‥ team-mates practising their speeches, peer-asses‥ in order to help each other speak with confidenc assertiveness, clarity, poise, etc. • Hold a competition, with a volunteer from staff ‥ (e.g. Philippa) and invite parents.

Catering for a range of abilities

• A vast range of skills exists in this class. By grouping similar abilities together, as opposing teams, I hope to create even com
• Within teams I plan to use mixed-ability groups so that they can support each other's learning, and build on each other's sug‥

Formative notes

N PLAN

Date: Term 4

Strand: Oral Language

and audiences:
understanding of how to shape texts for different purposes and audiences.
deliberate choice of content, language and text form, constructs a range of texts that demonstrates a developing
nding of
a variety of intentions, situations and levels of formality;
ndividuals or groups with varying characteristics and determinants such as backgrounds, interests and motivations.

ent activities:	Assessment for learning:	Resources:
assess the success criteria?	What happens next?	
bserving the debates. ider:	List the names of students needing learning support and what they need, here!	Teacher's own resources.
s each speaker aware to the elements of a debate?		
Have they written a persuasive argument?		
Can they rebut an argument spontaneously?		

osen:
solutions to traffic flow on
araoa Rd.

entranceway to new school.

eserve at Tiritiri-Matangi.

Bay Pier proposal.

luation

Children's learning: Students became very passionate about the issues they were debating. The L.I.s and S.C. discussions and displays made it much easier for students to focus and assist each other on the learning.

Their ability to organise a persuasive argument developed beyond my expectation. Their understanding of what a debate is and the roles of each participant was well cemented by the end of the unit.

I was very proud of the results that were witnessed by the parents.

Personal teaching: Structuring the unit around L.I.s and S.C. kept me and the students focused on the exact learning required each day. I found that it gave a natural flow to the unit, helped me organise the learning and helped me to redirect students to their learning.

I would structure a repeat in a very similar way.

BUILDING PARTNERSHIPS WITH FAMILY

Overview

Parents do influence student learning. What varies hugely from family to family is the extent to which this influence is positive and supportive. Schools and teachers are powerful agents in deciding and guiding family input, whether this agency is consciously exercised or not. This chapter describes how to consciously build parent support for learning by *all* students in *your* school and *your* classroom.

It's all about supporting student learning. The point of building partnerships with parents is to improve student learning. There is much research that clearly indicates that if teachers and schools can establish the right type of relationship, then student learning will be enhanced (for example, Biddulph et al., 2003). If all the previous chapters have made sense and you have implemented the principles and strategies described, then taking the step to build parental support will not prove too difficult.

Let's start by revisiting our guiding principles of relationships.

Building a partnership with the family is about building a sound, trusting, three-way relationship between the teacher, the student, and the student's family. We want this relationship with the home to be characterised by the same underlying principles as for our learning-focused relationship between teacher and student: openness, honesty and respect. If we achieve this then we will achieve an open relationship with parents, and the students, in which all parties will be able to raise issues of concern, have them addressed effectively, and have a strong commitment to supporting student learning. Openness means making information accessible to the parents, whanau and students — all of the information the school and the teachers use to shape powerful learning experiences for students, and which allows them to think about their progress and attainment.

Respect and honesty is offered when we want them to be properly informed about the progress and attainment of their child and we give them clear statements about exactly how we see progress and attainment. We do not avoid sharing information that they might misinterpret. We spend time helping them to interpret it. We don't patronise them with simplistic accounts of progress, we tell them the full story and respect their ability to understand if we have been clear enough. This does require that we have a good understanding ourselves. Also, we don't say anything to the parents that we would also not be quite happy to say to the students, or in front of the students. We would also ensure that the parents felt respected as parents, as people, as equals.

Parents, students and teachers have different roles in the partnership and want different things from the partnership that reflect those different roles. Normally the parent needs to know a lot more from the teacher than the teacher needs to know from the parent.

If there is an effective learning-focused partnership then each of the three members of the partnership will expect to know, and will know, a number of things.

The teachers will know

- that the parents trust their ability to provide for quality teaching and learning;
- that the parents will demonstrate to their child, through their actions, that they fully support the teaching and the curriculum;
- that the parent will raise immediately any concern about the child and their learning;

- that the parent will listen to any concern the teacher has about the child and their learning.

The students will know

- that they are supported by both teacher and parent to learn actively;
- that the teacher and the parents agree about the importance of school and of their respective roles;
- that both teacher and parents will really listen to any concern the students have about their learning and will help them to resolve that concern.

The parents/caregivers will know

- what the school and teacher are trying to achieve and that the teacher takes the education of their child very seriously and is strongly motivated to do whatever is necessary to enable their child to learn.
  - The parents need to know explicitly what the school is trying to achieve — what its mission and its vision are — what it stands for, what it is determined to achieve, how well it is achieving and why it will be brilliant for their child. If parents aren't aware of this, you haven't done the job. If they think it is just another school, just the one that is closest, it probably is. And that is not good enough. What is hard about being serious about having high standards in learning? And if you have them, how hard is it for the whole community to see that? Is your school driven or does it amble? Vision statements and charters are things that schools have in order to describe vision and purpose, but while they are necessary, they don't have any value unless the whole community knows that the school is really going for it. The school is known by its actions, not by its words.

'Wow, those two schools are almost side by side but they are so different. You go into one and it feels really alive, really organised and on to it. The kids are open-eyed, keen and respectful. The teachers act like professionals. And the other is just the opposite. The grounds are a mess and no one seems to care. The kids are bored, the teachers are bored, the principal is asleep. Everyone is bored. How can they be so different?'   Overheard in the neighbourhood

- that on a daily basis, the school works for the child
  - if their child is safe, happy, and learning at school;
  - if their child has a feeling of being respected, accepted and belonging;
  - if the teacher is respectful of the socio-cultural background of the family and holds high expectations of the child's ability to learn;
  - if the teacher takes responsibility for the quality of the teaching, the learning and the attainment and does not attempt to blame the parents for poor learning by their child.
- what is being taught — from big picture to small picture
  - The school must deliver the national curriculum. Parents need to know that they can see this if they want; and if they want, they need to be able to understand what it means for their child. Each school should be able to make the curriculum transparent for their parents. Every teacher should be able to give a three- to five-sentence summary of the essential

learnings intended in each curriculum that parents will understand clearly and also be able to describe what it means for their child's next steps. It is very puzzling and frustrating for parents if teachers, who are meant to be the experts, cannot easily describe what the school must teach their child. If it can't be described to them, how will their child find out?

- We also need to let parents know what the broad learning aims are for the next period ahead – maybe for a term at a time – and the types of learning experiences that their child is likely to be engaged with. This is normally easily managed with a newsletter from the teacher for the term ahead of what the class will be involved with.

- **how it is being taught**
  - Parents need to know the approach to pedagogy the school uses and why they use it. If the school uses the approach outlined in this book, then parents need to know what the essence of it is, and why the school has chosen this way; what the research says, how it differs from when they were at school. There should be simple statements about the pedagogy available as handouts, on the school's webpage, and there should be opportunity for parents to discuss the pedagogy with the teachers at information evenings. See page 213-14 for a possible statement.

- **how the parent can provide support**
  - The teacher/school needs to be clear about how they would like the parents to support the teaching and learning and offer support to the parents to be able to do it, or learn how to do it. For example, if the teacher wants the parents to listen to the child read, then it is important that the parents know how to do it in ways that supports the child's learning. They need to know how to give timely, useful feedback, and when and how to give praise. The teacher may need to organise some opportunities to help the parents learn how to do this.

- **how responsive the school is to discuss and resolve issues**
  - Parents want to know that the teacher is open and responsive to anything that the parents want to say, to any issues that they want to raise. They want to feel genuinely welcome at the school and, if they have concerns, that they can raise them and have them really listened to. They want to feel that there is a friendly, accessible, open, respectful and honest relationship between the school and themselves, and that this is there irrespective of the differences in socio-cultural backgrounds between parents and school and irrespective of the resources the parents can bring.

- **how the school informs about progress and attainment**
  - Most importantly, parents want to know how their child is getting on and that there are easy, accessible, two-way channels of communication available should they wish to talk with the teacher or senior management or vice versa, at any time. Schools and teachers tend to focus on this part of the relationship and find it the hardest to meet parental expectations with.
  - Of the lists above for teachers, students and parents, the one for parents is much longer. Why should this be when for an open, respectful relationship all three participants need access to the same information? It appears that the parents need to know more from the school than vice versa because so much of the information relevant to the child's learning

is generated in the school and the class. Because of this it is much easier for the teacher and the child to know it anyway, but the parent will not know it unless it is made available to the parent in one way or another. So let's have a look at how it might be all provided in simple ways.

Meeting parental expectations for information

Much of the information needed by parents to be equal and respected partners is easy for schools to make available through publications of one sort or another such as newsletters, charters, websites, brochures or prospectuses. But information directly about the child's learning, and about attainment and progress is another matter.

If the focus is to be kept on learning, and the ownership of the learning with the child, then the best person to talk about the learning is the learner. If the teacher does the talking, as is more conventional in a parent-teacher interview, then the message is that in fact the teacher is in charge of the learning, not the student. The teacher knows what has been taught *and* learnt (from assessment information), not the student. From a learning-focused perspective, the teacher has to know what has been learnt, but the student also has to know that they have learnt it. If the student has really learnt it, they should be able to describe, demonstrate or in some other way show evidence of that learning.

Student-led conferences

Not only is the student the best person to tell their parents what they have learnt, but if we believe that students build their knowledge by communicating what they know, then providing an opportunity for the students to tell their family what they know can significantly assist with that learning. But we cannot just ask students to do this; they need to know exactly what they have learnt, but they also have to have the skills to describe their learning to others, and they need the support to do this. What do we mean by student-led conferences?

We mean it as being a conversation between the student, parents and teacher that is focused on recent learning. The meeting set-up is managed by the school and teacher, but the conversation is led by the student.

All participants in well-planned and organised student-led conferences have found them to be powerful experiences for students, parents and teachers. The responsibility undertaken by the students to share and evidence their learning with their parents/caregivers, to show them what they have learnt, becomes a key factor in enabling rich communication between all parties and strong motivation for learning.

Why have student-led conferences?

Any activity that takes the time of teachers, or students, or parents needs to be justified in terms of the extent to which it supports improved student learning. In our view the conferences can be strongly justified in a number of ways in helping to achieve a range of outcomes that are associated with improved achievement. These outcomes for each group are listed over the page.

For students, student-led conferences are an opportunity to
- develop and extend their ability to talk about their learning;
- deepen their relationship with their parents around their school learning, to celebrate what has been learnt;
- shape their ability to clarify what they are learning and assess their own progress;
- reflect on their learning journey and modify it as a result of the reflection;
- set next steps in the form of goals and action plans.

All of these outcomes enable students to build motivation for learning, to enhance their self-esteem and self-efficacy and to confirm that they are taking significant responsibility for doing the work of learning.

For parents, student-led conferences are an opportunity to
- actively and meaningfully support their child in his or her learning;
- understand more fully what the child is learning and the progress they are making;
- help the child set positive goals;
- enjoy a rich, learning-oriented conversation with the child (and the teacher);
- be aware of how much the child is taking responsibility for his or her own learning and how the conference is a part of this; the students' talk reflects their thinking about how they learn and the type of learning conversations they have in class;
- understand better how learning and teaching happens 'these days'.

For teachers, the conferences enable them to accurately assess how students are progressing in developing the full archway of assessment for learning capabilities. That is, how well the student
- is shaping a genuine sense of partnership with the teacher, and the parents, in the learning;
- really understands what he or she is intending to learn and has learnt;
- is able to assess his or her progress in that learning;
- is able to request support for taking the next steps in learning;
- is able to reflect on the learning; what has worked, what has not, what have been the barriers and maybe outline the solutions;
- has a sense of what the next steps in the learning will be.

With the information from this informal assessment the teacher is able to support next learning steps. These may well occur during the conference itself by way of suitable prompts, or become the focus of subsequent teaching.

For teachers the conference also provides a powerful opportunity to build the partnership with both the student and the parents. In effect it is a plenary (reflection) on the recent learning with all three most relevant stakeholders present to celebrate success, to identify barriers, and to plan for actions to overcome any barriers (goal setting, etc). Teachers also see the interaction between the parents and their child, which in turn enriches their understanding of their student and the family context.

The conferences, when well organised, also become enjoyable for teachers due to the positive relaxed atmosphere created. Conferences also assist teachers, parents and students to better jointly understand the processes of classroom formative assessment practices, which in turn strengthen the sense of partnership between home and school.

For the principal and for senior management, the conferences enable them to

- see a high turn-out of parents — much higher than is often common in most schools for parent-teacher interviews;
- know that the parents are strongly supportive of the conference format;
- know that the support for the school itself is strengthened by the conferences;
- put in place a structure that creates support for parents to engage in conversations about learning with their children, that happens already in some homes but not all, that supports the use of a shared language of learning between teacher, student and family.

What does the research say?
There are strong claims, based on sizeable research, for the value of conferences.

- That strong partnerships between home and school supports student learning is shown by the many studies reviewed in Biddulph et al., 2003. This meta-study examined the evidence from many studies and concluded the following:
  - The research evidence suggests that effective school-home partnerships can enhance children's learning in both home and school settings. The positive impacts of such partnerships on children's achievement can be substantial, compared with school-based educational interventions alone. The benefits for children and young people can include better health and well-being, greater educational achievement, and increased economic well-being. These benefits can persist into adult life.
  - Strong school-home links are particularly important for children whose social class culture, and/or ethnicity and cultural heritages are different from those predominant in the practices of the school.
  - The research indicates that the majority of parents care about their children's education, want to support them, and are prepared to work in partnerships with others to do so. This includes parents from the lowest income families, and those with the least education. The evidence suggests that increased achievement is possible even in families with little formal education and/or limited facility in English. Parents (and whanau) across ethnic groups are often able to help their children make significant achievement gains despite experiencing very adverse economic conditions themselves, and despite having minimal power to effect improvements in their own circumstances.
  - There are various forms of partnership, but not all are effective. Those which are poorly designed, based on deficit views, and not responsive to the needs of families, can be ineffective and even counterproductive. Programmes which are effective respect parents and children, are socially responsible, and are responsive to families and the social conditions that shape their lives. Constructive partnerships empower those involved by

(a) fostering autonomy and self-reliance within families, schools and communities;

(b) building on the strong aspirations and motivation that most parents have for their children's development; and

(c) adding to (rather than undermining) the values, experiences and capabilities of parents and children.

– The evidence is that teachers can do much to initiate such constructive partnerships.

- Creating a context that casts the student in a legitimate and central role as an active and motivated participant in the learning process is fundamental to improved learning and is validated by all the research into assessment for learning (Black et al., 2002).

What needs to happen to establish successful student-led conferences?

In this section, we outline what we believe are the critical processes that a school needs to attend to over time if student-led conferences are to become an integral part of school life and substantially contribute to improved learning. Some of the processes we refer to cannot be put in place quickly and may require substantial staff professional development, as well as changes to schools' curriculum plan, assessment, personnel management, and reporting processes.

The following processes are not listed in an order of implementation but as a series of points that each school would need to consider and, where appropriate, plan to address over time.

- All teachers who will use conferences need to have good levels of skill in the use of assessment for learning strategies. The school needs to have in place processes for upskilling all new staff to the same level as current staff.

- All teachers need to understand the purposes of the conferences and what the students need to learn in order to fully play their role in making them work.

- All staff need to be very clear that the purpose of the conference is for the student to discuss their progress and achievement with their family, and that it is quite separate from any social, behavioural or family issues that the parent may want to talk about. Staff need procedures for enabling parents who want to raise other issues to make another time with the teacher to do that.

- The school needs to keep simple data about the success of the conferences — how many of the parents do come, how satisfied they are with them, how the students and the teachers rate them. The school also then needs to evaluate the data to identify any areas that need to be improved or fixed.

- The school needs to be clear about how this form of partnership communication with parents fits within the other forms of reporting so that there is not duplication of effort or messages.

- The school needs to gain the buy-in of the staff to the process and to resource any development needed to ensure that both teachers and students are properly skilled.

- For the conferences to provide maximum benefit for student learning they have to occur often enough for the plans set in one conference to have had a chance to have been completed and not to have been forgotten. Getting student-led conferences established firmly in a school takes time. In the first two years just one conference in the second term is likely to be quite sufficient. By the third year when most of the staff, students and parents are used to them it can be extended to an additional one in Term 4. If the student is well motivated they will have ongoing incidental conversations with both their parents and with the teacher about how the plans are being implemented. The student may decide to call a conference between those already planned if they feel that they need their 'learning partners' to come together again in the interests of best learning. Both the teacher and parents may also call such a conference.

What is the normal routine for the conferences?

- Senior management establishes the format and procedures to be used in the school, including the dates for the conferences for the year.
- Senior management needs to ensure that they are clear about the role of the teacher at the conference; that the student has the responsibility to run the conference, and the teacher is only there to support any difficult bits and to ensure that it starts smoothly.
- Senior management provides necessary professional development to ensure that all teachers have the necessary skills to positively promote the conferences and to teach their students the skills they need.
- It is important that *every* student have an opportunity to discuss their learning with a significant adult. (Some students may not have family that are in a position to attend. In these cases, so that the opportunity for the student to articulate their learning is not lost, it is important to organise for some other special person to be there. The teacher or a member of the senior management should ask the student who they would really like to tell about their learning. Often that person may turn out to be the principal. In these circumstances the person should act 'as the parent' in discussing the learning.)
- Each teacher discusses the purposes and format for the conferences with their class at the beginning of the year. The discussion also covers
  - the evidence students will need to have available to show their parents what they have been learning, what they have learnt, and what their next steps are;
  - how and when this evidence will be assembled – if portfolios are used then they must contain evidence of progress and achievement that is credible and easily followed by parents (samples of the type of student and teacher assessment sheets that meet this criterion can be seen on pages 216–21);
  - the roles each participant will have, particularly the major role the student takes;
  - what learning or practising each student will need to do in order to play their part fully before, during and after the conference, and when and how this learning will happen.
- At least four weeks before the first conference students need to begin to practise their roles. Becoming comfortable at describing to peers aspects of their current learning, what they have done well, what they are finding difficult, and where they

think they have reached with their learning will need to be practised to a greater or lesser degree depending on the extent to which they are used to self- and peer-assessment and reflection as a part of their routine learning approach. They will also need to develop confidence in greeting their parents in this context, which may be completely new to all of them. In adddition, they will need to develop their ability to explain the process to their parents, and to check that they understand it.

- Two to four weeks before the conference times, the school or each teacher sends letters home informing the parents of the conference times and the purposes and processes involved. The students also take responsibility for inviting their parents,

TABLE 13: ROLES AND RESPONSIBI

Teacher

Before

- Prepare any necessary letters or forms for parents explaining the intentions of the conference process – share them with the students.
- Ensure that any formal achievement information has been shared with students, along with your comments.
- Plan and provide opportunities for students to collect work samples that include learning intentions, success criteria self-assessments, peer-assessments as well as feedback and feedforward. (For example, in exercise books, curriculum folders, portfolios, etc.)
- Ensure students have experienced reflection about 'how their learning is going' as a natural and continually experiential part of their learning processes.
- Ensure they have not only reflected on their learning but they have also become comfortable about talking about their progress and achievement.
- Discuss student-led conferences with students.
- Practise using opportunities for students to role-play student-led conferences with one another.

During

- Verbally introduce the process to parents, particularly the role the parents should play.
- Help clarify student work samples if necessary.
- Act as encourager, clarifier as necessary to ensure conference runs smoothly.
- Encourage reflections and feedback from students, parents and self.
- Be aware of over-critical parents and have a plan to intervene if necessary.

After

- Read, summarise, and reflect on student and parent evaluation comments.
- Take debriefing sessions with the students to discuss the conferencing process and to get feedback from them.
- Support students with their personal goals.
- Debrief and evaluate the process with colleagues making agreed modifications, if necessary, for the next student-led conferences.

actually setting up the time for the meeting at the school and for explaining what it will be about.

- Before the conferences the students are given adequate time to prepare for the conferences by assembling their work (portfolios, e-portfolios, exercise books, annotated work, etc) and spending some time in small groups reflecting on how their recent learning has gone.
- During the conference the students lead the conversations with the parents to show them the learning achieved, the next steps to be achieved, and to discuss and set new goals. To support these conversations students use samples of work done (for

IN STUDENT-LED CONFERENCES

Student	Parent
Write invitations to parents/caregivers. Deliver and return communications between home and school. Collect work samples (for example, in exercise books, curriculum folders, portfolios, etc) that include learning intentions, success criteria, self- and peer-assessments as well as teacher feedback and feedforward. Practise reflection processes. Practise verbalising reflective thinking and insights with peers and teacher as a part of the learning process in the classroom. Rehearse student-led conferences through role-playing.	• Make an appointment with the teacher for another time if there are any concerns about the student's learning, behaviour. • Read material and invitations from the school, responding when appropriate using channels/systems provided. • Be positively supportive and give time to having supportive conversations with the student about what it is they are *learning* at school, rather than what they are *doing*.
• Do necessary introductions. • Share learning intentions and success criteria. • Share portfolio or exercise book contents or other evidence of learning. • Discuss strengths and challenges. • Set future learning intentions, state how you intend to work towards the learning. • Discuss ways to be supported with learning at home and at school.	• Listen carefully and ask clarifying questions. • View and provide encouraging comments on student work, progress and achievement. • Support goal-setting and learning intention opportunities.
• Complete conference evaluation form. • Write a thank-you note to parent/caregiver. • Undertake new activities related to new learning intentions.	• Complete conference evaluation sheet. • Monitor student's learning intentions and goal-setting plans. • Communicate with the teacher/school if you have any concerns as a result of the student-led conference.

example, portfolios, exercise books, curriculum folders) to exemplify their learning journey. The more students are able to discuss actual assessment results that they have access to and have used to promote their learning, the more parents are able to see for themselves where the students are actually at. Discussing running records, asTTle individual learning pathways reports, comparing their writing against the national exemplars are all ways in which students can use good assessment information with their parents. What is used is not important. How it is used is important. The teacher is not directly a part of this conversation but 'hovers' to ensure that the conversation does not 'freeze'.

- For the steps during the conference, see the role descriptions in Table 13 on pages 206–207.

Parents describing their experiences of student-led conferences

- 'Because my child was taking the lead I could comment and ask questions on an informal conversational level.' (Parent just as involved as child.)
- 'I wanted my child to have every opportunity to lead their conference and I spent the time listening and asking questions.'
- 'We spent about five minutes discussing each subject then we had about 10 minutes with the teacher.'
- 'I myself enjoyed my children telling and explaining what they have learnt at school.'
- 'I played a game with my son with pebble stones — it was great! Asking a lot of questions — very interested in my son's school work.'
- 'I felt my daughter did very well in explaining and understood what she was telling me. [She] was excited to show me her work and could answer my questions.'
- 'I like to hear my daughter explain things in her own way this way — she is sure to learn better and it reinforces her learning.'
- 'I support it very much because the child is responsible for their own learning and can best explain how they think their learning is going for themselves.'
- 'They have to take ownership for their work and be accountable.'
- 'I believe that if my son can explain his work to me it is proof to me that he is learning — not to mention the effect it has on his self-esteem.'
- 'It gives them confidence to speak about their work.'
- 'It gives the student pride and ownership of the process and their progress.'
- 'I enjoyed hearing from my daughter what she has been learning and having her explain it meant she had to have some understanding of what she was saying.'
- 'As my boy doesn't talk to me much about what goes on at school this was good for me to see his progress. Thanks.'
- 'At the end of his special evening he was proud of his work, of the tour, having his parents see his achievement and his future goals.'
- 'Learnt aspects from my son that I hadn't seen before — confidence I didn't realise he had.'
- 'It's like she's already on another level — it shows the knowledge of what she's learning.'
- 'It gives the student in future more confidence in "public speaking".'

Written reports on progress and achievement

Parents do want assurance from the teacher and the school that what their child has told them about their learning is actually correct, especially in terms of their rate of learning. Providing this assurance is relatively easy if the teacher and the school is on top of assessment, and can be done through a combination of verbal assurance at the student-led conference and by written report at other times.

What information do parents want from the school?

Parents will always have their own informal sources of information. These are useful in cross-checking and validating the information they receive from the school.

The school should provide illustrative evidence of learning in the form of portfolios, digital portfolios, exercise books or other products that are representative of the student's learning.

In addition to these sources of information there is also a need for clear formal information about actual student progress and achievement which is best given by

- reporting the actual level of attainment or measure the school itself uses to monitor progress — these might be the curriculum levels within which their child is working, reading ages, spelling ages, etc;
- illustrative comment about what this means in terms of progress and what the next learning steps might be.

Commitment by a school to formally report in this way will always need to be supported by additional information about how to understand the measures of progress used by the school and how to understand what standard of performance is indicated by the reported level of achievement (see the example of a school report on page 210). With all of this information, the parents then become able to enter into a learning-focused dialogue about how improved learning can be supported at home, or what learning goals might be most appropriate.

Written reporting to parents should

- be presented in a professional, meaningful manner and in a format that is appropriate for the age and stage of the student;
- be brief and constructive;
- be at intervals that parents feel are appropriate;
- be positive in tone;
- be easily understood;
- be responsive to cultural and language needs such as those for whom English is a second language;
- be based on substantive gathered and documented evidence;
- cover the essential learning areas and competencies of the New Zealand Curriculum;
- comment on attitudes, values, skills and knowledge;
- recognise student strengths and interests;
- be supportive of effective learning and teaching;
- clearly inform about *actual* student progress and achievement.

Education Review Office, 1996

Here is an example of a school report that meets all of the criteria listed on page 209.

NAME: **YEAR: 5**

ENGLISH

	Level	Effort	Comment
Speaking	3	B	Retells events in clear logical sequence. Is gaining
Listening	3	A	confidence with adjusting volume to suit the size of
Writing	3A	A	the audience. An attentive listener able to carry out a
Reading Age	11.5	A	series of instructions.
Spelling Age	13	A	Uses direct speech and descriptive vocabulary
Handwriting	4B	A	effectively in story writing, to capture audiences

LITERACY

Currently demonstrates academic levels consistent with, or better than, reasonable expectations for age. ☑

Does not currently meet general expectations in one or more areas. ☐

interest. Reworks adding and excluding words, phrases and sentences, where appropriate to improve text. Uses appropriate punctuation independently. Fluent reader but needs to make assumptions from the text in order to answer comprehension questions. Competent speller. Most written work is error free. Has a pen licence and is learning the conventions of joining in handwriting.

MATHEMATICS

	Level	Effort
Number	3A	
Measurement	3	
Geometry	3	A
Algebra	3	
Statistics	4	

NUMERACY

Currently demonstrates academic levels consistent with, or better than, reasonable expectations for age. ☑

Does not currently meet general expectations in one or more areas. ☐

Has sound knowledge and recall of basic facts. Has expanded the range of mental strategies used to solve problems in addition, subtraction, multiplication and division. Can record in an organised logical way and can talk about the results of a mathematical exploration.
Is developing the habit of 'Accuracy and Precision' by checking work with the opposite operation.
Makes reasonable estimates.
Is developing accuracy when performing measuring tasks using a range of units and scales.

SCIENCE

	Level	Effort
The Living World	4	
The Material World	4	A
The Physical World	4	
Planet Earth & Beyond	4	

Able to use information gleaned in a science experiment to suggest answers to questions and draw conclusions.

SOCIAL STUDIES

	Level	Effort
Social Organisation	4	
Culture & Heritage	4	
Place & Environment	4	A
Time, Continuity & Change	4	
Resource & Economic Activ	4	

Able to identify key words from information, make notes and formulate sequential paragraphs in own words, to present findings in social studies inquiry.

Able to transfer own knowledge and create, design, plan and make a board game that will teach others about a famous person.

TECHNOLOGY

	Level	Effort
Knowledge & Understanding	3	
Capability	3	A
Technology & Society	3	

HEALTH & PHYSICAL EDUCATION

	Level	Effort	Comment
Personal Health & Physical Dev	3		Discussed in DARE that that every decision has
Movement Concepts & Motor Skills	3	A	a consequence. Understands the importance of
Relationships with Others	3		physical fitness and a balanced diet for healthy
Healthy Communities & Env'mnt	3		living.

THE ARTS

	Level	Effort	Comment
Music	3	A	Confidently plays a part in tuned percussion with
Visual Arts	2	B	accompaniment. Is developing confidence in
Dance	2	A	own art ability. Exploring and identifying ways
Drama	2	B	to use symbolic colour in art works. Engages co-operatively in group role play.

ESSENTIAL SKILLS

Self-management & Competitive		Completes class work with effort and care.
Social & Co-operative		Prefers to work independently or in a pair but is
Work & Study		discovering the energy and advantages of working in a small group to achieve a common goal.

GENERAL COMMENTS

is self disciplined and hard working. He is learning to use his initiative and have faith and confidence in his own abilities. He has made sound academic progress across the curriculum. has neat work habits and takes pride in his presentation.

Teacher's Signature:_____

Principal's Signature:_____   December 2005

KEY:
Levels - In all cases current achievement levels are indicated.

Writing, Handwriting & Numeracy achievement:
Codes: B=Basic understanding; P=Gaining Proficiency; A=Advanced understanding
        at this curriculum level.
Science, Social Studies, Technology: Each strand is covered only once in a year. The achievement level indicated has been determined at the completion of units.
Effort: A = Works well consistently   B = Works well usually
          C = Works well sometimes   D = Greater effort needed

---

Guidelines for reading this Report

This report records the teacher's assessment of   progress and achievement during the current reporting period. The purpose of this report is to summarise   progress and achievement in relation to the New Zealand Curriculum.

Curriculum Achievement

The achievement levels in this report indicate   development relative to the New Zealand Curriculum. Because the levels are progressive and overlapping, all children are not expected to be achieving at the same level at the same time. The level shown for each aspect of the curriculum is that which, in the professional judgement of the teacher, best describes   achievement. This level is based on the assessment information collected and is intended to indicate   performance. The diagram below demonstrates how the levels straddle several years of schooling and indicates how children are achieving.

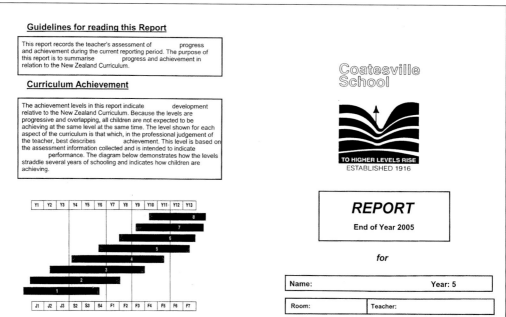

Coatesville School

TO HIGHER LEVELS RISE
ESTABLISHED 1916

REPORT

End of Year 2005

for

Name:		Year: 5
Room:	Teacher:	

TRY THIS!
What do we want to see?

We want to see this:

- 'Mum, you have to come to school so that I can show and tell you about what I have been learning.'
- 'But I don't need to because the newsletter from your teacher told me what you have been learning this term.'
- 'But Mum, that just told you what we were intending to learn over the term. I want to show you what I have learnt! And anyhow, we have to set some goals for next term!'

And this:

- 'When Wiremu asked me to come to his conference at his school I did not want to at first because I thought that it would be another interview with his teacher like the ones that I have been to in the past. At those I just felt told off for having a stink son. But this time he was so keen I knew that I had to turn up for him. It was awesome. He was so proud of what he has been learning, he spoke so well about it. I was so proud of my son. And best of all, we set some goals that he and I are going to work on next term. It is so good to know that I can actually help my boy to learn.'

And this:

- 'The written reports we get from the school are great. They only come once a year, but that is fine 'cos we have the interviews during the year and we see lots of our kids' work during the year. They show us how our kids are learning in relation to all the other kids in the country, and they have good comments about what they have learnt in each subject too. And they are written in a simple, friendly manner that tells us that the teacher really does know and care about our child. What I like best about them is that my child, despite learning at a much slower pace than others, is proud of his report. If they ever have any concerns about him they let us know so quickly!'
- 'We talk with our children about their reports and the areas that they need to work harder in. We pop up to school occasionally to look at their work and see if things are going along well. Each time we get a new report we can see that progress is being made and that's what's important. Most of the time everything is fine and, on the odd occasion that there's a problem, we're always made aware of it.'
- 'I thought that the one they sent us in March was good. It told us where there was no problem and, in the section where there was a problem, it was quite specific about what that was; we were able to talk about it with our daughter and help her at home.'
- 'I like the main reports where there are levels given. You can look at the progress graph on the back and see where your child fits in on the national scale.'
- 'Having a level mark and an effort mark that are backed up by a comment is very useful. I think you need all three things to get a good overall picture. There is a balance between the promotional positive and the objective.'
- 'I want to know how well my child is doing compared to other children. As long as they are average, or above average, I am happy. But whether I like it or not, I want to be told the truth; and I am.'

Using the scales below, place a cross in the square to show your answer

		How important is this to you?					How satisfied are you with our current performance?				
		Unimportant				Important	Not at all satisfied				Very satisfied
		1	2	3	4	5	1	2	3	4	5
1.	This school really believes in high standards.	❑	❑	❑	❑	❑	❑	❑	❑	❑	❑
2.	My child's teacher really believes in high standards.	❑	❑	❑	❑	❑	❑	❑	❑	❑	❑
3.	My child's teacher really believes that my child can achieve.	❑	❑	❑	❑	❑	❑	❑	❑	❑	❑
4.	My child enjoys school.	❑	❑	❑	❑	❑	❑	❑	❑	❑	❑
5.	The school supplies clear information about what my child is going to be learning.	❑	❑	❑	❑	❑	❑	❑	❑	❑	❑
6.	The school supplies clear information about how they teach.	❑	❑	❑	❑	❑	❑	❑	❑	❑	❑
7.	The school staff are always friendly and open – it is easy to talk to them about anything.	❑	❑	❑	❑	❑	❑	❑	❑	❑	❑
8.	My child's teacher is always friendly and open – it is easy to talk to her about anything.	❑	❑	❑	❑	❑	❑	❑	❑	❑	❑
9.	The school always contacts me quickly if they have any concerns about my child (before the concerns get too big).	❑	❑	❑	❑	❑	❑	❑	❑	❑	❑
10.	My child is very proud of what he/she is learning at school.	❑	❑	❑	❑	❑	❑	❑	❑	❑	❑
11.	The information I get from the school makes it very clear what progress is being made and how well my child is achieving.	❑	❑	❑	❑	❑	❑	❑	❑	❑	❑
12.	It feels like a really good partnership between the school and our family about my child's learning.	❑	❑	❑	❑	❑	❑	❑	❑	❑	❑

TRY THIS!

Check out how your parents feel about the partnership with the school. Get the okay from your principal and then send the short survey (on the page opposite) home on an A4 sheet of paper along with a covering letter explaining why you want your parents to complete it. Do not ask them to put their name to it. Fill one out yourself in terms of how you would like your parents to complete it so that you can see if they see things the same as you. Rewrite it if you like so that you are confident your parents will know what you are getting at.

See if there are gaps between how important they think an issue is and how satisfied they are. If there are any items where there is a big gap (a negative difference of more than −1) between the average satisfaction rating less the average importance rating, it indicates a problem area. For example, if parents, on average, rate the statement, 'the school really believes in high standards' as a '5' in importance, but as a '3.5' in their satisfaction, this gives a 'gap' of −1.5, which is big enough to try to reduce.

How we teach at our school!

We have chosen to teach a particular way at our school. We have looked closely at the research into how children learn best and we want to teach so that all children learn best. What the research tells us is that in order to learn best, schools must recognise

- the profound influence the motivation and self-esteem of learners have on learning;
- the importance of active involvement of learners in identifying learning goals and criteria for knowing when these are achieved;
- the necessity to adjust teaching to take account of the results of assessment;
- the need to provide effective, timely feedback to learners;
- the need to support learners to be able to assess themselves, reflect on their learning and to understand how to improve.

What students should be doing in every class:

- All students should be obviously learning — they should be engaged in their learning tasks with very little distracted time.
- All students should be able to describe what they are learning, and why it is important for them to learn it.
- All students should be able to describe how they will know when they have learnt something properly.
- All students should find what they are learning challenging but within their reach.
- All students should be able to describe how they know what progress they are making and what they will learn next.
- All students should describe the process of their learning as a partnership between the teacher and themselves (with help from their friends and peers and family).

- All students should find their classroom a vibrant and enjoyable place in which to learn.
- All students should be happy to tell you, their parents, what they are learning and why.
- All students should know their current achievement levels and what their next goal should be based on this.

What teachers should be doing in every class:

- All teachers should be making what is to be learnt, and why it is to be learnt, very clear to children so that the children can see the importance of learning it, how they will learn it, and when.
- All teachers should be ensuring that every child is challenged with learning at a level that is appropriate for them so that every child experiences success and feels able as a learner.
- All teachers should be talking with students about their work, assessing their work, and giving them help and support that they find useful, encouraging and enabling them to think deeply about what they are learning.
- All teachers should be managing the classroom so that all children are engaged in learning with very little wasted time.
- All teachers should be talking with the students regularly about what they are finding difficult about their learning and helping them to overcome those difficulties.
- All teachers should describe the process of teaching and learning as a partnership between themselves and the students (and the families).
- All teachers should be sharing information about progress and achievement with students.

If all these things are happening, your child will know it, and you will know it. If you have doubts, if you don't think they are happening; come and see us and talk about them. Please.

PORTFOLIO STUDENT AND TEACHER ASSESSMENT SHEETS

Portfolio assessment sheet
Maths: number

Global learning intention
We are learning how to solve simple addition problems.

Specific learning intentions:
We are learning how to read and write the numbers from 0–100.
We are learning how to skip count in 2s, 5s, and 10s.
We are learning how to solve addition problems to 20 by counting in our heads.
We are learning how to solve simple addition by counting on from the biggest number.

I can:
Read and write the numbers from 0–100

Skip count in 2s, 5s and 10s

Work out adding problems to 20 by counting in my head

Work out adding problems by counting on from the biggest number

Teacher comment on number progress:

_____

_____

_____

_____

_____

Current ENP **(Early Numeracy Project)** stage: _____
(See best fit criteria)

Current achievement level: **(See bench-mark information)**

'At Risk' two or more stages below expected	Below expected stage	At expected stage	Above expected stage	Two or more stages above expected stage

Portfolio assessment sheet
Recount writing

Global learning intention
We are learning how to write a recount.

Specific learning intentions:
We are learning how to start our story by saying
- when we went;
- who we went with;
- where we went.

We are learning how to use capital letters and full stops in the right places.
We are learning how to write events in order.

I can:
Start my story with when, who and where.

Use capital letters and full stops in the right places.

Write the events of my story in order.

Teacher comment on writing progress:

_____

_____

_____

_____

_____

Current writing stage _____
(See best fit criteria)

Current achievement level: (See bench-mark information)

'At Risk' two or more stages below expected	Below expected stage	At expected stage	Above expected stage	Two or more stages above expected stage

Portfolio assessment sheet
Writing: Years 4–8

Global learning intention
We are learning how to . . .

Reflection on my writing:
In writing I have been practising . . .

I have got better at . . .

The thing that I like most about this writing is . . .

If I was to do it again I would . . .

My next goal is . . .

Teacher comment on writing progress:

_____

_____

_____

_____

_____

Current writing stage _____
(See best fit criteria)

Current achievement level: **(See bench-mark information)**

'At Risk' two or more stages below expected	Below expected stage	At expected stage	Above expected stage	Two or more stages above expected stage

Portfolio assessment sheet
Writing: Years 1–3

Global learning intention:
We are learning how to write letters and sound out words.

My goal:
I am learning to make spaces in my writing.

☺   ☺   ☺   ☺

Teacher comment on writing progress:

_____

_____

_____

_____

_____

Current writing stage _____
(See best fit criteria)

Current achievement level: (See bench-mark information)

'At Risk' two or more stages below expected	Below expected stage	At expected stage	Above expected stage	Two or more stages above expected stage

Portfolio assessment sheet
Number: Years 4–8

Global learning intention:
We are learning how to . . .

Reflection on my mathematics:
In number knowledge I have been learning . . .
    I have got better at . . .
    This is helpful because . . .

In number strategies I have been learning . . .
    I have got better at . . .
    This is helpful because . . .

My next goal is . . .

Teacher comment on progress in mathematics:

_____

_____

_____

_____

_____

Current numeracy stage _____
(See best fit criteria)

Current achievement level: **(See mathematics bench-mark information)**

'At Risk' two or more stages below expected	Below expected stage	At expected stage	Above expected stage	Two or more stages above expected stage

Portfolio assessment sheet
Number: Years 1–3

Global learning intention:
We are learning how to count . . .

I can:
Count to 10

Match 1 to 1

Add two numbers using objects

Add two numbers using fingers

Teacher comment on progress in mathematics:

_____

_____

_____

_____

_____

Current numeracy stage _____
(See best fit criteria)

Current achievement level: (See mathematics bench-mark information)

'At Risk' two or more stages below expected	Below expected stage	At expected stage	Above expected stage	Two or more stages above expected stage

Bibliography

Alton-Lee, A. (2003) *Quality Teaching for Diverse Students in Schooling: Best Evidence Synthesis*. Ministry of Education, Wellington.

Alton-Lee, A. (2005) 'Shifts towards evidence-based teaching: Quality Teaching for Diverse Students in Schooling.' Unpublished think-piece-in-progress, Ministry of Education, Wellington.

Argyris, C., & Schön, D.A. (1974) *Theory in Practice: Increasing Professional Effectiveness*. Jossey Bass, San Francisco.

Assessment Reform Group (2002) *Assessment for Learning: Ten Principles*. www.assessment-reform-group.org.uk

Bandura, A. (1986) *Social Foundations of Thought and Action*. Prentice Hall, Englewood Cliffs, New Jersey.

Berliner, D. (1991) 'What's all the fuss about instructional time?' In Ben-Peretz, M., & Bromme, R. (Eds) *The Nature of Time in Schools: Theoretical Concepts, Practitioner Perceptions*. Teachers College Press, New York.

Biddulph, F., Biddulph, J., & Biddulph, C. (2003) The complexity of community and family influences on children's achievement in New Zealand. *Best Evidence Synthesis, 6.*

Black, P., & Wiliam, D. (1998) *Inside the Black Box: Raising Standards through Classroom Assessment*. King's College School of Education, London.

Black, P., Harrison, C., Lee, C., Marshall, B., & Wiliam, D. (2002) *Working Inside the Black Box*. Department of Education and Professional Studies, King's College, London.

Borkowski, J.G., Carr, M., Rellinger, E., & Pressley, M. (1990) Self-regulated cognition: Interdependence of metacognition, attributions, and self-esteem. In Jones, B. & Idol, L. (Eds) *Dimensions of Thinking and Cognitive Instruction*. Lawrence Erlbaum, Hillsdale, New Jersey (pp. 53–92).

Boston, C. (2002) *The Concept of Formative Assessment*. www.ericdigests.org/2003-3/concept.htm:6

Brophy, J. (2004) *Motivating Students to Learn*. Lawrence Erlbaum Associates, Mahwah, New Jersey.

Clarke, S. (2003) *Enriching Feedback in the Primary Classroom*. Hodder & Stoughton, London.

Clarke, S. (2005) *Formative Assessment in the Secondary Classroom*. Hodder Murray, London.

Clarke, S., Timperley, H., & Hattie, J. (2003) *Unlocking Formative Assessment — Practical Strategies for Enhancing Students' Learning in the Primary and Intermediate Classroom*. New Zealand edition: Hodder Moa Beckett, Auckland.

Clay, M.M. (2005) *Literacy Lessons Designed for Individuals*. Heinemann, New Hampshire.

Crooks, T.J. (1988) The impact of classroom evaluation practices in students. *Review of Educational Research, 48* (pp. 438–81).

Crooks, T.J. (2002) Assessment, Accountability and Achievement: Principals, Possibilities and Pitfalls. Keynote address presented at the 24th annual conference of the New Zealand Association for Research in Education, 5–8 December 2002, Palmerston North.

Darr, C. (2005) Five questions worth asking about self-regulated learning. *SET: Research Information for Teachers*, 2.

Delpit, L. (1988) The silenced dialogue: power and pedagogy in educating other people's children. *Harvard Educational Review*, 58:3 (pp. 280–98).

Department for Education and Skills (2004) *Excellence and Enjoyment: Learning and Teaching in the Primary Years*. DfES Publications, Annesley, Nottinghamshire.

Dweck, C.S. (1999) *Self Theories: Their Role in Motivation, Personality and Development*. Psychology Press, Philadelphia.

Education Review Office (1996) *Reporting Student Achievement*, 3:Autumn.

Elbow, P. (2004) Writing First! *Educational Leadership*, 62:2 (pp. 9–13).

Gilbert, J. (2001) It's Science, Jim, but not as we know it: Re-thinking 'Old' discipline for the Knowledge Society. *SAME Papers* (pp. 174–90).

Harvey, A. (1983) *A Journey in Ladakh*. Cape, London.

Hattie, J. (1999) Influences on Student Learning (Inaugural lecture: Professor of Education, University of Auckland).

Jones, B. & Idol, L. (1990) *Dimensions of Thinking and Cognitive Instruction*. Lawrence Erlbaum Associates, Hillsdale, New Jersey.

Leven, T. & Long, R. (1981) *Effective Introduction*. Association for Supervision and Curriculum Development, Washington D.C.

McCallum, B. (2000) *Formative Assessment — Implications for Classroom Practice*. www.qca.org.uk/downloads/formative

McClune, H.F., & Lord, G.H. (1916) *Democracy in the Schoolroom: A Guide to Primary School Work, with Special Reference to Sole Charge Schools*. Whitcombe & Tombs, Auckland.

Marsano, R. (2004) *Building Background Knowledge for Academic Achievement: Research on What Works in Schools*. Association for Supervision and Curriculum Development, Alexandria.

Ministry of Education. (1995) *Developing Science Programmes*. Learning Media, Wellington.

Ministry of Education. (2003a) *Effective Literacy Practice in Years 1 to 4*. Learning Media, Wellington.

Ministry of Education. (2003b) *Planning for Better Student Outcomes*. 16:September.

Ministry of Education. (2003c) *Planning for Better Student Outcomes*. 16:November.

Ministry of Education. (2003d) *The New Zealand Curriculum Exemplars*. Learning Media, Wellington.

Ministry of Education. (2004) *Curriculum Update*, 54:20.

Nuthall, G, & Alton-Lee, A. (1997) 'Understanding Learning and Teaching Project 3'. Report to the Ministry of Education, Wellington.

OECD (2005) The Definition and Selection of Key Competencies: Executive Summary. www.oecd.org/dataoecd/47/61/35070367.pdf

Palincsar, A.S. (1986) *Teaching Reading as Thinking*. North Central Regional Educational Laboratory, Oak Brook, Illinois.

Palincsar, A.S. & Brown, A.L. (1984) Reciprocal teaching of comprehension-fostering and comprehension-monitoring activities. *Cognition and Instruction, 2* (pp. 117–75).

Palmer, P.J. (1983) *To Know as We Are Known: A Spirituality of Education*. HarperCollins, San Francisco.

Qualifications & Curriculum Authority, UK. (2005) www.qca.org.uk/296.html#sharing

Rychen, D. & Salganik, L.E. (2003) *Key Competencies for a Successful Life and a Well Functioning Society*. Hogrefe & Huber, Gottingen.

Sadler, D.R. (1987) Specifying and promulgating Achievement Standards. *Oxford Review of Education, 13* (pp. 191–209).

Sadler, D.R. (1989) Formative assessment and the design of instructional systems. *Instructional Science, 18* (pp. 119–44).

Schön, D. (1987) *Educating the Reflective Practitioner*. Jossey-Bass, San Francisco.

Schwarz, R. (2002) *The Skilled Facilitator: A Comprehensive Resource for Consultants, Facilitators, Managers, Trainers and Coaches*. Jossey-Bass, San Francisco.

Senge, P.M. (1992) *The Fifth Discipline — The Art and Practice of the Learning Organisation*. Century Business, London.

Stewart, D. & Prebble, T. (1993) *The Reflective Principal: School Development Within a Learning Community*. ERDC Press, Massey University, Palmerston North.

Stiggins, R.J. (2002) Assessment crisis: the absence of assessment for learning. *Phi Delta Kappan* (pp. 758–80).

Stiggins, R.J., Arter, J.A., Chappuis, J., & Chappuis, S. (2004) *Classroom Assessment for Student Learning*. Assessment Training Institute, Portland, Oregon.

Timperley, H., & Parr, J. (2004) *Using Evidence in Teaching Practice — Implications for Professional Learning*. Hodder Moa Beckett, Auckland.

Waterman, A.S. (1981) Individualism and Interdependence. *American Psychologist, 36* (pp. 762–73).

Weiman, C. (2005) Powerpoint presentation: A New Vision of Science Education. University of Colorado, Colorado. http://wiki.wsu.edu/wsuwiki/Teaching_Large_Classes

www.tki.org.nz/r/esol/esolonline/classroom/teach_strats/consensus_e.php

Zimmerman, B. (2001) 'Theories of self-regulated learning and academic achievement: An overview and analysis'. In Zimmerman B. & Schunk D. *Self-Regulated Learning and Academic Achievement Theories: Theoretical Perspectives* (2nd ed). Lawrence Erlbaum Associates, Hillsdale, New Jersey.

Index